hotels • resorts • spas • trains • cruises • destination weddings

honeymoonchic ■ asia

hotels • resorts • spas • trains • cruises • destination weddings

honeymoonchic ■ asia

text joe yogerst • julia clerk • eliza teoh • joanna greenfield

thechiccollection

THIS PAGE: *A bride holding a bunch of lotus flowers at Four Seasons Resort Koh Samui.*

OPPOSITE: *The private deck overlooking the Indian Ocean at Coco Spa.*

PAGE 1: *Coco Spa at Coco Palm Bodu Hithi in the Maldives.*

PAGE 2: *A newly wed couple stroll hand in hand at the Diva Maldives.*

PAGE 6: *The water villa at Shangri-La's Villingili Resort affords its occupants the view of a calm sea.*

PAGES 10–11: *A refreshing view starts the morning at AYANA Resort & Spa.*

PAGES 108–9: *Minimalist chic at the Alila Villas Uluwatu framed against the stunning backdrop of the Indian Ocean.*

PAGES 216: *View of the outside lounge of Tropical Oasis, one of the many chic rooms at W Retreat Koh Samui.*

Editor
Valerie Ho

Assistant Editor
Akemi Hoe

Managing Editor
Francis Dorai

Designer
Chan Hui Yee

Production Manager
Sin Kam Cheong

Sales and Marketing Director
Antoine Monod

Sales and Marketing Managers
Suresh Sekaran
Daniel Tolentino
New Bee Yong
Meliana Salim
Kate Tan

Sales and Marketing Consultant
Patcharee Youngcharoen

Editions Didier Millet Pte Ltd
121 Telok Ayer Street, #03-01
Singapore 068590
telephone : +65.6324 9250
facsimile : +65.6324 9251
enquiries : edm@edmbooks.com.sg
website   : www.edmbooks.com

©2011 Editions Didier Millet Pte Ltd

Printed by Tien Wah Press (Pte) Ltd, Singapore.

isbn: 978-981-4260-34-3

COVER CAPTIONS:

1: *The spacious outdoor deck is a feature of the Escape Water Villa at Coco Palm Bodu Hithi, Maldives.*

2: *A romantic dinner in the jungle at Shangri-La's Villingili Resort & Spa, Maldives.*

3: *Fresh flowers adorn the property at Raffles Grand Hotel d'Angkor, Siem Reap.*

4: *Enjoy a cocktail at the lounge of Four Seasons Resort Koh Samui.*

5: *The newlyweds enjoy a dhoni ride at Conrad Maldives Rangali Island.*

6: *The lavish Puri Le Mayeur suite at Tugu Bali.*

7: *The contemporary style villas at Let's Sea Hua Hin Al Fresco Resort.*

8: *An inviting bath awaits in the private resort at the W Retreat Koh Samui.*

9: *A couple chill and relax at sunset at Shangri-La's Villingili Resort & Spa, Maldives.*

10: *A bride enjoying the sea view at Four Seasons Resort Koh Samui.*

11: *Count the stars on the moon bed at Let's Sea Hua Hin Al Fresco Resort.*

12: *Take a walk among nature at the Mandarin Oriental Dhara Dhevi in Chiang Mai.*

13: *Be prepared to laze and enjoy at Bali's AYANA Resort & Spa's river pool.*

14: *The sun sets over the private villa at Coco Palm Dhuni Kolhu, Maldives.*

15: *An Azamara Club Cruise has the amenities of a five-star hotel.*

16: *An aerial view of the Lagoon Villas at Coco Palm Dhuni Kolhu, Maldives.*

17: *An Eastern & Oriental Express train passes through the Thai countryside.*

18: *A luxe villa overlooks the calm sea at Four Seasons Resort Koh Samui.*

19: *A unique Dine by Design set up on the beach at Shangri-La's Villingili Resort & Spa, Maldives.*

20: *Enjoy a couple spa at AYANA Resort & Spa, Bali.*

contents

honeymoonideas 10

Introduction 12

Honeymoon Tips & Ideas 16

Asia's Best Mainland Beaches 20

Island Hopping Holidays 24

Bright Lights, Big Cities 30

Gourmet Getaways 40

Cultural Destinations 46

Action & Adventure 52

Ocean & River Luxury Cruises 60

Romantic Train Journeys 68

Spas & Wellness Retreats 74

Eco Chic Escapes 82

Winter Vacations 88

High-altitude Holidays 94

Destination Weddings 100

honeymoonescapes

Trains & Cruises
Azamara Club Cruises 110
Eastern & Oriental Express 112
Road to Mandalay 114
Royal Caribbean International 116

Bhutan
Amankora 118
Uma Paro 120

Cambodia
Song Saa Private Island 122
Raffles Hotel Le Royal 126
Raffles Grand Hotel d'Angkor 128

China
Brilliant Resort & Spa, Chongqing 130
Brilliant Resort & Spa, Kunming 132
Grand Hyatt Shanghai 134
JW Marriott Shanghai 136

Indonesia
Amanusa 138
AYANA Resort & Spa 140
Komaneka at Bisma 142
Matahari Beach Resort & Spa 144
Maya Ubud Resort & Spa 146
Tugu Bali 148
Uma Ubud 150
Villa Babar 152
Villa de daun 154
Villa Sungai Bali 156
Tugu Lombok 158

Laos
Amantaka 160

Malaysia
Avillion Port Dickson 162

Maldives
Coco Palm Dhuni Kolhu & Coco Palm Bodu Hithi 166
Cocoa Island 168
Shangri-La's Villingili Resort & Spa 170

Philippines
Amanpulo 172

Singapore
Capella Singapore 174

Sri Lanka
Amanwella 176

Thailand
Aleenta Resorts & Spa 178
Siri Sathorn 180
Four Seasons Resort Chiang Mai 182
Kaomai Lanna Resort 184
Mandarin Oriental Dhara Dhevi 186
Four Seasons Tented Camp Golden Triangle 188
Let's Sea Hua Hin Al Fresco Resort 190
Four Seasons Resort Koh Samui 192
SALA Samui Resort & Spa 194
ShaSa Resort & Residences 196
W Retreat Koh Samui 198
Pimalai Resort & Spa 200
Paradise Koh Yao 202
Amanpuri 204
JW Marriott Phuket 206
Renaissance Phuket Resort & Spa 208
SALA Phuket Resort & Spa 210

Picture Credits & Acknowledgements 212
Index 213

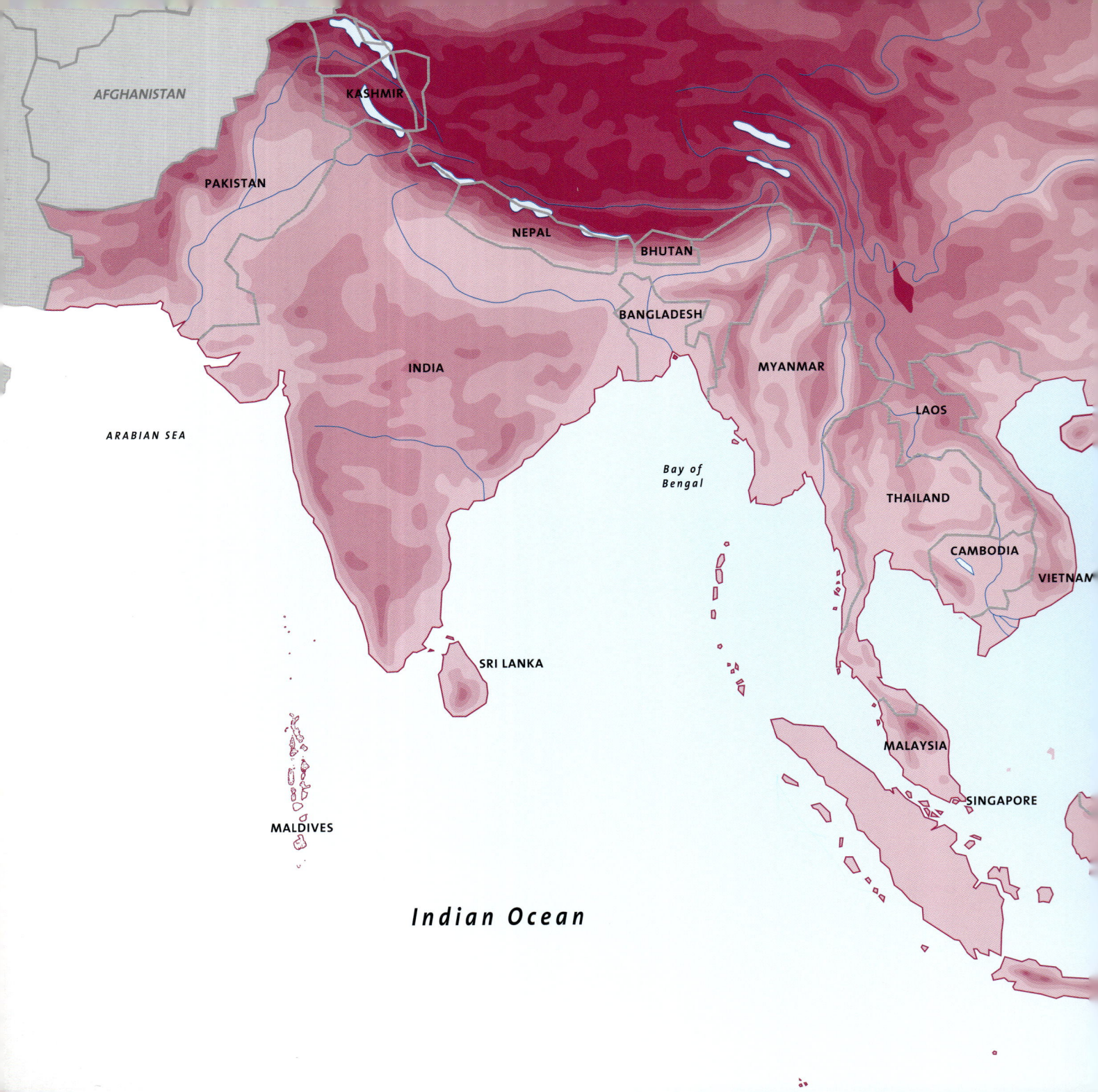

AFGHANISTAN

KASHMIR

PAKISTAN

NEPAL

BHUTAN

BANGLADESH

INDIA

MYANMAR

LAOS

THAILAND

CAMBODIA

VIETNAM

MALAYSIA

SINGAPORE

MALDIVES

SRI LANKA

ARABIAN SEA

Bay of Bengal

Indian Ocean

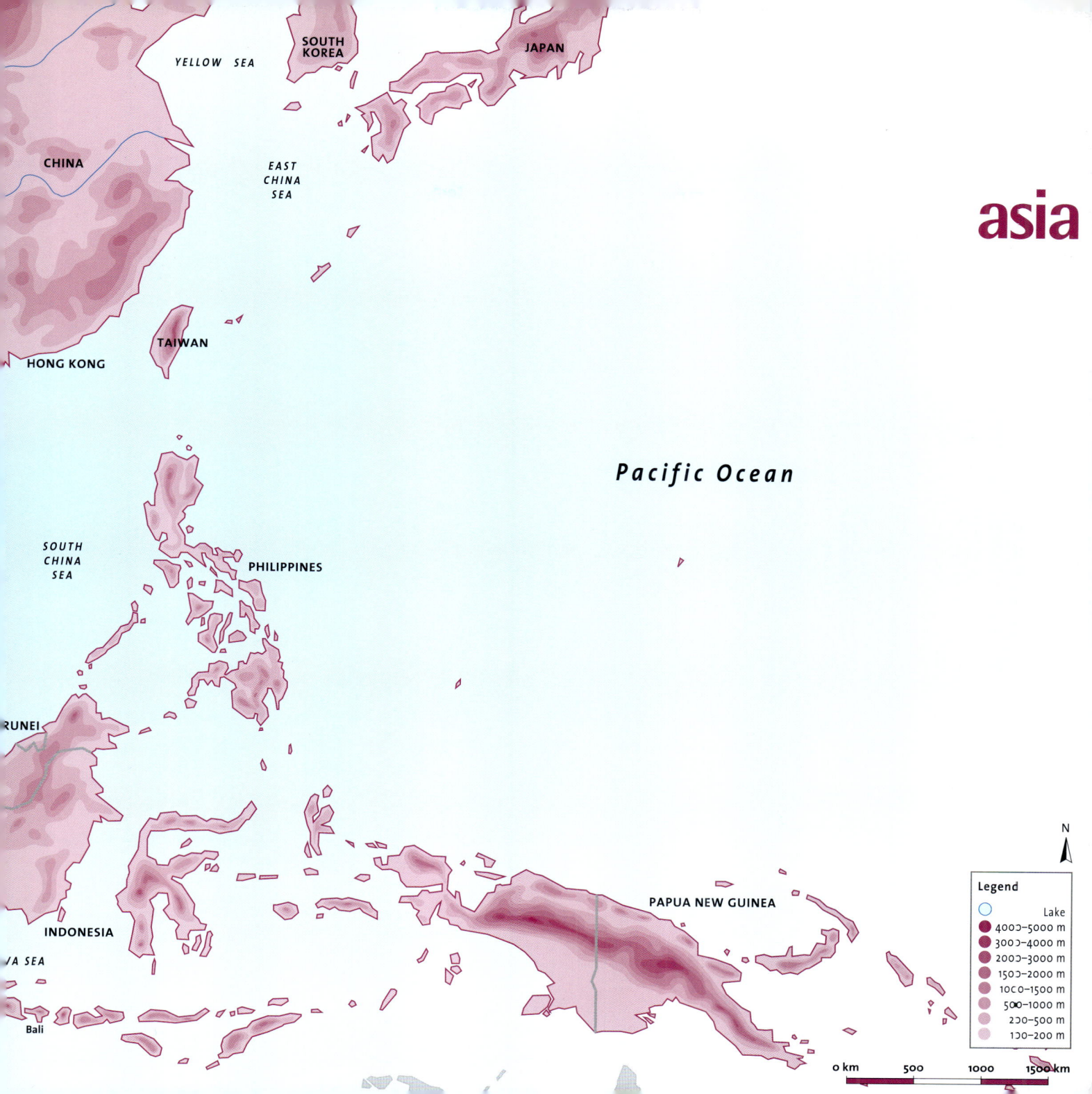

asia

YELLOW SEA

SOUTH KOREA

JAPAN

CHINA

EAST CHINA SEA

TAIWAN

HONG KONG

Pacific Ocean

SOUTH CHINA SEA

PHILIPPINES

RUNEI

INDONESIA

...A SEA

Bali

PAPUA NEW GUINEA

N

Legend

⬡	Lake
⬤	4000–5000 m
⬤	3000–4000 m
⬤	2000–3000 m
⬤	1500–2000 m
⬤	1000–1500 m
⬤	500–1000 m
⬤	200–500 m
⬤	100–200 m

0 km   500   1000   1500 km

honeymoon**ideas**

Asia abounds with options for that perfect honeymoon or amorous getaway. In this section are chapters on romantic holiday ideas – from beach and gourmet getaways to action-packed ski trips and eco-friendly escapes – plus useful tips on how to add extra spark to your honeymoon.

Introduction

Honeymoons and romantic holidays come in all shapes and sizes, and what you and your lover end up doing on your getaway depends on what you enjoy together – walking along an empty beach, discovering a new city, climbing a mountain, exploring the wilderness, or experiencing a hybrid of several locations and activities. As the old Doris Day song goes, "Everybody loves a lover". You will be amazed to find that no matter where you go, other people often get swept up in your enthusiasm for one another. It is the perfect opportunity to make the most of the romantic vacation possibilities on offer throughout Asia.

There is no denying that some Asian destinations are particularly made for romance. Bali has it all: chic resorts, secluded beaches, terraced rice fields and lush green highlands with enough mysticism, culture and traditions to impress even the most jaded traveller. The abiding sense of history, beauty, culture and refinement found in ancient places such as Kyoto, Angkor Wat and Luang Prabang put them in a league of their own. Huge cities like Hong Kong, Bangkok, Seoul and Singapore offer an excitement, vibrancy and bustle that are infectious. Moreover, who could deny the appeal of one of the great testaments to love ever built, the Taj Mahal?

Some couples relish traditional romantic activities. Walk hand-in-hand along a deserted beach in the moonlight while sharing your dreams and wishing upon stars. Soak in a bathtub with scented bubble bath, surrounded by the glow of lots and lots of candles. Take a sleigh ride through the snowy countryside and then warm up by a roaring fireplace. Active outdoor couples are more likely to dive straight into adrenaline adventures like skydiving, mountain climbing, bungee jumping or snowboarding. Still others choose the glam route: gourmet dinners, all-night dancing and endless shopping offered by big cities.

Honeymoons through the Ages

Nobody really knows where honeymoons originated, but there is certainly no lack of theories or legends. From earliest times, and in just about every major world culture, the period immediately following a wedding was considered special or sacred. The Book of Deuteronomy in the Bible advises that newly married men should abstain from fighting and be exempt from military duty in order to "bring joy to the wife he has married".

But honeymoons were not always happy occasions for the betrothed couple. The Vikings and many of the Eastern European and Central Asian nomadic tribes were prone to kidnapping their future wives from nearby settlements, an act that required them to go into hiding until the bride's family no longer had murderous intentions. The Norse people called this period of hiding – and presumably getting to know one another in the Biblical sense – the *hjunottsmanathr*, which is believed by some to be the root of the word "honeymoon".

THIS PAGE: With its alluring blend of sand and sea, Coco Palm Bodu Hithi resort in the Maldives has plenty of secluded spots for couples to share intimate moments.

OPPOSITE: The natural surroundings around the Mandarin Oriental Dhara Dhevi near Chiang Mai provides opportunities for couples to explore paddy fields, plantations and rainforests.

Another origin for the period directly following a wedding might be the ancient practice of drinking honeyed wine or mead to celebrate nuptials. It could simply symbolise that life is sweet right after a couple first ties the knot. Being highly practical people, the ancients figured this episode of bliss lasted around a month or one lunar cycle. The first use of "honeymoon" in the English language is believed to be from the mid 16th century, derived from the word moon. "The one loveth the other at the beginning exceedingly," wrote Richard Huloet of marriage in 1552, "the likelihood of their exceeding love appearing to assuage, the which time the vulgar people call the honey moon."

Asia also claims that the term "honeymoon" has its origins in this continent. Members of the Indian elite would go away together post marriage, a tradition that enamoured the British colonials, who took it back to the motherland, England. By the early 19th century, British couples were also taking "bridal tours" after their wedding, a trend that soon spread to France and the rest of the continent. The most popular places for Victorian-era honeymoons were Italy and the French Riviera; or Niagara Falls in the case of the United States and Canada.

21st-century Romance

Honeymoons have become much less structured in recent years. The rule these days is "No rules". Do anything, go anywhere and stay as long as you like. And while you and your other half could certainly spend the holiday guzzling copious amounts of mead, you are free nowadays to create your own honeymoon tradition. It could be something as simple as making a scrapbook together, a combination of photos, ticket stubs, postcards and other mementoes from your trip. Or, for the more digitally inclined, making your own honeymoon photo book that you can actually present to family and close friends.

Another way to keep your honeymoon memories alive long after the trip has passed is doing the same thing or visiting similar types of places on subsequent trips, especially those that mark your wedding anniversary. Maybe you learned to scuba dive or went trekking on your honeymoon – activities that easily lend themselves to repeating and sharing on future vacations. Or perhaps the highlight of that initial trip was a candlelit dinner for two on the beach. Just think of the number of beaches (in different parts of Asia) where you can replay that romantic scene over and over again.

You and your future spouse might also contemplate a "secret honeymoon" wherein one of you volunteers to choose the place, plan the details, make all the bookings and then get the other to the airport on time. More than anything else, turn off the mobile phone, leave the computer at home and just bask in one another's company without interruptions or interference from the outside world. The most romantic part of any romantic trip is the time that you give to each other.

THIS PAGE: Some hotels offer the most imaginatively discreet dining options, like a "Jungle Dinner" in the heart of the island's forest at Shangri-La's Villingili Resort in the Maldives.

OPPOSITE: The ultra-luxurious, two-and-a-half-hour Diamond Miracle Treatment at AYANA Resort & Spa in Bali includes a Creme de la Mer facial with sea quartz and diamond dust, as well as an ocean splash rose bath with petals from 500 red roses.

Honeymoon Tips & Ideas

From choosing an idyllic destination and booking the honeymoon suite to sweet nothings whispered in your lover's ear, there are plenty of ways to make your honeymoon or couple's holiday the experience of a lifetime.

Advance preparations can make a huge difference to the romance factor of your couple's getaway, honeymoon or anniversary trip. It could be something small, like arranging for the airline to make a mid-flight congratulatory announcement, or asking for a flower-covered bed or bath upon arrival at your hotel; or something more complex, like surprising your partner with a Balinese-style wedding or blessing ceremony.

Pack with Prudence & Passion

Pack little surprises for your lover, one for each magical day of your honeymoon or holiday. Depending on your budget, these could range from jewellery to perfume, bubble bath to a bottle of wine, or it could be just your thoughts and feelings, written down and presented in adorned boxes.

When packing for your special time abroad, don't forget to bring along the right clothing. Even if you are headed for a fairly casual destination, it sets the tone if you take the time to dress up for each other.

There is nothing worse than getting sick on a romantic getaway. Take some basic precautions to stay healthy, like checking whether or not the local tap water is safe to drink, staying away from street food stalls (in some locations) and making sure you are protected with the required vaccinations.

Romantic Rooms & Rituals

Always check out the honeymoon suite in advance, especially if there is more than one available at your hotel. You want to make sure the suite really does offer something extra in the way of romantic décor, ambience or amenities, and is not just an ordinary room with the word "honeymoon" stuck on the door. Even if there is no honeymoon suite, romantic features in ordinary rooms or suites might make all the difference to your amorous getaway, like booking one with a private pool or an outdoor shower.

If going away on a cruise, you can probably pre-book something special to be delivered nightly to your cabin, including a bottle of champagne or wine, canapés or cupcakes, special robes, spa services, flowers or candy – whatever you know your sweetheart will love. Some liners will even decorate your cabin with balloons, streamers and other trimmings.

Credit card concierge teams are a good source of information on how to make your vacation special. Many credit card companies have special perks and benefits to lure more affluent customers, and their teams of call centre professionals can help you hunt down good offers on activities and special events at your choice of destination. Check to see if the hotel or resort you are staying at have honeymoon or special romance packages. It may suggest creative ideas like a dawn or dusk hot-air balloon ride, watching the sunrise from a mountaintop or simply breakfast in bed.

Some hotels offer special rituals for honeymooners. Upon arrival at some hotels in Bali, for example, couples are treated to their own special musical serenade or prayer and have to cut through a string of flowers to get into the honeymoon suite (symbol of the new life together) and are given special "wedding costumes" to wear to a private dinner in a romantic location.

Wherever you stay, be sure to tell the hotel employees what your special occasion is, as it could mean reservation of a private poolside cabana, an in-room gift like champagne and chocolate-covered strawberries or even a room upgrade.

His & Her Pampering

Get a couple's massage – being pampered together is a sensuous delight. Most hotels and resorts now offer in-room spa treatments and services. Those that don't have their own spas will gladly bring in an expert from elsewhere. Be sure to check out the signature treatments.

If you and your partner really like spa services, choose hotels which are dedicated spa resorts, featuring a vast array of spa services, and sometimes even yoga, Pilates and tai chi sessions. These resorts may be situated near natural hot springs and guests can enjoy these, on top of nature walks and hikes.

Feed Your Feelings

Discreet dining has become readily available and hotels are certainly getting more creative about where they set up secluded dinners for two. Unspoilt beaches, private islands, rocky headlands, exotic tropical gardens, in the shallows of a lagoon – these are some choices you can pick from. Many hotels will let you design the menu, tailor-made with your

favourite dishes. And to set the tone, don't forget to ask for fresh flowers, candlelight and entertainment.

But dinner isn't your only option. Hotels can also arrange, for example, pre-dinner canapés and champagne aboard a private boat, complete with butler service. During the cruise, you can also ask to include an onboard couple's massage. If you enjoy the outdoors, pack a lunch takeaway or order a picnic. Then find your own spot for a meal out with nature.

For some couples, a shared cookery lesson could be the height of romance. Many hotels now offer some sort of culinary experience. Usually your lesson will start with actually procuring the raw ingredients you are going to cook. Buying fish fresh directly from the fishermen and vegetables from the local markets will be both interesting and educational, but it will probably mean an early morning. These culinary lessons often give out a certificate of completion, signed by the executive chef, to include in your honeymoon scrapbook. Hotels also provide a complimentary apron for participants.

Swept Away by Love

The type of accommodation you choose, of course, depends on your personal preferences and there are many choices available throughout Asia. Numerous hotels are built beside, over and sometimes even under water to take advantage of the inherent beauty of lakes, seashores and other waterfront locations. Some villas in the Maldives and Malaysia hang right over the ocean and feature private

THIS PAGE (FROM TOP): The Banyan Tree Bintan resort in Indonesia provides magically discreet dining venues; bathrooms at the Four Seasons Tented Camp in northern Thailand are designed for romance; water is an essential part of the Coco Palm Bodu Hithi experience in the Maldives.

OPPOSITE: The posh Water Villas at the Conrad Maldives on Rangali Island boast glass floors for full enjoyment of the teeming sea life below.

THIS PAGE (FROM TOP): Houseboats allow couples to plan their own itinerary; the cosy Tibetan Spa Suite at the Banyan Tree Ringha in southern China exudes a comfortable warmth; a handcrafted Tibetan bathtub in a Banyan Tree Ringha suite.

OPPOSITE (FROM TOP): Honeymoons can coincide with special events, like Thailand's Loy Kra Thong festival; celebrate your matrimonial bliss under the magical lanterns at an ancient temple in Shanghai.

sundecks with infinity-edge pools, as well as open-air bathtubs with steps leading directly down to the azure water. Inside, some have glass-panelled floors to provide fascinating views of the exotic marine life that flourishes right below your bungalow.

Beach destinations are always popular, and that's fine for couples seeking relaxation and romance. For those looking for more activities, there are the less developed destinations such as Cambodia, India, Sri Lanka and Vietnam, which offer a wider range of travel experiences.

Cosy Countrysides

Not all romantic vacation spots need to be situated near or on water. Seeking out really different hotel experiences is romantic in itself. The diverse range that is available in Asia is astounding – from resorts set on large expanses of land, on or abutting nature preserves in India, tea plantations in Sri Lanka to luxury-tented resorts near elephant camps in upcountry Thailand. There is something for one and all.

That's not all: there are retreats that specialise in yoga or vegetarianism in India, and cosy renovated farmhouses located at high altitude in China, where you can snuggle up by the romantic open fireplace on cold winter nights, with a private balcony offering breathtaking views of distant snow-capped peaks.

Staying in a Japanese *ryokan* (inn) is another magical experience. Many are arranged in the traditional *sukiya* style tea ceremony pavilion with *tatami* walkways. Original painted screens, fine works of pottery and antique *tansu* pieces adorn the hallways and spaces of many of these inns. Stylish boutique hotels also abound in Asia, offering the luxuries of a private villa with the service of a five-star hotel.

Asia's Love Boats

A cruise is another idea for a no hassle, romantic getaway. Once onboard, you and your lover can do as much or as little as you want. There are many options to choose from in Asia. The big cruise lines tend to change their ships and itineraries often as they move their vessels around the world by season and demand, so it's best to check the cruise company websites.

As a general rule, larger ships boast more onboard facilities and activities (like multiple restaurants, spas and round-the-clock entertainment); smaller vessels offer more personalised service and dock at more remote ports of call.

Small boats are best for exploring the region's inland waterways. Luxury riverboats ply the exotic waters of the Irrawaddy River in Burma (Myanmar), the Yangtze in China and the Mekong through Laos, Cambodia and Vietnam. Itineraries often include stops at ancient cities, temples and pagodas. Other boats are available for just the two of you or for a very small party.

Amorous Festivals

Arrange your romantic getaway to coincide with a particular holiday or celebration in your destination. Asia observes hundreds of festivals and holidays that you could enjoy as a participant or spectator.

Held on the first full-moon night of the lunar year, the Lantern Festival is commonly regarded as one of the most important and romantic festivals in many countries in Asia, including China, Taiwan and Hong Kong. Streets, temples and buildings are decorated with lanterns of all descriptions and local celebrants wander the streets carrying paper lanterns. The holiday differs somewhat from country to country. For example, at Tainan Yanshui in southern Taiwan, authorities release an explosion of firecrackers to thank the gods for blessings. In the village of Pinghsi, tens of thousands of sky lanterns are launched to line the sky with twinkling wishes from spectators.

Thailand's Loy Kra Thong festival fully embodies the amorous feelings of Thailand's young men and women as they take to the closest sea, river or lake to launch

their *kratong* and see what luck the following year will bring. *Kratong* are lotus-shaped receptacles, complete with a candle and incense, that can float on the water. Buy one and find a romantic place to set it adrift. Or better yet, make one for your lover. As the sun dips below the horizon and the full moon begins to hover in the night sky, release it with the outgoing tide or current. Your *kratong* will become part of thousands of twinkling lights floating off into the unknown distance. According to legend, if the *kratong* floats away from you, the coming year will bring good fortune; if it floats back towards the shore, then perhaps your luck may not be quite as you hoped. ~ **JC**

Vegetarian Getaway

Couples on a vegetarian diet may find the Vegetarian Festival, which takes place in Takuapa Old Town on Thailand's west coast, thrilling. Celebrated during the ninth month of the Chinese lunar calendar, the festival honours this lifestyle, and includes colourful religious processions, traditional ceremonies, a magnificent lantern display and lots of tasty vegetarian dishes, of course. Local residents of Chinese ancestry strictly observe a nine-day vegetarian or vegan diet and perform ancient rituals for the purposes of spiritual cleansing and merit-making. It is believed that good fortune is bestowed upon all who observe these religious rites.

Asia's Best Mainland Beaches

Asia's long and deeply indented mainland means rich pickings for beach aficionados, with hundreds of different places where couples can stroll alone, nuzzle up on an empty beach or sneak a kiss in the waves.

Given the fact that it's the largest and most populous continent, maybe it shouldn't come as a surprise that Asia also has the longest coastline – more than 62,000 km of mainland shore ranging from snow-covered Siberian sands to coconut and palm-shaded tropical strands. Be it walking along a secluded beach strewn with driftwood and shells or diving into a tropical lagoon, every Asian country with a shoreline offers some kind of coastal experience for couples on their honeymoon or romantic getaway. Most places offer a wide choice of seaside resorts to choose from. But no matter where you decide to stay, it's hard to resist an amorous beach getaway. The combination of sea, sun and sand is bound to set your romance aflame.

Vietnam: The Next Big Thing

Geography has blessed the long, thin strip of land that is **Vietnam** with hundreds of beaches of all shapes and sizes. But the country's tumultuous history means that very few of them were developed into resorts until recently. As such, Vietnam offers many quiet virgin beaches.

Even during bygone days, **Nha Trang** was a popular coastal escape for French colonials, the local aristocracy and even the royal family, who stayed in a whitewashed villa overlooking the southern end of the beach strip. The broad, white-sand strand in central Vietnam curls around a sapphire bay protected from the South China Sea by a cluster of 20 barrier islands. The seafront promenade (Tran Phu Street) is bustling night and day, a heady blend of local teenagers and souvenir hawkers, foreign backpackers and well-heeled international travellers searching for the next "big thing" in beach destinations. Hobie cats and parasailing are available along the main strand, and there are plenty of choices in boat trips to the outlying islands.

Nha Trang's underwater hub is the Hon Mun Marine Park. Dives can be organised through the **Coral Reef Dive Center** (6/0 Quan Tran-Hung Vuong St, Nha Trang; +84.58.352 4993; vietnamcoralreef.net) or **Scuba Dive Vietnam** (8A Biet Thu St, Nha Trang; +84.58.352 1586; scubadivevietnam.com). Those who don't dive can catch a glimpse of many of the same sea creatures, including potentially lethal local denizens such as sharks and lionfish at the **Nha Trang Oceanography Institute** (1 Cau Da St; +85.58.359 0034; www.vnio.org.vn).

Given its position as Vietnam's premier beach locale, Nha Trang now boasts a number of high-end resorts, like the **Six Senses Ninh Van Bay** (Ninh Van Bay, Ninh Hoa, Khanh Hoa, Vietnam; +84.58.372 8222; www.sixsenses.com), perched on its own crescent-shaped patch of sand on a rugged peninsula north of the city. The most romantic of the four different types of accommodation are the secluded Rock Villas at the western end of the bay. Tucked amongst giant boulders and accessed by a hillside staircase, the thatched-roof bungalows feature a private plunge pool, mini wine cellar, handcrafted bathtubs and spacious beds that offer panoramic water views over the tips of your toes. The resort's three or four night Romance Package includes a sunset cruise and candlelit four-course dinner for two in the wine cellar or on the jetty.

Thailand: "Royal" Beach Vacations

Thailand's love affair with beaches started in the early 1920s when King Rama VII built a seaside summer palace for his beloved Queen Rambai Barni at **Hua Hin** on the Gulf of Thailand. The king dubbed it Wang Klai Kangwon ("Far From Worries") and that fairly well describes the mood of modern Hua Hin, probably the most low key and laid back of all the major Thai beach resorts. The nation's first golf course took shape nearby and a new railway line brought eager bathers from Bangkok, the start of a beach boom that has now lasted for nearly a century.

The royals still frolic in Hua Hin (behind very high walls, mind you), but there are plenty of ways that mere mortals can entertain themselves, including a hot new sport – kiteboarding. Other options include bare-back horse riding along the strand and half a dozen excellent golf courses. There's even a winery, **Hua Hin Hills Vineyard** (204 Moo 9, Baan Khork Chang Patana, Nong Plup, Hua Hin, Prachuap Khiri Khan, 77110 Thailand; +66.81.701 0222; huahinhillsvineyard.com) on the grounds of a former work elephant training camp in the jungle highlands behind the coast.

Located near the southern end of the beach strip, the **Let's Sea Hua Hin Al Fresco Resort** (83/188 Soi Talay 12, Khaotakieb-Hua Hin Rd, Hua Hin, 77110 Thailand; +66.32.536 888; www.letussea.com; see pages 190–191) can easily be described as a modern take on the royal beach treatment. And while you and your darling may not get as much pampering as the king and queen, it comes pretty close. Take your pick between Moon Deck Suites with private rooftop retreats

THIS PAGE: Southern Thailand's mainland coast is renowned for its sheer limestone cliffs, caves and other "karst" formations.

OPPOSITE: Luxurious Water Villas tucked between giant boulders at the Sixth Senses Ninh Van Bay, not far from Nha Trang along Vietnam's central coast.

Asia's Best Mainland Beaches

THIS PAGE: *Beaches along the east coast of Peninsular Malaysia are a nesting place for several sea turtle species including the giant leatherback.*

OPPOSITE: *A one-hour flight south of Mumbai, the old Portuguese enclave of Goa is now India's hippest beach resort area.*

couples who want to combine a beach holiday with something more organic, like wildlife watching, trekking and taking a dip in the jungle pools at the bottom of waterfalls found in nearby Khao Phanom Bencha National Park. Krabi is also a jump-off spot for daytrips to several dozen idyllic islands. Caving and rock climbing in the area's iconic karst terrain is also popular. Krabi-based **Andaman Adventures** (23/8 Moo 2, Ao Nang, Krabi 81000, Thailand; +66.84.627 6779; www.andamanadventures.com) can organise a number of adrenaline-packed outdoor activities, including kayaking tours through the nearby islands, white-water rafting in Khao Sok National Park, and a new sport known as deepwater soloing, which is free climbing up a sheer cliff face to a place where you can leap into the deep blue sea.

Malaysia: Coast to Coast

Peninsular Malaysia also boasts a long and varied coastline. Literally picking up where Thailand leaves off, the northwest coast is dramatic "karst" topography – sheer limestone cliffs and deeply indented bays framed by warm turquoise waters. Further south along the fabled Strait of Malacca, the shoreline alternates between sandy strands and rich mangrove habitats. The east coast, on the other hand, looks more traditionally tropical – coconut palms and casuarinas along golden sands that seem to stretch on forever. Given Malaysia's efficient highway system and relatively short distances, you and your lover could conceivably take in both sorts of coast during a honeymoon or holiday.

The stretch between Malacca and Port Dickson is an ideal place to base a west coast beach getaway because this area allows you to combine fabulous sea and sand with history, shopping and delicious local cuisine. Highlights of this coast include the whitewashed colonial lighthouse at Tanjung Tuan and its resident monkey troupe; the 18 km of uninterrupted beach around Port Dickson; and the old colonial city of Malacca with its 500-year-old treasure trove of Portuguese, Dutch and British architecture.

Modelled after a traditional Malay fishing village, **Avillion Port Dickson** (3rd Mile, Jalan Pantai, 71000 Port Dickson, Negeri Sembilan, Malaysia; +60.6.647 6688; www. avillionportdickson.com; see pages 162–165) offers a wide variety of coastal accommodation – from beach chalets that open right onto the sand to classic over-water chalets with private decks and outdoor showers, as well as posh water villas. Couples can slant their stay towards spa treatments or a yoga retreat, or splurge on a "Drive Me to Avillion" romance package that includes limousine transfers from Kuala Lumpur, a spa treatment, candlelit dinner, sparkling wine and chocolates.

Over on the other side of the peninsula, the coastal stretch between Kuantan and Kuala Terengganu presents a combination of scenery, beaches and activities. Nature lovers flock to Cherating Beach to watch giant leatherback turtles lay their eggs. You can also visit the government-run turtle sanctuary at Pantai Chendor.

where you can make wishes upon the starry skies, or Studio Piers with direct access to the resort pool. Each room comes with an expansive terrazzo bathroom and oversized tub, and separate rainshower for two. In addition, the mood lighting, coupled with the Let's Sea "laZzzzz" bed creates the ideal ambience and comfort for a beach vacation.

Over on the other side of the peninsula, **Krabi** and its beaches face the Andaman Sea, flanked by towering limestone mountains and rainforest. The town makes an excellent base for

A number of handicraft centres in and around Kuala Terengganu produce and sell a wide variety of traditional Malaysian arts and crafts, from *kris* and *batik* paintings to *songket* and colourful kites.

Given its traditional look and feel, the **Tanjong Jara Resort** (Batu 8, Off Jalan Dungun, 23000 Dungun, Terengganu, Malaysia; +60.9.845 1100; tanjongjararesort.com) could easily be mistaken for another artisan cluster. "Unmistakably Malay" is the motto of this tranquil beachfront retreat, designed to reflect the grandeur and elegance of the region's 17th-century royal palaces. Its traditional Malay cuisine is amongst the best you will find along the east coast. In addition to more modern resort activities, Tanjong Jara also offers couples the opportunity to try *batik* painting, kite-making, Indera Deria (Malay-style yoga) and cookery classes together.

Goa: From Hippies to Hip

Founded just six years after Columbus landed in the Americas, **Goa** was created by the Portuguese as one of their gateways to the subcontinent. In modern times the Indian Ocean enclave has transformed into India's premier beach resort. Blame it on the Western hippies who flocked here in the 1960s and 70s in search of free love, cheap highs and beach parties that raged from dusk till dawn. The flower children are long gone, but they were around just long enough to ignite the transformation of Goa into a hip and upscale choice for Indians and chic jetsetters from overseas.

Parading up and down Anjuna Beach and the other main strands is Goa's main activity, followed closely by hanging out at the waterfront bars and cafés. The usual array of water sports is also available: scuba diving and snorkelling, windsurfing and sailing. If you and your significant other dig culture, then take a stroll around old Goa town and its collection of UNESCO World Heritage colonial buildings. The body of St Francis Xavier rests in a silver casket inside the 16th-century Basilica of Bom Jesus, across from the massive Sé Cathedral. The locally based **Heritage**

Network (+91.83.2395.2097; www.heritagenetworkindia.com) offers guided walking tours of the old town, as well as traditional dinners and folk dance performances in local historic homes.

It may not be the swankiest digs, but **Elsewhere... The Beach Houses & Otter Creek Tents** (www.aseascape.com) certainly has the most interesting name of any Goan hotel. It might just be the most romantic – colourful bungalows spread along a golden beach and canvas-roof cottages strewn along a mangrove creek that leads down to the same strand. And talk about seclusion: Elsewhere is actually beyond the end of a road in North Goa, reachable via a bamboo bridge and sandy track. Book out the entire compound and bring your whole wedding party along. ~ **JY**

From Bloomers to Bikinis

It wasn't until the early 18th century that mankind began to consider the seaside as a place of relaxation and recreation. Men generally swam naked back in those days. In fact, male skinny-dipping wasn't outlawed in Britain until 1860. But from the onset of beach vacations, there was an effort to cover up as much of the female anatomy as humanly possible. Early women's bathing costumes stretched all the way down to the wrists and ankles and generally included some sort of head cover.

After the turn of the 20th century, female swimsuits quickly evolved from long-sleeved bloomered bathing dresses to the surprisingly sexy 1920s one-piece suits. The bikini was born after World War II and named after a South Pacific atoll where the atomic bomb was tested because its impact on the beach vibe was so explosive. Bikinis also became skimpier as time went on, culminating in Brazilian string bikinis that leave very little to the imagination.

Island Hopping Holidays

With the alluring combination of sun, sea and sand, tropical islands have long proved popular with romantics of every persuasion, perfect for a honeymoon, anniversary trip or even a first date. With over 25,000 islands to choose from, Asia offers plenty of paradise.

Islands have always occupied a special niche in the human imagination, dreamy visions of some far-off place where we can leave our worries behind, indulge our wildest fantasies, and slink into the arms of some exotic civilisation as the sun sinks beyond the coconut trees. Certainly, alpine meadows, desert oases and northern seascapes have their appeal, but how can anything top a combination of warm sun and a cooling sea breeze, coconut palms shading an endless white-sand strand, and turquoise water that's always a perfect temperature when it comes to setting an amorous mood. It's no wonder that so many romantic books and movies have been set on tropical isles, and likewise, why so many crooners have penned songs that summon up that same dreamy, exotic vibe.

Asia's islands also offer a vast array of vacation options. Mega resorts and chic boutiques are certainly not in short supply, especially on the better known islands such as Bali and Phuket. At the end of the day, Asia is the perfect location – maybe not a private strand for every single couple, but certainly a beach for every taste.

Indonesia: Bali & Lombok

Bali has been the quintessential island of romance since the 1920s, when foreign visitors were first swept away by the island's lush landscapes and rich culture. Nearly a century later, Bali remains a captivating island that's modern and ancient, crowded and compellingly empty, familiar and outlandishly different all in the same breath. What sets this volcanic isle apart from its Indonesian neighbours is the enduring strength of Balinese civilisation – a seething mass of painters, carvers, musicians and dancers who have transformed everyday life into one huge open-air drama that plays out in black-rock Hindu temples, thatched-roof villages and even along the island's vaunted beaches.

Like the geckos you find clinging to Balinese walls, the island is always changing colour, switching its spots. With its rowdy bars and dance clubs, **Kuta** is an all-night party city. **Nusa Dua** is for those who crave slick modern resorts with their own beaches and golf courses. **Seminyak** has always had the best eats and beach life, and **Sanur** is pleasantly relaxed. **Ubud** in the central highlands – with its emerald-green rice terraces and rapids – is all about solitude and luxury. Tee off inside a volcano; raft a white-water river; surf the famous break at **Uluwatu** – one Bali, many different moods.

Tucked up in the central highlands near Ubud, **Komaneka at Bisma** (Jalan Bisma, Ubud, Gianyar 80571, Bali, Indonesia; +62.361.971 933; www.komaneka.com; see pages 142–143) is typical of the hospitality couples find throughout the island. A contemporary take on traditional Balinese style and architecture, the rooms are decorated with rich fabrics and exquisitely crafted local furnishings. Echoing the nearby rice terraces, the resort crawls up a lush jungle hillside, each level affording another take-your-breath-away view of the highlands. The nine villas come with their own private terraces and plunge pools, although the long, thin pool that slices through the heart of the resort also invites you to take a dip. Komaneka's honeymoon package includes cultural activities, shuttle services, spa treatments for two and plenty of tasty treats.

At the cutting edge of the Bali beach experience are chic boutique hotels like the **Jamahal Private Resort** (Jalan Uluwatu 1, Jimbaran, Bali, Indonesia 80364; +62.361.704 394; www.jamahal.net). The name is a hybrid of the Sanskrit word for "precious" and the Indonesian word for "time". And that's exactly how this resort in **Jimbaran** treats couples seeking precious time together. Lush gardens transform each of the spacious, Balinese-style villas into a tropical oasis of privacy and intimacy. In addition to a swimming pool that backs onto many of the villas, Jamahal also has its own private beach club with lounge chairs, sun umbrellas and a waterfront bar with drinks and snacks. For couples who crave even more adventure, the world-famous surfing breaks of Uluwatu are minutes away.

Neighbouring **Lombok** is what Bali must have been like half a century ago – still largely undiscovered and thoroughly unspoilt, an unusual blend of Muslim and Hindu influences side by side. The best example of this cultural harmony is the 18th-century temple complex at **Lingsar**, which caters to both faiths. Lombok is ripe for freelance exploration, roaming back and forth across the island to places like the traditional Sasak village of **Karangbayan**, the sprawling Sweta market (where all the various arts,

crafts and foods of Lombok are sold) and the **Sukarare** district where traditional *songket* fabric is spun. Pack a picnic lunch and dine on the grounds of the Mayura Water Palace, built by the Balinese kings who ruled over Lombok during most of the 18th century.

Overlooking miles of almost always empty beach on the island's northwest coast, the **Tugu Lombok** (Jalan Pantai Sire, Sire Beach, Lombok, Indonesia; +62.370.612 0111; www. tuguhotels.com/lombok; see pages 158–159) epitomises what this island is all about. A place where bygone grace and tranquillity blend easily with modern indulgence and luxury in a setting that blows your mind – Bali looming across the water and volcanic Mount Rinjani soaring up from behind. A Buddhist meditation room, daily yoga sessions, spa trips to a nearby waterfall, an 18-hole golf course and expansive wine cellar are all part of the Tugu experience. The pièce de résistance, however, is the dining experience: couples can choose to have private meals in the gardens, on the beach, or in the room. Instead of restaurants, the resort arranges cultural dining experiences based on local rituals, costumes and cuisine.

Malaysia: Langkawi & Penang

The largest island off Peninsular Malaysia, **Langkawi** unfolds as a sweeping expanse of jungle-covered mountains, villages and rice paddies surrounded by the aquamarine waters of the Andaman Sea. Located about halfway between Penang and Phuket, the island is 40 minutes from

THIS PAGE (FROM TOP): The lavish Puri Dadap Merah suite at the Tugu Lombok resort is modelled after the architecture of an ancient temple; Matahari Beach Resort & Spa in Bali is framed by rice paddies, volcanic mountains and the deep blue sea.

OPPOSITE: Over-water bungalows (with very private balconies) are just one of the beguiling aspects of Coco Palm Bodu Hithi resort in the Maldives.

Island Hopping Holidays

restaurants and clubs that rocks around the clock, as well as the best place to catch boats to outlying islands like Pulau Singa Besar and Pulau Dayang Bunting, both part of a marine national park. The best beaches, though, are on the north shore, the secluded strand of Datai Bay, the black sands of Pantai Pasir Hitam, and the bright white Tanjung Rhu with its limestone bluffs and dreamy views up the coast to Thailand.

Langkawi is all about getting wet, on a couple's day at the beach or the various outdoor sports options. Just about everyone's favourite outing on the island is Telaga Tujuh (Seven Wells), a series of seven cool jungle pools linked by spectacular waterfalls, the surrounding jungle inhabited by monkeys notorious for pinching picnic lunches. The **Damai Indah** (Royal Langkawi Yacht Club, Jalan Dato Syed Omar, Kuah, Langkawi, 07000 Kedah, Malaysia; +60.17.584 9353; www.damaiindah.com) is a traditional Bugis-style teakwood sailing craft that makes both private and shared cruises through the Langkawi archipelago. You can charter the vessel just for the two of you for the whole day or only a sunset cruise. **Langkawi Kayak** (2 Taman Vokasional, Kuah, Langkawi, 07000 Kedah, Malaysia; +60.4.967 2259; www.langkawikayak.com) specialises in guided trips to the outlying islands and through the island's rich mangrove ecosystem.

Penang is all the various secrets of the Orient rolled into one. Cloud-shrouded mountains and crowded markets that reek of Indian spices. Mysterious temples where snakes

crawl around golden idols and whitewashed churches that might have been plucked from a village green in England. Palm-shaded beaches, jungle waterfalls, the call of a *muezzin* at the break of dawn – Penang is more like a dozen lands than a single spot off the west coast of Peninsular Malaysia.

Perched on the island's north shore, **Batu Feringgi** is the place to head for outdoor seafood eateries, luxury waterfront resorts and a long,

Honeymoon with Headhunters?

It's possible in the Malaysian state of Sarawak on Borneo island, especially along the wilder reaches of rivers where the indigenous Iban people live and welcome visitors for overnight or multi-day stays. To be honest, they gave up headhunting a generation ago. But there are Iban who remember the ways of the past and will gladly spin stories about the good old days. The Skrang is the closest wild river to the state capital of Kuching. Reaching an Iban village along its banks involves a half-day drive along the Trans-Sarawak Highway and then a one-hour canoe trip. Accommodation is either on the floor of the communal area in the main longhouse, or in simple wood-framed beds in a special longhouse for guests. The Iban will gladly share their food and *tuak* (a potent rice wine), and they will be delighted to demonstrate various aspects of their jungle culture: weaving, fishing and poison blowpipe hunting. The Sarawak branch of Diethelm Travel (www.diethelmtravel.com/malaysia) organises several river safaris and longhouse stay experiences.

THIS PAGE: A series of seven cascades that tumble through the jungle, Telaga Tujuh is a major draw on the Malaysian island of Langkawi.
OPPOSITE: The turquoise waters and dramatic limestone landscape of Koh Phi Phi are typical of the islands found along the Andaman Sea coast of Thailand and Malaysia.

the mainland by ferry and about half an hour's flight from Kuala Lumpur. Called the "Island of Legends" because of the amazing wealth of fables and folktales, Langkawi is also renowned for its natural beauty and pristine beaches.

There's a beach for just about every mood. Pantai Chenang is the busiest strand, a long strip of resorts, white strand of beach. Taking pride of place here is **Shangri-La's Rasa Sayang Resort & Spa** (Batu Feringgi Beach, 11100 Penang, Malaysia; +60.4.888 8888; www.shangri-la.com), one of the hotels that proved that Southeast Asia could do beach resorts as well as anybody on the planet. Three decades later, the resort's island paradise vibe seems as fresh as ever, especially the lagoon pool area with its massive shady trees and dreamy sea views. The modern tropical décor has often been updated, and Shangri-La's reputation for impeccable service is complemented by a wide array of couple-friendly activities such as spa treatments and golf.

Georgetown, the island capital, nestles on the northeast corner of Penang with narrow streets lined by shophouses and magnificent British colonial architecture around the Padang, the city retains a bygone air, almost as if it were left behind in a different era. Georgetown is so well preserved it often "doubles" for other cities in Hollywood versions of Asian history (like the recently released *Beyond Rangoon*). There are many ways for couples to while away a day in Penang, including a visit to the **Penang Butterfly Farm** (830, Jalan Teluk Bahang, 11050 Penang, Malaysia; +60.4.885.1253; www.butterfly-insect. com), the world's largest living butterfly menagerie, and a glide to the top of **Penang Hill** on the recently refurbished funicular railway with plenty of time for lunch, tea or desserts at the **David Brown Restaurant** (Strawberry Hill, Penang Hill, Penang, Malaysia; +60.4.828 8337; www.penanghillco.com.my).

Thailand: Phuket & Koh Samui

Phuket is the consummate jet-set retreat, a gorgeous island on the edge of the Andaman Sea that continues to attract the rich and famous in droves as well as ordinary tourists who have an eye for the extraordinary. Where else in Asia can you frolic through the waves on the back of an elephant? Or visit a beach made famous by the legendary James Bond? Much of the island is picture-postcard perfect: white-sand beaches framed in turquoise water, water buffalo set against a backdrop of emerald rice fields and sheer limestone cliffs that rise straight up from the water at **Phang Nga Bay** and the offshore islets of **Koh Phi Phi**.

The southern Thai island is also known for water sports. The King's Cup Regatta, Southeast Asia's most prestigious boating event, takes place off Phuket every December, starting with a candlelight ceremony at **Kata** beach. Some of the region's most spectacular scuba spots are within easy reach of Phuket, including the submarine caves at **Koh Dok Mai** and the spectacular **Similan Islands** in the Andaman Sea where divers often spot manta rays, leopard sharks and moray eels. Hardcore diving couples could easily wrap a honeymoon around one of the four-day liveaboard scuba trips offered by **Similan Diving Safaris** (13/19 Moo 7, Khaolak, Kukkak, Takuapa, Phang-Nga 82190, Thailand; +66.76.485 470; www.similan-diving-safaris.com).

Phuket's other claim to fame is some of the region's oldest and most luxurious beach resorts. Along with Bali, this is where the modern beach holiday phenomenon started 30 years ago. With more than 900 resorts –

many of them breathtaking – it's often hard to decide where to stay on the island. **SALA Phuket Resort & Spa** (333 Moo 3, Mai Khao Beach, Thalang District, Phuket, Thailand 83110; +66.76.338 888; www.salaresorts.com/ phuket; see pages 210–211) on the northwest shore consistently ranks amongst the best. Ensconced amidst an old coconut plantation, the resort overlooks the golden sands of **Mai Khao** beach. Starkly modern and refreshingly white, the pool suites and villas feature an air-conditioned indoor area adjacent to an al fresco area with private plunge pool, a full-size daybed and a two-person bathtub.

Koh Samui floats like an emerald gem in a turquoise sea called the Gulf of Siam. Pioneered by hippies in the 1970s and inhabited by upscale dropouts in the 90s, the island blends everything couples love about

Thailand – golden beaches, lush scenery, beach bungalows, boisterous clubs and spicy Thai food. The Samui vibe is being as individual as you want to be. If that means party, party, party, you can find it in abundance. That whole backpacker scene in *The Beach* starring Leonardo DiCaprio is abundant here.

The higher end of the resort market is personified by **Four Seasons Resort Koh Samui** (219 Moo 5, Angthong, Koh Samui, Surat Thani 84140, Thailand; +66.77.243 000; www.fourseasons.com/kohsamui; see pages 192–193), which crawls up a jungle hillside on the island's northwest shore. Suites and villas offer an amphitheatre view of the sea, sky and far-off islands. The secluded forest spa specialises in ancient and alternative treatments and therapies including the New Moon Ritual, Earth Goddess experience, Chakra Crystal massage and even one treatment that blends astrology and palm reading. Couples can book a private spa sala with twin indoor and outdoor Thai-style massage beds, outdoor shower and bathtub, and a steam room or indoor rainshower.

Indian Ocean Escapes: The Maldives & Sri Lanka

The ancient land of Serendib is a teardrop-shaped island at the tip of the Indian peninsula. It has been an important centre of Buddhism since the 6th century AD and is the only predominantly Buddhist nation among the Indian Ocean islands. Sri Lanka is a kinder, gentler version of India, with a population of about 18 million people. The landscape is incredibly diverse: coral reefs and palm-fringed beaches along the west coast, tea plantations in the highlands and thick elephant- and tiger-infested jungle in the far south. The feeling of the British Raj lives on in much of the island, especially places like the old hill station at Nuwara Eliyia and the fortress at Galle.

The late Geoffrey Bawa – one of Asia's most influential architects – designed many of Sri Lanka's more notable hotels. Couples can admire his unique "tropical modern" style in the island's cultural triangle, the capital Colombo and the fabulous beaches down south. Among Bawa's many stunning waterfront hotels is the **Jetwing Lighthouse Galle** (Dadella, Galle, Sri Lanka; +94.91.222 3744; jetwinghotels.com), perched on a bluff above a wild stretch of coast near the historic city of **Galle**. Every colour, every column, every view was created to accentuate the site's natural shoreline beauty. And if you should want to renew your vows – or have a second wedding Sri Lankan style – the resort can arrange all the local trimmings including a *poruwa* (raised platform) decorated with flowers, local girls to sing devotional songs , Sri Lankan drummers, dancers and an *ashtaka* (holy man) to perform the ceremony in Sinhalese.

Divers have long sought the **Maldives** for the lavish coral reefs that surround the 19 atolls that comprise this tiny nation. In recent years the islands have also been discovered by showbiz celebrities, international sports stars and an increasing number of honeymoon

couples. Like a string of pearls dangling from the tip of India, the archipelago stretches due south into the middle of the Indian Ocean. The vast majority of the country's 300,000 people live in **Malé**, the lively little capital, and a handful of other populated islands. That means that most of the Maldives is virtually empty, a perfect place for couples to escape the rat race and get far away from the madding crowds.

Couples have nearly a hundred resorts from which to choose, most of them located on private islands and reachable only by float plane or private boat. **Cocoa Island** (Makunufushi, South Malé Atoll, Maldives; +960.664 1818; www. cocoaisland.como.bz; see pages 168–169) personifies the Maldives experience, a stunning boutique resort on a sliver of sand in what seems like the middle of nowhere. The spacious over-water Dhoni Suites hover above a turquoise lagoon, their wooden architecture inspired by the traditional dhoni sailing boats that still ply these islands. You and your lover can literally walk out the back door and down a flight of steps into the sea.

The Philippines: Palawan

Palawan in southern Philippines offers something that has largely vanished from the rest of the island nation: unspoiled nature. It comes in myriad forms including vacant beaches, vast tracks of virgin forest, secluded turquoise coves, nature reserves, marine national parks, sparkling coral reefs and underground rivers. Stretching 425 km from north to south, Palawan is flanked by the Sulu Sea on one side and the South China Sea on the other. It has more than 1,700 "outriders" – smaller islands, sand bars and coral reefs that wrap around the coast – a utopia for scuba divers, snorkellers and kayakers.

The coast features towering cliffs that plunge straight into the sea, majestic rock outcrops and secluded white-sand coves that can only be reached by foot or boat. Limestone formations predominate both above and below ground, including St Paul's Subterranean River, an 8-km stretch of limestone cavern that spills into the South China Sea. Locally based **Sakura Charters** (Rizal Ave Extension; Puerto Princesa City, Palawan, Philippines 5300; www.sakuracharter.com) runs liveaboard dive trips to the nearby Tubbataha Reefs marine World Heritage Site and day cruises to the underground river.

The region's swishest digs is **Amanpulo** (Pamalican Island, Philippines; +63.2.976.5200; www. amanresorts.com; see pages 172–173), a private island resort in the Sulu Sea off the northeast coast of Palawan. The only way to reach the resort – short of piloting your own boat – is by scheduled charter flight from Manila. The 40 casitas, perched right on the beach or in the lush gardens behind, are a modern take on the traditional Filipino *bahay kubo* house. Tucked in the forest at the back of the resort, these villas feature sensuous two-person bathtubs next to floor-to-ceiling windows that give soaking couples a panoramic view of the jungle outside. ~ JY

Bright Lights, Big Cities

From posh restaurants and boisterous nightlife to theme parks and cultural icons, world-class cities like Hong Kong, Shanghai, Singapore and Tokyo present boundless opportunities for couples to explore, encounter and be entertained together.

Asia's urban areas are the stuff of legend, cities that are justifiably world famous from many different points of view. They flaunt unsurpassed shopping and thriving after-dark scenes, with both highbrow culture (theatre, dance and music) and lowbrow high jinks (bars, nightclubs and casinos). Many of Asia's best theme parks – like Hong Kong Disneyland and Universal Studios Singapore – are also located within the cities, as are many of the region's top museums, religious shrines, royal palaces and gardens.

Cities can be explored in several different ways. Some prefer to wander about aimlessly, without any sort of set plan; each day is a new adventure that unfolds. Others opt for a much more structured approach, a slate of guided tours and scheduled events that get them from place to place. No matter how you and your partner decide to discover a metropolis, it's likely to be an unforgettable experience.

Tokyo: Japan's Eclectic Capital

Tokyo could be the hippest town on the entire planet, as well as one of the more exciting cities for a romantic urban getaway. The Japanese metropolis is huge and sprawling, and often daunting to first-time visitors. But in recent years it has become much more user-friendly thanks to an explosion of English-language signs and local English speakers. In addition, there's an urban transit network (subways and trains) that can whisk you to the most popular neighbourhoods and sights in a matter of minutes.

Much of Tokyo lends itself to couple-outings, places that can take an entire day to explore together. **Akihabara** is called "Electric City" because of its neon lights and electronics shops, but the high-rise neighbourhood is also ground zero for Japan's thriving comic book (manga), animation (anime) and "cosplay" (costume play) crazes. The eight-storey department store **Yodobashi** (Hanaoka Kanda, Chiyoda-ku, Tokyo; +81.3.5209 1010; www.yodobashi-akiba.com) sells 300,000 different electronic items and gadgets including cameras, computers and just about anything that plugs in or uses batteries. The place is like a circus, salesmen standing on footstools,

Asia's Tallest Buildings

With structures like the Empire State Building and Willis (Sears) Tower, the United States long dominated the other "race into space" – constructing the world's tallest buildings. That is now changing – the economic boom that started in the 1980s brought increasingly taller structures to Asian cities. Asia currently boasts the world's six tallest buildings and 16 of the top 20. Towering over everything else is the 828-metre Burj Khalifa in Dubai, a pencil-thin high-rise completed in 2010 and more than twice as tall as the Empire State Building. The current runner up is Taiwan's Taipei 101 (508 metres); followed by the Shanghai World Financial Center in China (492 metres); the International Commerce Centre in Hong Kong (484 metres); and the Petronas Twin Towers in Kuala Lumpur (452 metres).

shouting out the latest deals through megaphones. **Tsukumo Robot Kingdom** (3rd Floor, Tsukumo Denki Building, 1-9-7 Soto-kanda, Chiyoda-ku, Tokyo; +81.3.3251 0987; robot.tsukumo.co.jp) hawks a wide range of automated druids, from a Hello Kitty robot that responds to Japanese language commands to a Kondo KHR-2 robot that plays air guitar and kicks a football.

Harajuku is the hub of Japanese youth fashion and style, a place to shop for the latest outfits and accessories or merely people watch. "Harajuku Girls" gather here on weekends to flaunt their offbeat fashions and bizarre personas. They linger on the bridge near Harajuku train station or parade along super-trendy Omotesando boulevard, where most of the international designer shops are located. Funky local boutiques – like Device, N°44 and the original Bathing Ape store – are more often found on back lanes like Takeshita-dori. Escape the crowds in nearby Yoyogi Park, one of the city's largest green spaces and home to the revered Meiji-jingu shrine. On weekends, the park hosts live bands and a flea market.

Overlooking the Imperial Palace grounds and located near the Ginza shopping district and main railway station, the **Peninsula Tokyo** (1-8-1 Yurakucho, Chiyoda-ku, Tokyo 100-0006; +81.3.6270 2888; www.peninsula.com/tokyo) offers an ideal place to base your Japanese honeymoon. The sleek modern décor goes hand-in-hand with multiple high-tech amenities. Guests can monitor lights, curtains, room temperature and

THIS PAGE (FROM TOP): The Imperial Palace in Tokyo is one of several spectacular royal abodes that grace Asia's big cities; Tokyo's fashion-savvy Harajuku Girls add a splash of excitement to the already hip city.

OPPOSITE: Spectacular new skyscrapers like the Burj Khalifa in Dubai – the world's tallest building – have pushed Asian cities into the sky.

average humidity from a wireless remote control. Another LCD screen instantly tells you the weather conditions outside. The bathroom features a wall-mounted TV that you can watch while soaking in the tub, and boasts a robotic toilet with more than a dozen different flush settings. Yet, there are plenty of romantic corners: a penthouse bar with views over the Royal Palace grounds, a handcrafted chocolate shop off the lobby, an indoor pool that looks like something out of *Star Trek*, or the neighbourhood in which you can take a romantic stroll with a his-and-her iPod tour garnered from the front desk.

Seoul: The Korean "Heart"

With a population of over 11 million, **Seoul** has grown into the globe's fifth largest metropolitan area, a thoroughly modern city of glass-and-steel façades with 21st-century attitudes. Its residents are among the world's most frequent users of mobile phones, computers and interactive cyber games. "PC bangs" (Internet parlours) are now more prevalent than kimchi stalls. Yet beneath this futuristic façade lies something far different, a kinder and much more gentle Seoul that nearly got swept away in the rush to modernise.

As the long-time base of Korea's powerful Joseon Dynasty, Seoul boasts a wide array of ancient gardens and palaces where lovers can stroll and imagine the romances that unfolded within during ancient times. The 15th-century **Changdeokgung** (110-360 Yulgok-ro, 99 Jongno-gu, Seoul; +82.2.762 8261; eng.cdg.go.kr) was a hub of imperial

power for more than 500 years. The last empress of Korea lived here until her death in 1966 and members of the royal family lingered until the late 1980s, living in seclusion in a section of the palace originally built for a royal concubine.

Another trip down memory lane is the daily changing of the guards at **Deoksugung** (5-1 Jeong-dong, Jung-gu, Seoul; +82.2.771 9955; www.deoksugung.go.kr), a spectacular event that runs for more than half an hour. After over a century on hiatus, the ceremony was resurrected in the 1990s as a means to celebrate the city's past. Korean scholars researched the flamboyant costumes and accessories in an attempt to portray history with as much accuracy as possible. Armed with royal banners and menacing weapons, several dozen guardsmen march through the palace's main gate to the blare of horns and conch shells, and a clash of cymbals and drums – a tremendous din that might have driven enemies away all on its own.

Located between these two palaces, funky **Insadong** is like a Korean version of Greenwich Village, a neighbourhood of students, artists and fashion mavens. Locals flock here to browse the art galleries and antique shops, munch their way through food stalls and watch a wide variety of street performers. Insadong is also renowned for its teahouse restaurants. Founded by a former monk, **Sanchon** teahouse (Jongno-gu, Gwanhun-dong 14, Seoul; +82.2.735 0312; www.sanchon.com) serves authentic Korean food prepared along strict

Buddhist guidelines, and eaten from little lacquered gingko wood "alms bowls" with dark wooden chopsticks. Some of the dishes are familiar (tofu and kimchi) but others alien. Among the exotic concoctions is the flat pancake-like *jeon* made with lotus root, pumpkin and corn; a fiery stew called *jjigae* heaped with radish, mushrooms and chilli peppers; and the deep-fried *yugwa*, a dessert fashioned from rice flour, honey and mugwort.

Perched on the edge of leafy **Namsan Park**, the elegant **Shilla Seoul** (202 Jangchung-dong 2-ga, Jung-gu, Seoul; +82.2.2233 3131; www.shilla.net) feels more like a resort than a traditional big city hotel. The Shilla boasts one of the capital's best swimming pools and its own sculpture garden, plus easy access to trails that lead through thick forest to the top of Namsan for panoramic views of Seoul. Couples can choose from chic modern rooms or traditional Korean-style suites with low tables and floor cushions.

Shanghai: Love On the Bund

Shanghai is growing faster than just about any major city in the world, a remarkable building boom and economic gold rush fuelled by the city's homegrown drive to get ahead. It's also the only big city in China (other than Beijing and Hong Kong) that can stand alone as a honeymoon destination or romantic escape, thanks to an exotic blend of old and new on either side of Shanghai's Huangpu River.

Old Shanghai is on the western side of the river, an area called **The Bund,** once the heart of the European concession. The waterfront buildings once housed foreign banks, trading houses and consulates, one of the world's great treasures of Art Deco architecture and other bygone European styles transplanted to the East. A stroll along the Bund

THIS PAGE: Shanghai blends futuristic architecture with a meticulously restored old town called The Bund along the western bank of the Huangpu River.

OPPOSITE: Seoul has revived its royal traditions in recent years with events like the daily changing of the guards at Deoksugung Palace.

Bright Lights, Big Cities

THIS PAGE: Form meets function at the Shanghai Museum, a storehouse of Chinese artefacts inside a building designed like an ancient bronze cooking pot.

OPPOSITE (FROM TOP): Reflected in the harbour both night and day, Hong Kong's skyline remains one of the world's most photogenic; British colonial-era trams still cruise between Causeway Bay and other parts of Hong Kong Island.

Promenade is the first thing that anyone should do on arrival, especially when the diffused light casts the riverfront in a romantic glow at dusk.

The iconic **Peace Hotel** (20 Nanjing Rd East; +86.21.6321 6888; www.fairmont.com/peacehotel) overlooking The Bund has been a hangout since the 1930s, one of the few places where one could find nightlife even during the dark days of the Cultural Revolution. Recently revamped by Fairmont into a luxury boutique hotel, Peace Hotel has regained its former elegance and standing as one of the world's great hotels. Even if you don't stay at this hotel, be sure to enjoy the cocktails and live music at the famous Jazz Bar.

Nanjing Road has turned into something of a mini Ginza, a three-mile-long pedestrian street lined with boutiques, flashy nightclubs and electronics stores. More than 600 shops cater to a wide variety of goods, prices and styles, from ageless Chinese souvenirs and factory overrun clothing to chic international boutiques like **Tiffany** (618 Nanjing Xi Lu; +86.21.6288 278; www.tiffany.com). One of the road's retail anchors is the 10-storey **Westgate Mall** (Nanjing Xi Lu 1038; +86.21.6218 7878; www. westgatemall.com.cn), home to Isetan department store, numerous restaurants and dozens of brand-name shops. A small tram ferries passengers along the boulevard.

Designed in the shape of an ancient bronze cooking vessel, the **Shanghai Museum** (201 Renmin Avenue; +86.21.6372 5300; www. shanghaimuseum.net) is probably the best of its kind in China, a priceless storehouse of ancient treasures from the various dynasties and one of the city's "must-see" locations.

Modern Shanghai sits on the eastern banks of the river. Rising from what used to be rice paddies and vegetable plots a generation ago, the futuristic Pudong district is now home to stunning 21st-century icons like the **Oriental Pearl TV Tower** with its giant spheres and the 101-storey **Shanghai World Financial Center** (100 Century Ave, Pudong; +86.21.3867 2008; swfc-shanghai.com) which lays claim to the world's highest observation deck – a sky-high 474 metres above street level.

Hong Kong: An Intoxicating Blend

Like its Pacific Rim sisters Sydney and San Francisco, **Hong Kong** is an intoxicating blend of water and hillsides, cutting-edge skyscrapers and Victorian-era architecture, views that seem to stretch forever, and tiny snapshots of local life. In other words, it is a city rife with romance; one that provides the ideal setting for a honeymoon or an amorous getaway. And like the other two cities, one of the best ways to sink into the Hong Kong vibe is simply sitting somewhere: in a park or along the waterfront, and watching the world go by.

Of course, there are plenty of things for the two of you to do, starting with local transportation. Ride the historic **Star Ferry** (+852.2367.7065; www.starferry.com. hk) back and forth between **Hong Kong Island** and the **Kowloon** side, or the other ferries to the outlying islands like **Lantau** and **Cheung Chau**. Hop on the Peak Tram to the summit of Victoria Peak, gawk at the views, grab a bite to eat, and if you've got the time (and the energy) walk all the way back down to the harbourside. Get a top-deck seat on one of the old double-decker street trams that still

rumble between Wanchai and Western District. Glide between Central District and Mid-Levels on the world's longest escalator, hopping off here and there to explore the antique shops of Hollywood Road or the trendy bars and restaurants of the hillside SoHo district. Get a bird's-eye view of the city on one of the vertigo-inducing "flightseeing" tours offered by **Heliservices** (+852.2523 6407; www.heliservices.com.hk).

Sooner or later, you and your partner will not be able to resist shopping. The glitzy malls may get all the press, but street markets are still the life and soul of Hong Kong, helter-skelter places where both locals and resident expats browse for bargains after work and on weekends. They range from the legendary Stanley Market on the south side of Hong Kong Island (best on Sunday mornings when you can combine shopping with a pub crawl along the waterfront); to the dark and brooding lanes of Western District (where foreigners are usually few and far between); to Kowloon's mischievous Night Market where knock-offs are still the rage.

The waterfront **Hotel InterContinental Hong Kong** (18 Salisbury Rd, Kowloon; +852.2721 1211; hongkong-ic.intercontinental.com) could be the world's most feng shui-friendly hotel, with an elongated entrance and glass-walled lobby allegedly designed to facilitate the passage of the "nine dragons", said to dwell in the mountains that flank Kowloon district. Whether it's the iconic rooftop pool terrace (with its spa cabanas) or the floor-to-ceiling

Bright Lights, Big Cities

THIS PAGE (FROM TOP): The legendary Emerald Buddha lies inside the golden-domed Wat Phra Kaeo temple in Bangkok; paintings of Buddha images for sale in the sprawling Chatuchak Market.

OPPOSITE: Sri Srinivasa Perumal temple in Singapore's Little India district, one of several ancient neighbourhoods that make the Lion City a mosaic of old and new Asia.

windows of the corner suites, the InterContinental offers the city's most spectacular harbour and skyline views, especially at sunset when the lights start to twinkle on the other side of the water. A number of the suites feature private terraces with outdoor plunge pools, where a twosome can contemplate the skyline in absolute privacy.

Bangkok: Buddhas & Bustling Markets

Thailand's "City of the Angels", **Bangkok**, is a huge, hip metropolis where the action never seems to stop. Although ancient temples and glittering royal palaces still dominate the heart of the city, the rest of Bangkok has morphed into a flashy city of the future where high-rise towers, elevated freeways and air-conditioned malls are the norm. Yet beneath this Blade Runner façade, traditional Thai customs continue to flourish – a city of Buddhist shrines, ever-present smiles and food that will knock your socks off.

First rule of touring Bangkok – wear a pair of shoes that is easy to slip on and off – because you're going to be cruising through a whole lot of places where footwear is strictly verboten. Start with the most important shrine in all of Thailand, the Temple of the Emerald Buddha (Wat Phra Kaeo) inside the Grand Palace complex (Na Phra Lan Rd near Sanam Luang, Bangkok). Adjacent to the palace is the rambling Wat Pho or Temple of the Reclining Buddha (Sanam Chai Rd at Maharaj Rd, Bangkok; +66.2.225 9595; www. watpho.com), famous for both its

huge statue and a massage school where the young monks will gladly soothe your aching muscles. Watch the sunset from the golden mount of Wat Saket (Ratchadamnoen Klang and Boripihat Roads, Bangkok) and then take a boat across the **Chao Praya River** before dawn the following morning to watch the sunrise from the steps of the glass-covered Wat Arun, on the west bank of Chao Praya River.

Although air-conditioned malls are where the hip, young Thais tend to hang out, Bangkok's famous street markets are alive and thriving. You could easily spend a whole day at the weekend Chatuchak Market – over 15,000 stalls that sell just about anything you could ever want to buy (including monkeys). If fake bling is your thing, browse for brand name knock-offs at the Patpong Night Market in the heart of the "wicked" entertainment district.

The Sukhothai Bangkok (13/3 South Satthorn Rd; +66.2.344 8888; www.sukhothai.com) may be the only hotel on the entire planet based on a fabulous ancient civilisation – the eponymous ruined city in northern Thailand. Often ranked amongst the best hotels in the world, The Sukhothai sprawls across several acres of tropical gardens in the middle of modern Bangkok, looking more like a royal palace than a place where mere mortals might actually sleep. The regal lobby, the palatial hallways and the reflecting pond with its stone stupas add to the illusion that you have stepped into the past rather than a modern hotel.

Singapore: Romance in the Lion City

Singapore may be a futuristic high-tech wonderland, but it's also one of the region's most romantic destinations, an island that blends old British colonial charm and exotic Asian neighbourhoods with some of the most incredible modern architecture anywhere on the planet. Throw in great shopping, good nightlife and an increasing menu of outdoor options and you've got all the makings of an astonishing tropical honeymoon. Anyone who thinks the "Lion City" isn't passionate should drop in on Valentine's Day, when much of the shopping district is draped in pink and reservations must be made at restaurants for their romantic meals.

Despite its sleek high-rise skyline, Singapore has preserved many of its colourful old neighbourhoods – 200-year-old ethnic enclaves where you can sample the sights and sounds of several distinct Asian cultures. Dig into curry served on a banana leaf or get your fortune told by a psychic parrot in Little India. Browse for *batik sarongs* and beautiful Persian carpets in the myriad shops along Arab Street. Treat yourself to a traditional massage at an oriental spa or light joss sticks at the ancient Thian Hock Keng (Temple of Heavenly Bliss) on Telok Ayer Street, near Chinatown.

Singapore's abundant green space includes ordinary parks and gardens ripe for a romantic stroll, rainforest reserves with hardcore hiking trails, and several world-class wildlife attractions. **The Singapore Zoo** (80 Mandai Lake Rd, Singapore 729826; +65.6269 3411; www.zoo.com.sg) boasts the world's largest orang-utan colony and an incredible walk-through exhibit named Fragile Forest where you can get up close and personal with Asian rainforest creatures like orang-utans and tigers. The adjacent **Night Safari** is a unique after-dark zoo that showcases (and breeds) nocturnal animals from around the globe.

Singapore also flaunts a surprisingly good party scene. The century-old **St James Power Station** (3 Sentosa Gateway, Singapore 098544; +65.6270 7676; www.stjamespowerstation.com) has morphed from an electricity generator to an eclectic nightlife hub. The entertainment hotbed prides itself on its 11 different venues under one roof, including a jazz club, wine bar, sports bar, Mando pop dance venue and Latin music club where salsa, merengue and tango take over the floor each night. Other after-dark party spots include the beach side of **Sentosa Island** and **Singapore River**, and hangouts like **Clarke Quay** and **Boat Quay**. One of the island's other stylish clubs is **Zouk** (17 Jiak Kim St, Singapore 169420; +65.6738 2988; www.zoukclub.com), which sprawls through several old waterfront godowns. The first local club to play house music and host international DJs, Zouk features several distinct sections, including the surreal **Velvet Underground** (with its velvet-covered walls) and a club-within-a-club called **Phuture** that could easily double as the Starship Enterprise.

Tucked away in the middle of Singapore's Chinatown, the

sensuous **Scarlet Hotel** (33 Erskine Rd, Singapore 069333; +65.6511 3333; www.thescarlethotel.com) is the perfect antidote to the humdrum high-rise abodes that dominate the Singapore sleeping scene. Every one of the 84 rooms is distinct – a fresh and often shocking blend of Oriental touches and over-the-top California design themes like golden sunburst beds and fuchsia fabrics. Pairing Scarlet's out-of-the-world ambience is a pair of dreamy eateries, a breezy rooftop café with stunning city views

and the outlandish Desire – where browsing the menu is enough to rouse your senses.

Jakarta: Exotic Urban Delights

Up against tropical paradise islands like Bali and Lombok, bustling **Jakarta** is often overlooked as a holiday destination. For couples willing to take the time to explore, Indonesia's capital offers its own exotic delights. While it may not be the sole focus of a honeymoon or

romantic weekend, Jakarta makes a great stopover to an Indonesian beach getaway.

Start your exploration with a stroll through Merdeka (Freedom) Square, the largest park in the city centre, a massive area of trees and lawns surrounded by historic buildings. Over on the square's western edge is the National Museum (Jalan Merdeka Barat No 12; +62.21.381 1551), one of the finest in Southeast Asia. The collection covers nearly every epoch of Indonesian

history from the Stone Age and the early Buddhist and Hindu kingdoms, through the advent of Islam and Dutch colonial times. Highlights include the ancient Hindu stonework in the main courtyard; an exhibition of model houses from all around the archipelago, and the treasure rooms upstairs.

Another interesting amble is the old colonial neighbourhood of **Kota** in north Jakarta not far from the harbour. The Dutch are long gone but much of their architecture survives around a small square called the Taman Fatahillah. With a collection that ranges through several periods of Indonesian painting, the **Balai Seni Rupa** (Fine Arts Museum) (Jalan Pos Kota 2, Tambora, Jakarta, 11110; +62.21.690 7062) now occupies a lovely Greek-style building that served as a law court during colonial times. The gabled structure on the square's western flank is the **Museum Wayang** (27 Jl. Pintu Besar Utara, Mangga Besar 11110, Jakarta; +62.21.692 9560), showcasing traditional Indonesian puppets from around the archipelago. If you are there on Sunday, you can catch the puppet performances or watch how puppets are made. If you feel thirsty, duck into the beautifully restored Café Batavia (+62.21.691 5531; www.cafebatavia.com) on the north side of the square.

Then you can either drive or walk the short distance to Sunda Kelapa, Jakarta's oldest wharf, where hundreds of colourful Bugis schooners dock each day. The sailors are friendly – more than willing to have their photo snapped – and small boats can be hired for a tour of the harbour. A short drive to the east is Ancol Dreamland, a sprawling waterfront entertainment and recreation complex that includes a theme park with thrill rides, an oceanarium with marine animal acts, a water park with giant slides and a wave pool, arts and crafts market, 18-hole golf course and Indonesia's largest bowling alley.

Jakarta has plenty of sleek, modern five-star hotels, but the city's most romantic abode has to be **The**

Dharmawangsa (Jalan Brawijaya Raya No 26, Kebayoran Baru, Jakarta 12160; +62.21.725 8181; www.the-dharmawangsa.com) in the swanky Kebayoran neighbourhood. The design blends classic Indonesian Art Deco and modern touches, the structure wrapped around an expansive garden with a tree-shaded pool and outdoor bar. The hotel spa features private suites equipped with sauna, hot tub, steam room and massage beds for two, where couples can spoil themselves with a signature caviar facial or chocolate spa treatment. ~ JY

Theme Park Honeymoons

Couples with a shared interest in thrill rides and cute characters could easily create a honeymoon that revolves around urban theme parks in Tokyo, Hong Kong and Singapore.

In 1983, Disney sparked the trend with the launch of Tokyo Disneyland, its first venture outside of the United States and the third most popular theme park on the planet.

Another of Asia's oldest play zones is Ocean Park Hong Kong, a combined oceanarium, zoo and amusement park with over three dozen rides and attractions. Hong Kong Disneyland, on Lantau Island, features four classic Disney zones: Main Street, Adventureland, Tomorrowland and Fantasyland.

The latest addition in Singapore is an integrated resort, Resorts World Sentosa, a huge amusement and entertainment complex that includes a theatrical circus show *Voyage de la Vie* and the only Universal Studios theme park in Asia.

THIS PAGE (FROM TOP): *A dramatic lightning pierces the sky near Merdeka Square in the heart of Jakarta; three-wheeled rickshaw taxis are one of the many ways to get around the Indonesian capital.*

OPPOSITE: *Clarke Quay is one of several former commercial areas along the Singapore River that have been restored into modern eating, entertainment and shopping hubs.*

Gourmet Getaways

Food is one of Asia's eternal allures. An array of regional and national cuisine transforms the freshest ingredients from forest, field and sea into dishes that are often as artful as they are delicious. And it doesn't seem to matter what the source is: Asia's street stalls and five-star restaurants are equally skilled when it comes to creating gourmet fare.

Whether it's haute cuisine or hole-in-the-wall street fare, "food glorious food" is the major draw card of Asia's gourmet destinations. Tokyo and Hong Kong have already joined the ranks of international cities with Michelin star restaurants to their credit, but every Asian city has hidden gems that don't always make the culinary headlines. Asia's dining venues boast an almost infinite variety. Tokyo's sprawling fish market; Singapore's numerous hawker stalls; Shanghai's countless restaurants and India's former palaces count among the myriad of places in Asia where couples can enjoy romantic meals.

Japan: Outdoor Eating & Artful Meals

Japan is one of the few places where you can literally plan an entire honeymoon around eating. In Tokyo, start with the **Tsukiji Fish Market** in Tokyo (+03.3547 8011; www.tsukiji-market.or.jp/tukiji_e.htm), where the world's best tuna is landed each morning, transferred straight from fishing boats into the auction hall, from where the giant fish are whisked away to local restaurants and supermarkets. Get there early. Visitors who make their way to the market before 7 am can watch the whole process unfold before their very eyes, from the frenzied auctions to the master fishmongers who hawk more than 400 kinds of seafood from the 1,500 stalls scattered through the maze-like market pavilions. Afterwards, duck into one of the market cafés, like **Ryuzushi** (5-2-1 Tsukiji, Chuo, Tokyo Prefecture; +81 3-3547-6894) where fishermen and tourists alike wash down their fresh sushi breakfast with piping hot sake.

Another great Tokyo dining treat – almost unknown to tourists – is the outdoor *yakitori* restaurants in the **Yurakucho** district, near the train station of the same name in central Tokyo. Some are tucked down narrow alleys, others beneath old brick railway arches that somehow managed to survive World War II. While some are proper restaurants, others are no more than chairs and tables strewn across the sidewalk. Nevertheless, they all serve the most amazing barbecued meats – chicken, pork, beef and seafood grilled to perfection, with traditional side dishes like potato salad, green peppers, cucumbers, eggplant and leeks. Wash these meats down with copious amounts of local draft beer.

Japan's most sumptuous dining treat is *kaiseki*, a traditional multi-course meal with ingredients that change by the season and are rarely found outside the land of the rising sun. Often called "edible art", *kaiseki* dishes often resemble tiny gift packages that should be safeguarded in a jewellery box rather than eaten. The number of courses can run as high as 14 for a single meal, most of them vegetarian or seafood. *Kaiseki* chefs create hundreds of different courses for selection and are continuously thinking up completely new dishes.

Kaiseki reaches the height of perfection in **Kyoto** restaurants such as **Kikunoi** (459 Shimokawara-cho, Yasakatoriimae-sagaru, Higashiyama-ku, Kyoto; +81.75.561

0015; kikunoi.jp/english) where hostesses clad in pea-green kimonos escort patrons to private *tatami* rooms just big enough for two, with a window in each looking out onto a burbling brook or miniature Zen garden. Among Kikunoi's many *kaiseki* dishes are *hozuki* tomatoes fashioned into small pods containing a portion of *ayu* fish, sea cucumber, Japanese mountain peach and gingko beans; *Shiizakana* hotpot with boiled eggs, roasted eggplant, fish seasoned with *mitsuba* (Japanese wild parsley) and *sansho* (pepper powder); and a *Mukozuke* seafood course of thinly sliced *onaga* (red snapper) and *hamo* (conger eel) sashimi served on a lotus leaf with *ume* (sour plum sauce) and wasabi mustard.

China & Hong Kong: Meals with a View

A dozen different food cultures wrapped into one, China boasts the region's most diverse cuisine scene, a mouth-watering gamut that runs all the way from Cantonese seafood and spicy Sichuan hotpots to Shanghai noodles and classic Beijing duck. But when it comes to romance, nothing trumps a meal with a spectacular view.

Shanghai offers several sky-high treats. **Club Jin Mao** (Jin Mao Tower, 22 Century Ave, Pudong; +86.21.5047 1234 Ext. 8778; www.shanghai.grand.hyatt.com) is one such restaurant on the 86th floor of the Grand Hyatt Shanghai in the futuristic Pudong District. The views alone are enough to take your breath away, especially at the window tables. The restaurant's contemporary

THIS PAGE (FROM TOP): Shanghai has become one of the world's most exciting food cities thanks to restaurants like the sky-high Jade on 36 French gourmet restaurant at the Grand Hyatt Shanghai; the aptly named Cloud 9 bar at Grand Hyatt Shanghai.

OPPOSITE: The gourmet Neel Kamal restaurant and a flower-strewn barge are among the romantic dining options at India's Taj Lake Palace hotel in Udaipur.

THIS PAGE (FROM TOP): Dining at one of the floating restaurants in Aberdeen Harbour remains a quintessential Hong Kong culinary experience; afternoon dim sum and tea is another Hong Kong tradition.

OPPOSITE: Romantic "Dinner of the Spirit" beneath a banyan tree and the "Sanya Rak" dinner cruise at the Banyan Tree Phuket.

décor complements the sleek modern architecture you see outside. But the menu is firmly anchored in old-time Shanghai: drunken chicken and rich soups, steamed pork dumplings and sautéed eight treasures in sweet and spicy sauce.

Hong Kong offers plenty of choice in that regard, from spectacular penthouse and mountaintop eateries that overlook the city to incredible waterfront locations where you and your dinner date can watch the ferries cruising back and forth, and the skyline reflected in the harbour. One of the more distinctive venues is the **Oyster & Wine Bar** at the top of the Sheraton Hong Kong (20 Nathan Rd, Tsim Sha Tsui; +852.2369 1111; www.starwoodhotels.com) on

Kowloon side, where the cosy booths and subtle lighting complement the scenic views. The menu here includes more than two dozen types of oysters from all around the globe.

Higher still is **Hutong** (1 Peking Rd; 28F, One Peking Building, Tsim Sha Tsui; +852.3428 8342; www. aqua.com.hk), a northern Chinese eatery that hovers on the 28th floor of another Kowloon skyscraper. The décor is old-school China: wooden tables, silk curtains, antique screens and Buddha busts. The menu, however, is a modern take on traditional favourites. You could easily call Hutong's innovative cuisine nouvelle Beijing – dishes like braised prime beef wrapped in lotus leaves, fried pork tendon with scallions and dried prawn roe, sugar

cane prawns in lemongrass chilli sauce. But the pièce de résistance is the view, especially from a dimly lit table-for-two beside a window.

Locals swear by the ramshackle seafood eateries on the outer islands, especially the ones on **Lamma Island** and **Po Toi Island** that hang out over the water on stilts. Steamed garoupa, black-pepper squid and baked lobster with cheese sauce count amongst the specialities on these islands. Public ferries make the run from Central District, but the most romantic way to reach the outer isles is hiring your own junk for a full-day excursion that leaves plenty of time for hiking, swimming and beachcombing along the outer edges of Hong Kong. Several companies charter junks with skippers, one of which is **Saffron Cruises** (+852.2857 1311; www.saffron-cruises.com). Saffron also arranges sampan dinner cruises for two in Aberdeen Harbour on the south side of Hong Kong Island. The two-hour voyage includes a three-course meal with champagne.

Thailand's Offbeat Eats

Thai restaurants around the globe might all look the same, but not back home where offbeat restaurants are the rule rather than the exception. Whether one is high in the sky, at the end of a dock or lost in the jungle, Thailand is a world leader when it comes to unusual romantic dining.

In Bangkok, perched 61 floors above the central city and Chao Praya River, Bangkok's aptly named **Vertigo Grill & Moon Bar** (Banyan Tree Bangkok, 21/100 South Sathon Rd,

Sathon, Bangkok; +66.2.679 1200; www.banyantree.com) bills itself as one of the world's highest open-air restaurants. It's impossible not to get butterflies in your stomach while being escorted from the entrance to a table that seems to float above the Thai metropolis. Grilled seafood and steak are the house specialities. Afterwards, grab an after-dinner drink at **Moon Bar**. At the opposite end of Bangkok's dining scene in terms of ambience and elevation is **The Royal Dragon** (35/222 M.4 Bangna-Trad Rd; Bangna, Bangkok; +66.2.398 0037; www.royal-dragon.com), certified by the Guinness people as the world's largest restaurant. Waiters zip around on skates and fly through the air at this three-ring-circus of a restaurant, which also features kick-boxing, folk dancing and live music.

In **Phuket**, couples who are interested in cooking together can study the fine art of Thai cuisine at **Mom Tri's Kitchen** (12 Kata Noi Road, Kata, Phuket; +66.76.330 0157; www. boathousephuket.com). The popular waterfront eatery is the most renowned on the island, both for its wine cellar and a menu that overflows with wonderful local dishes – *tom yum* soup, *pad thai* and stir-fried prawns – and recipes that Executive Chef Tummanoon Punchun will teach. The chef has produced a cookbook of his recipes, available at the restaurant.

Four Seasons Tented Camp Golden Triangle (PO Box 18, Chiang Saen Post Office, Chiang Rai; +66.53.910 200; www.fourseasons. com/goldentriangle; see pages 188–189) in **Chiang Rai**, northern Thailand, offers a number of rustically romantic dining experiences. Among the choices are a private barbecue for two under the stars, a gourmet picnic at some secluded spot in the jungle, or al fresco dining around the campfire with elephants standing guard nearby. In keeping with the resort's Golden Triangle location, the menus blend Thai, Laotian and Burmese influences.

India's Geographical Feast

Much like its neighbour on the northern side of the Himalayas, **India** is large enough to host a number of distinct culinary cultures. Northern India and Punjab are known for their tandoori oven specialities; *biryani* rice dishes and creamy curries derived from Mughal days. The south is known for its coconut-based curries, copious spices and delicious rice-flour pancakes. Seafood is the operative word along India's long and varied coastline. Aside from these, there are the many regional cuisines: Portuguese-influenced Goan food; mutton dishes and a feast called *wazwan* in Kashmir; and fish cooked a dozen different ways in Bengal.

One way for couples to sample a wide range of Indian food on their honeymoon is a culinary tour that takes them to different regions – literally eat your way across the subcontinent while soaking up famous sights like the Taj Mahal. Luxury travel outfitter **Horizon** (www.horizon-co.com) organises two-week epicurean journeys across northern India with stops in Delhi, Agra, Jaipur and elsewhere. The

itinerary includes private cookery sessions, visits to local food markets, eating at gourmet restaurants and digging into home-cooked meals with local families.

You don't have to join a culinary tour to eat like a Mughal. India's palace hotels boast majestic dining rooms where the days of the rajahs live on in the décor, service and cuisine. One of the most amorous venues in Asia, the **Taj Lake Palace** (PO Box 5, Udaipur, Rajasthan 313 001, India; +91.294.242 8800; www.tajhotels.com) in the middle of Lake Pichola in **Udaipur** offers several romantic dining locations, including

Neel Kamal with its royal ambience and sumptuous Rajasthani cuisine. Couples staying at the hotel can also arrange intimate dining experiences anywhere they want on the property. Perhaps it's worth considering dinner on a marigold-bedecked royal barge floating on the lake.

Equatorial Eating Experiences

Asia's equatorial nations – Singapore, Malaysia and Indonesia – also have rich food cultures. Common popular dishes like nasi goreng (spicy fried rice), laksa (spicy noodle soup) and satay (barbecued skewered meats)

cross national boundaries and maritime barriers. Worthy of note, however, the three countries each have their own unique treats over and above these.

While **Singapore** certainly has its fine dining, the Lion City is world-famous for its hawker centres, which are clusters of small open-air eateries that often tout a variety of dishes. Historically they arose near public housing estates or transportation nodes (like Newton Circus). While Chinese food predominates, Indian and Malay cuisine are also found at these places. The mouth-watering spread includes Hainanese chicken rice, chilli

crab, char kway teow (fried rice noodles in black sauce) and oyster omelettes. Today, hawker centres (many air-conditioned) have spread across the island. Singapore has several dozen, ranging from old-style, high-rise hubs such as **Chinatown Complex** (335 Smith Street) to romantic waterfront **East Coast Seafood Centre** (1220 East Coast Parkway), where you can bookend your meal with a walk along the shore to admire the twinkling lights of the Singapore Strait.

Couples craving more upscale eats might want to check out the new **Ku Dé Ta** (SkyPark at Marine Bay Sands North Tower, 1 Bayfront Ave, Singapore

018971; +65.6688 7688; www.kudeta.com.sg) perched at 200 metres above the city on the top floor of the **Marina Bay Sands** casino hotel. If you can tear yourself away from the vertigo views, the menu unfolds as a feast of modern Asian cuisine, with dishes such as bamboo roasted black cod in red miso, steamed Sri Lankan crab claws, or lemongrass poached foie gras terrine. For dessert share a slice of steamed palm sugar cake, order another round of lychee martinis, and then take turns ogling each other and the panorama.

Firefly Suppers in Bali

For a completely different take on Indonesian dining, make a pilgrimage to Big Tree Farms (+62.361.461 978; www.bigtreebali.com) in upland Bali between May and September, when the world-renowned organic grower organises its Firefly Supper Series beneath the stars. The menu changes according to what's in season and includes selections from a bounty of more than 80 varieties of fruit and vegetables. The six-course dinner also features foods grown or raised by other local organic or sustainable farmers. Lit by hundreds of coconut-oil torches, the dining pavilion stands in the middle of an ancient coffee plantation and the view from your table is a sweeping panorama of highland Bali, including the island's last stand of old-growth forest. Big Tree spreads across the slopes of Mount Batukaru, Bali's second highest peak, in the Jatiluwuh area. As the area is so remote, the farm provides return transportation from your hotel to the Firefly location.

Hawker stalls are also a staple in **Penang**, the favourite foodie destination in Malaysia. The island also boasts one of Asia's best food blogs (makanpenang.blogspot.com), especially helpful to anyone who isn't well acquainted with local food. Penang's other claim to fame is a savoury hybrid of Chinese and Malay culinary influences – Nonya cuisine. Also found in Malacca and Singapore, Nonya cooking blends Malay spices and condiments with Chinese ingredients and cooking techniques to produce dishes found nowhere else on the planet. Among the many unique Nonya dishes are otak otak (a coconut-flavoured fish paté wrapped in banana leaf) and sambal sotong (chilli squid). One of the island's premier Nonya restaurants is **Hot Wok** (124-E & F Jalan Burma, 10050 Penang; +60.4.227 3368; www.hotwok.com.my), located in an old shophouse in historic Georgetown.

Bali may have more restaurants per capita than anywhere else in Asia, it's one of those places where it's hard to choose where you are going to eat on any given night. But when it comes to intimate dining, it's hard to beat the **Tugu Bali** (Jalan Pantai Batu Bolong, Canggu Beach, Bali; +62.361.731 701; www.tuguhotels.com; see pages 148–149) and its myriad eating venues. A traditional Balinese, open-air kitchen lies at the heart of the resort's **Waroeng Tugu** restaurant, where patrons eat at rustic antique tables while watching the chef prepare their chicken curry or beef satay right in front of them. Couples can also arrange a seafood barbecue on the beach for two, with only the

moon, the stars and a single torch for illumination, the black sand tingling your toes. Other très romantic venues include a private pavilion hovering above the lotus pond or a Peranakan-style room called the Black Chamber, decorated with local antiques, a single table for two and just enough room for Balinese dancers to entertain you during dinner. ~ JY

THIS PAGE: *Tugu Bali offers a number of intriguing dinner options, including a restaurant with a traditional Balinese open-air kitchen.*

OPPOSITE: *Singapore's highest dining venue is the breathtaking Ku Dé Ta on the roof of the new Marina Bay Sands hotel.*

Cultural Destinations

From the jungle-shrouded temples of Angkor to the giant stupa of Borobudur, from the Forbidden City to the Taj Mahal, Asia overflows with world heritage sites and time-honoured cultural gems that appeal to the serious history buffs, intrepid travellers and couples with a heightened sense of romance.

Anyone who thinks culture and honeymoons are poles apart needs a quick-potted lesson in history. The quest to discover history (with a huge dose of culture) is how modern travel started in the early 19th century. A group of young writers, painters and poets called the Young Romantics roamed Europe, North Africa and the Middle East in search of the historical icons of Western civilisation – the Great Pyramids, the Acropolis and the ruins of the Roman Forum. Along the way they often guzzled too much wine, munched too many olives and fell in love with one another, as well as locals they met in exotic foreign lands. Quite naturally, they romanticised the places where all of the wonderful encounters took place in books, poems and paintings that are now considered the classics of that era.

Extrapolate the concept by two hundred years and a couple of thousand miles farther east, and what we have today is Asia, the perfect place for a romantic journey back in time and amongst exotic cultures. What is more romantic than walking hand-in-hand amongst the ruins of Angkor Wat; watching a live performance of the *Ramayana* beneath a full moon at the Prambanan temples in Indonesia; sleeping in a real palace in Jaipur; or sneaking a kiss in one of the manifold temple gardens of Kyoto? Asia is ideal for a honeymoon or romantic getaway that combines culture and romance.

Love Amid the Ruins

Hue, in central Vietnam, is like a hologram: the image depends entirely on your angle of view. It is an intriguing city, and one of the most dazzling in all of Asia: a city of gardens filled with lotus ponds, tree-shaded avenues and the tantalising smell of flower blossoms; a city of the arts that gave birth to an architectural style that mixes mythical creatures, chromatic colours and ostentatious decoration, a sort of Oriental baroque; as well as a water town that spreads along the banks of the slow-flowing Perfume River (Song Huong).

The city's sprawling Citadel – home of the Vietnamese monarchy until 1945 – is now a huge open-air museum; while some of the palaces are left in ruins, others have been restored to their former glory. Upstream from the city, and best reached by riverboat, are the opulent royal tombs, every bit as impressive as Egypt's Valley of the Kings, and far less crowded. For the adventurous at heart, journey from Hue to Hoi An on a motorbike with **Hue Riders** (www.hueriders.com) or go on a surfing safari down to Lang Co Beach with its long, white-sand strand and turquoise lagoon.

Southeast Asia's most celebrated ruins, and one of the great treasures of human civilisation, is **Angkor** in northwestern **Cambodia**. Most of the attention goes to a single landmark: the massive Angkor Wat. The ancient metropolis actually sprawls across an area of 200 sq km, which includes hundreds of temples and palaces built between the 9th and 14th centuries AD when Angkor was the centrepiece of the mighty Khmer civilisation.

A visit to the main temple is highly recommended, but the best sunsets at Angkor are from the summit of Bakheng Hill, where you can snuggle up beneath a temple dedicated to Lord Shiva to watch the golden orb slowly sink over the Cambodian rainforest. Couples can choose to walk to the top or share a howdah on the back of an elephant. If you feel like having a picnic amid the ruins, it's best to choose one far away from the madding crowds, like jungle-shrouded Ta Prohm temple, where the roots of the giant kapok trees grow around the ancient stone walls like lovers locked in immortal embrace.

THIS PAGE (FROM TOP): The ruined city of Bagan (Pagan) in northern Burma (Myanmar) comprises over 5,000 temples, shrines and palaces; among Angkor's many ancient monuments are the solemn stone faces of Bayon Temple.
OPPOSITE: A magical dusting of snow covers Beijing's Forbidden City, once the seat of China's imperial dynasties and now a leading cultural tourism attraction.

THIS PAGE (FROM TOP): A kimono-clad geisha strolls through one of Kyoto's many gardens; visitors wash their hands before entering a Japanese Shinto shrine.

OPPOSITE (FROM TOP): Fashioned in the shape of a giant mandala, Borobudur is the world's largest Buddhist stupa; the nearby temples of Prambanan were built during a period when Java was the domain of Hindu rulers.

Nearly everyone who visits Angkor bases themselves in the nearby lakeside town of **Siem Reap**, where a wide range of accommodation can be found. The chic boutique **Hotel de la Paix** (Sivutha Blvd, Siem Reap, Cambodia; +855.63.966 000; www. hoteldelapaixangkor.com) blends ancient Khmer and modern Art Deco motifs into a gorgeous modern abode that offers a perfect focal point for exploring the ruins. The hotel's three-night "Intimate" experience is designed for dreamers, lovers and anyone wanting to capture the passion. It includes a romantic candlelit dinner for two, a hands-on "pamper-your-partner" massage lesson and a decadent breakfast in bed.

Nearly as large as Angkor, and far more remote, is the ruined city of **Bagan** (Pagan) in northern **Burma** (Myanmar). The numbers are overwhelming – more than 5,000 temples, stupas, palaces and shrines spread along the eastern bank of the Irrawaddy River, the bulk of them constructed between the 11th and 13th century AD. The golden-domed Ananda Temple is the most famous of these, but the upper levels of the terraced Thatbyinnyu Temple are the best place to watch sunrise over the misty Irrawaddy floodplain.

Book a hot-air balloon flight for two with **Eastern Safaris** (Business Suite 03-06, Sedona Hotel Yangon, Myanmar, +95.165 2809; www. easternsafaris.com) and glide across the sacred ruins. Alternatively, enjoy the view at ground level from the back of a pony cart driven by a local guide. Rather than staying ashore, couples can also explore the ruins on a luxurious **Road to Mandalay** river cruise (www.roadtomandalay.com; see pages 114–115).

Living History Enclaves

Three hours south of Tokyo via bullet train (Shinkansen) lies the ancient city of **Kyoto**, where so much of medieval Japanese culture was born and continues to thrive. The city's old **Gion** neighbourhood looks much the same as it did 400 years ago, a maze of narrow lanes flanked by delicate wooden buildings sheltered by bamboo blinds. Gion is the last remaining stronghold of the geisha, many of whom live in *okiya* (lodging houses) on the upper floors of these buildings. Visitors gather at twilight to watch the geisha commute to their places of work in small restaurants, bars and *ochaya* (tea houses) within the neighbourhood. Elsewhere, Japan's culture capital overflows with ancient temples, gardens and museums.

While Kyoto has some fine hotels, couples also have the option of staying overnight in an authentic *machiya* or townhouse – historic wooden structures with *tatami* bedrooms, sliding rice-paper doors and tiny Zen gardens where you can contemplate your love. **Iori Machiya Stay** (Sujiya-cho 144-6, Takatsuji-agaru, Tominokoji-dori, Shimogyo-ku; +75.352 0211; www.kyoto-machiya. com) has 10 different *machiya* to offer (choose from a selection of Meiji-era merchant homes to the deep, narrow Taisho-era homes).

Scattered in and around the Gion area, the *machiya* are fully restored with modern bathrooms and even kitchens for those who want to whip up their own romantic meals.

On the south side of Java island in Indonesia is the royal city of **Yogyakarta** and Kraton palace, home of the only autonomous monarchy left in Indonesia. The Javanese consider the Kraton (and its royal tenant) a direct spiritual link between heaven and earth, an architectural interface with the powers that be. Around 40,000 royal retainers live in and around the Kraton, and on any given day visitors can see them going about their duties as royal guards, dancers and musicians. Royal patronage also extends to the craft villages in the countryside around Yogya – Kota Gede is known for its silversmiths; Kasongan for its clay maestros; Pendowoharjo for its wooden maskmakers; and Gendeng for the men who make wayang puppets from thin strips of leather. The villages make great places to browse and buy honeymoon souvenirs, especially unique items that will summon memories of your romantic interlude long after the trip is over.

Just outside of the city stands Borobudur, the world's oldest and largest Buddhist stupa, erected between 775 and 840 AD. The huge circular temple was built in the shape of a mandala. Buried for centuries beneath volcanic ash, Borobudur was rediscovered in modern times and restored to its former glory. More than two million pilgrims and tourists trek to the summit each year. On moonlit nights between May and October the royal opera troupe performs the *Ramayana* epic on a massive outdoor stage in front of nearby Prambanan, a 9th-century Hindy temple complex about 18 km east of Yogya. This is an incredibly romantic way to punctuate a getaway to south Java.

Sprawling across a thumb-shaped peninsula between the Mekong and a slow-flowing tributary, **Luang Prabang** is an Asian version of Havana, a city preserved in an almost pristine state through a combination of politics, poverty and what some might call karma. Nowhere in Southeast Asia is there a more exotic skyline, a panorama of golden stupas and steeply pitched temples built during the time when Luang Prabang was the royal capital of Laos. *Tak-bat* – ritual alms collection – unfolds at dawn each morning, as a supernatural drumbeat summons hundreds of monks in flowing orange robes from their monasteries.

UNESCO declared the city of Luang Prabang a World Heritage Site in 1995, "the best preserved traditional town in Southeast Asia". Since then, many of the ramshackle old French colonial villas have been converted into lovely guesthouses and broken-down shophouses into cafés, galleries and trendy outdoor eateries, many of them perched on bluffs above the Mekong. From the muddy banks below, boats set off on the upriver journey to Thailand and the Golden Triangle. **Mekong Cruises** (50/4 Sakkarine Rd, Ban Vat Sene, Luang Prabang, Laos; +856.71.252 553;

Cultural Destinations

Khajuraho: The Kama Sutra in Stone

As much as Taj Mahal is a monument of love, Khajuraho is a shrine to unbridled sensuality. Built between the 9th and 12th centuries AD, the north Indian temple complex is world renowned for its erotic artwork, sandstone statues and carvings of naked *apsaras* and couples making love in just about every imaginable position. Very little is left to the imagination in this medieval masterpiece. Listed as a UNESCO World Heritage Site, Khajuraho remains the subject of intense speculation about why the ancient Hindus rendered such life-like erotic art. Was there a spiritual significance? Was it merely a guide to Tantric sex? The mystery adds to the shrine's timeless carnality. Don't forget to pack a copy of *The Complete Kama Sutra*, Alain Daniélou's modern translation of the classic, both for the insight it affords into ancient Indian culture and the tips it might give you for the honeymoon suite.

mekong-cruises.com) makes the upriver journey in two days on vintage teakwood riverboats, stopping overnight at an eco-lodge in a secluded hilltribe community.

One of the old colonial buildings has transformed into an elegant all-suite hotel called the **Amantaka** (55/53 Kingkitsarath Rd, Ban Thongchaleun; +856.71.860 333; www.amanresorts.com; see pages 160–161), the central courtyard now occupied by a swimming pool and sun chairs. Best for lovers are the two standalone Amantaka Pool Suites, replete with private verandah, spa treatment room, personal plunge pool and a large, indoor bathtub that can be lit up with candles and incense sticks.

Wonders of the World

Forsaking his homeland on the Mongolian steppes, Genghis Khan established Beijing as the capital of a united China in the 13th century AD, although the city wasn't called **Beijing** ("Northern Capital") until Ming Dynasty times. The Forbidden City arose between 1406 and 1420, hundreds of thousands of workers labouring night and day to create one of the world's great landmarks. Covering an area of 100 hectares, the heavily fortified domain includes six main palaces, dozens of minor palaces and more than 9,000 rooms.

Many of Beijing's other important sights were also fashioned during the Ming Dynasty,

including Tiananmen – the world's largest public square. Not far away stands the blue-roofed Temple of Heaven, a masterpiece of Ming architecture and once the scene of an annual Winter Solstice ceremony during which the emperor prayed for a good harvest. The Sons of Heaven normally spent the scorching summer months in the hills northwest of the capital, a vast garden area with lakes and hills called the Summer Palace. More than anywhere else in Beijing, the palace lends itself to romantic liaisons – strolling down the Long Corridor with its incredible paintings, over the 17 Arch Bridges or along the leafy shore of Kunming

Lake; paddling out to the Marble Boat where the Empress Dowager once watched Chinese opera performances; or dining on revived imperial court dishes at the restaurant inside the Ting Li Guan (Pavilion for Listening to the Orioles). And, of course, right outside the capital looms the Great Wall of China.

Drift back in time at **Kaorou Ji** (No 14, Qianhai Dongyan, Shishahai, Xicheng District, Beijing; +86.10.6404 2554), a 150-year-old restaurant renowned for its grilled meats and romantic location overlooking the canal that connects Qian Hai and Hou Hai lakes just north of the Forbidden City. The house speciality is barbecued lamb marinated in soy sauce, rice wine and coriander. Couples can dine inside the traditional Qingzhen (Muslim) eatery or opt for a romantic "floating" dinner on a flat-bottomed boat rowed around the lakes by your personal oarsman. The two-hour eating adventure also includes music and a chance to launch candles across the water on miniature boats. Afterwards, stroll across Yinding Bridge and grab an after-dinner drink at the trendy waterfront bars lining Qian Hai's north shore.

Nothing prepares you for your first glimpse of the **Taj Mahal** in the northern Indian city of **Agra**. Like so many other things that attract heaps of praise, you really do expect to be disappointed; the global icon can't possibly be as stunning as everyone says. But it actually is, especially at dusk and dawn, when the white marble turns a soft pink.

As everyone knows by now, the Taj was built as a monument of love, commissioned by the Mughal emperor Shah Jahan as the last resting place of his most cherished wife, Mumtaz Mahal. She died at the age of 38 while giving birth to their 14th child. The domed structure looks as fresh today as it must have been in the middle of the 17th century when it was originally built, its perfect symmetry reflected in a long man-made pond and the slow-flowing Yamuna River. The Taj is especially enchanting on full moon nights, when the grounds are open until midnight, the perfect time for an amorous stroll around the world's most romantic building.

If you're going to splash out on a hotel room during a honeymoon in India, then save your pennies for the astonishing Kohinoor Suite at the **Oberoi Amarvilas** (Taj East Gate Rd, Agra 282001, India; +91.562.223 1515; www.oberoihotels.com). Perched on the fifth floor, the suite's spacious living room opens onto a private balcony that floats just 600 metres from the Taj Mahal. Mirroring the famous landmark, the suite's white marble bathroom is made for romance, including a large, old-fashioned bath that is easily large enough for two, with its own picture window looking out onto the Taj. ~ **JY**

THIS PAGE: The ultimate tribute to love, India's Taj Mahal glows soft pink in the early morning light beside the Yamuna River.
OPPOSITE (FROM TOP): Beijing's Forbidden City basks in the glow of a full moon; the Pak Ou Caves and their myriad Buddha statues are one of the main attractions along the Mekong River between Luang Prabang and the Golden Triangle.

Action & Adventure

Asia overflows with adrenaline-pumping activities for couples who like to take their honeymoons with a huge dose of action – from white-water rafting in Borneo and wildlife safaris in India to trekking in Nepal and diving in Indonesia or in the Maldives.

Some couples just cannot while away their time or laze around even when they are on holiday. The idea of having a romantic dinner on an isolated beach or enjoying a couple's massage in a chic spa will hold no allure for them. The good news is that there are plenty of options for go-getting couples who need their adrenaline fix while on holiday – whether they are looking for speed, height, sensation, exertion or the ultimate a no-holds-barred mind-blowing experience.

With new adventure activities shaking up the scene every year, the variety and choices are limitless. For adrenaline junkies, opting for an adventure honeymoon could mean accomplishing a feat they will likely never get (or dare!) to do again, or visiting a place they might never return to. But don't forget, it's your honeymoon, so make sure there is a nice hotel and good food to return to at the end of the day. Finding a good travel agent to make the bookings and plan the logistics is vital.

Go Climb a Mountain

Mountaineering might not be the first activity that comes to mind when one thinks of honeymoons, or Asia. But if this sounds like your idea of newlywed bliss, the region offers abundant opportunities for mountain climbing, from easy day hikes that are suitable for just about anyone, to highly technical climbs that are amongst the most challenging in the world.

One of the region's most popular climbs is **Mount Kinabalu** in the Malaysian state of **Sabah**. It's easy to reach the base of the mountain from Kota Kinabalu and its international airport, and the terrain is varied enough to cater to both seasoned climbers and casual trekkers.

Mountain Torq (Unit 3-49, Asia City Complex, 3rd Floor, Jalan Asia City, 88000 Kota Kinabalu, Sabah, Malaysia; +60.88.268 126; www.mountaintorq.com) is making climbing much more accessible for people who don't have the technical skills. Situated in Kinabalu National Park, this outfit offers rock climbing, rappelling, mountaineering courses and the world's highest via ferrata. Italian for "iron road", the via ferrata is a series of steel rungs, rails and wire cables set along a mountain face which climbers scale with the aid of safety harnesses hooked onto the cables that line the route. The via ferrata, which takes three to four hours to complete, is set on the sheer Panar Laban rock face between 3,411 and 3,776 metres above sea level, topping out at just 325 metres short of the mountain's highest summit.

Mountain Torq also offers Mount Kinabalu trekking itineraries that run from a short "Walk the Torq" (two days and one night) to customised programmes for more experienced trekkers and climbers. If you and your partner decide to tackle Kinabalu on your own, do keep in mind that having an authorised guide is compulsory, and porters are widely available. More information is available on the **Sabah Tourism Board** website (www.sabahtourism.com). Summit round trip treks usually take two days, but couples can take an extra

day if they wish to fully appreciate the rarefied air and expansive views.

Annapurna in **Nepal** is one of Asia's most storied summits, and also one of the most dangerous. The climb is best tackled as part of an experienced guided party like those offered by **Explore Himalaya Travel & Adventure** (GPO Box 4902, Thamel, Kathmandu, Nepal; +977.1.441 8100; www.explorehimalaya. com) or **Alpine Ascents International** (109 West Mercer St, Seattle, WA 98119, USA; +1.206.378 1927; www.alpineascents.com). It takes about two weeks to scale the 8,091 metres of Annapurna I, the highest peak. There are two climbing seasons during the year – from March to May, and from September to November.

Another legendary peak is **Kilash** in **Tibet**, the highest mountain in the western part of Gangdise Shan, which carries significant meaning in several different religions. To Hindus it is the throne of Shiva, to Buddhists the "precious jewel of the snows"; Jain pilgrims call the mountain Asthapada, the place where their first prophet attained enlightenment; to the followers of Bon, Tibet's oldest religion, the peak is Yungdrung Gutse, the "nine-storeyed swastika mountain".

Due to its religious significance, climbing the peak is considered off limits, but you can join a three-week pilgrimage trek around the base of Kailash with experienced outfitters like **Summit Climb** (PO Box 123, Lakebay, WA 98349, USA; +1.360.570 0715; www.summitclimb.com). But be warned, this is not a luxury trip. The trek starts off with visits to the

THIS PAGE (FROM TOP): Asia offers an array of mountaineering opportunities from easy daytrips to intense multi-day climbs; rappelling allows for a safe, controlled but thrilling descent down cliffs or into caves in places like southern Thailand and the Malaysian state of Sarawak.

OPPOSITE: Once the hunting grounds of the Maharajas of Jaipur, Ranthambore National Park now offers tiger safaris during which you can get up close to these amazing beasts.

Action & Adventure

cities of **Lhasa** and **Kathmandu**, then turns into the hinterland, under Mount Everest, onto the strikingly barren Tibetan plateau and later follows the ancient pilgrims' trek around Mount Kailash. The climb is said to bring forgiveness for a lifetime of sin. The tour then crosses the border into Nepal, following yak trails and visiting remote outposts and bustling towns, until it's time to return to the Kathmandu valley through the Nepalese mountains.

White-water Wonderlands

Traverse Tours (Lot 227-229, 2nd Floor, Wisma Sabah, Jalan Tun Fuad Stephen, 88000 Kota Kinabalu, Sabah, Malaysia; +6.88.260 501; www.TraverseTours.com) in Sabah organises white-water trips down the Padas River, the longest rafting route in **Borneo**. Said to have the best class III and IV rapids in Southeast Asia (don't be fooled by their names like Merry-Go-Round, Break Point, Scooby Doo, Cobra, Curve, Lambada and Head Hunter), the route covers a distance of about 30 km. As an added bonus, couples get to enjoy a 90-minute drive from Beaufort town to the starting point on an antique train. A locally owned and operated outfit, Traverse Tours is fondly referred to by natives as the "River Bug" crew. Guides are all trained in swiftwater rescue and white-water safety and are certified by the New Zealand Canoeing Association.

Sumatra also offers many rafting-worthy rivers to satisfy both beginners and experts. The Bingei River, only a couple of hours from **Medan**, is largely peaceful but there is a section as it enters a canyon where the rapids are almost non-stop. The typical three-hour rafting trip culminates with the three-metre "Dragon's Tongue" drop. The Asahan River, which begins at Porsea with the beautiful 220-metre-high Siguragura Waterfall, has four rafting sections. The upper section (below Tangga Dam) consists of a long, continuous stretch of class IV rapids. But the going gets even wilder with a stretch of river nicknamed "The Nightmare" because of its violent V and VI-grade rapids. The various waterfalls along the way provide calm swimming holes. The Asahan Valley is also a great place to spot local wildlife, including screaming gibbons, hornbills, flying foxes, monitor lizards and freshwater crocodiles. Rafting trips on this river can be arranged at many travel agencies in Parapat.

Green Discovery (PO Box 9811, Hang Boun Rd, Ban Hay Sok, Vientiane, Laos; +856.21.264 528; www.greendiscoverylaos.com) offers one of the most spectacular white-water routes in **Laos** – a two-day expedition through the Xaisomboun Special Zone, running grade V rapids on the Nam Ngum River and paddling through steep-sided gorges where only the most intrepid venture. Internationally trained river guides lead every trip. For couples who prefer a multi-sport honeymoon, Green Discovery also offers a two-day "Secret Eden" journey of trekking, caving and kayaking on a wilderness route between the villages of Pha Thao and Vang Vieng.

Leaps of Faith

Few activities beat bungee jumping when it comes to giving you an instant burst of adrenaline. In **Phuket**, Thailand, **Jungle Bungy** (61/3 Wichitsongkram, Kathu, Phuket 83120, Thailand; +66.76.321 351; www.phuketbungy.com) offers lovers a chance to leap from the top of 50-metre-high towers over a beautiful lagoon. In **Chiang Mai**, **Chiang Mai X Centre** (263 Moo 1, Mae Rim-Samoeng Rd, T. Mae Rim, Mae Rim District, Chiang Mai, Thailand; +66.53.297 700; www.chiangmai-xcentre.com) offers bungee jumping, together with paintballing, off-road buggies, trail biking and a newfangled adventure sport called zorbing, in which couples roll down a slope while being tossed around (in each other's arms) inside a giant, translucent plastic ball.

New Zealander AJ Hackett, the father of bungee jumping, was on hand in 2006 to open the **Macau Tower Sky Jump** (Largo da Torre de Macau, Macau SAR, China; +853.2893 3339; www.macautower.com.mo), which holds the Guinness World Record for World's Highest Commercial Decelerator Descent. Described as a hybrid between bungee jumping and skydiving, participants dive into a 75 km per hour, 20-second "flight" from an outer rim of the 233-metre-high Macau Tower, which ends in a gentle landing at ground level. And if that is not enough of a thrill, you can sign up for the tower's spectacular bungee jump (in which you attain a speed of up to 200 km per hour (during the freefall) or the Skywalk X

THIS PAGE (FROM TOP): Takeoffs and landings at Lukla Airport in the Himalayas are made more dramatic by the surrounding mountain ranges; adrenaline junkies can choose between wet, dry, straight, zigzag, single and multi-person Zorb globe rides.

OPPOSITE (FROM TOP): Mountain biking offers accessibility to fascinating areas of Asia not accessible by other means; spending time acclimatising at base camp is essential for a successful climb of mountains like Everest.

Action & Adventure

THIS PAGE (FROM TOP): A BASE jumper launches off the KL Tower in Malaysia, one of only a handful of destinations worldwide where the edgy sport is legal; rock climbers test the cliff faces at Thailand's Railay Bay.

OPPOSITE (FROM TOP): The only strictly marine herbivorous mammal in the world, the dugong is one of the fascinating creatures you may encounter in Indo-Pacific waters; couples may come face to face with bottlenose dolphins while diving near Subic Bay in the Philippines.

around the main outer rim of the tower along a thin catwalk without handrails. Meanwhile, the two-hour Mast Climb allows you and your lover the satisfaction of climbing up and down the 100-metre-high ladders of the building's mast.

The rugged **Phra Nang Peninsula** near Krabi Beach Resort is Thailand's hottest rock-climbing area thanks to a multitude of steep cliffs, limestone crags, deep-pocketed walls, gnarly overhangs and hanging stalactites. Since climbers first discovered this area in the 1980s, over 650 routes have been developed using the French grading system (from easy 5a routes all the way up to extreme 8c). Most routes are accessed by boat, others by a long jungle walk or even abseiling from above. The most popular climbs include Tonsai, East and West Railay and Phra Nang Beach. Spring and autumn are generally the best times if you want to escape the baking heat or the wet monsoon seasons. Guided climbs and instruction are available at beachfront hotels and bungalows in nearby Ao Nang and Railay East Beach. **King Climbers** (next to YaYa Resort, West Railay Beach, Krabi, Thailand; +66.75.637 125 or +66.75.1476 0270; www.railay.com/railay/climbing/climbing_courses.shtml) offers single as well as multi-day rock climbing courses.

Caves abound in the porous limestone terrain of southern Thailand and northern Peninsular Malaysia. One of the best places for a subterranean adventure is a massive trans-border protected area formed by the 5,000-hectare Perlis State Park

in **Malaysia** and the 20,000-hectare Thaleban National Park in **Thailand**. **Jungle Walla** (88 Jalan Telok Datai, 07000 Langkawi, Malaysia; +60.19.225 2300; www.junglewalla.com) offers a three-day, two-night trip inside the labyrinth of the Gua Wang Burma cave system with its honeycombed passages and underground streams. This is no lightweight trip. Be prepared to get muddy and squeeze through some tight spaces in order to see the amazing natural sculptures, as well as exotic species of insects and fungi which could include giant toads, whip scorpions, centipedes, bats and striped cave racers. The tour also includes a trek through thick jungle to the summit of a 553-metre limestone peak for stunning views of Langkawi and Ko Tarotau.

BASE (Buildings, Antennae, Spans and Earth) jumping must be one of the craziest and most dangerous sports in the world. Jumpers hurl themselves off the top of buildings, towers or bridges, deploying a parachute that hopefully breaks their fall. Shanghai and Kuala Lumpur are among the handful of cities where BASE jumping is legal. In fact, they celebrate it. **Shanghai** was the location for the 2004 BASE Jump show, staged from the top of the Jin Mao Tower. **Malaysia** hosts two annual BASE jump competitions: the KL Tower International BASE Jump, directly followed by the Sibu BASE Jump. There are currently no BASE jumping schools in Asia. People who want to learn this sport can sign up for courses in North America and Europe, with **FJC BaseEuphoria**

(+351.93.889 5084; www.baseeuphoria.com) which offers courses in Switzerland and Portugal; or **Apex Base** in Colorado (126 Old Post Office Rd, Boulder, CO 80302, USA; +1.303.442.3537; www.apexbase.com). Most schools insist that learners complete at least 200 skydives before taking a BASE course.

Asia's Wild Blue Yonder

The 915-metre sea wall off **Sipadan Island** is considered one of the world's top ten dives, and the main reason for Malaysia's popularity as a scuba destination. There are about 12 dive spots around the island – including Barracuda Point, named for its concentration of barracudas. Divers in this area also regularly report sighting whitetip sharks, grey reef sharks, eagle rays and sea turtles, as well as bumphead parrotfish. If you want to try and spot rarer sharks like hammerheads or threshers, South Point is probably your best bet, but they are normally only seen around the 40-metre depths. Divers need to be warned of strong currents in these areas. **Pulau Sipadan Resort & Tours** (1st Floor, 484 Bandar Sabindo, Tawau, Sabah, Malaysia; +60.89.765 200; www.sipadan-resorts.com) is one of the few dive operators permitted to bring divers to Sipadan Island.

Asia offers some relatively untouched scuba territory. Some divers have started to rave about the waters off **Sihanoukville** on Cambodia's gulf coast. Dugong and whale sharks are known to inhabit these waters, and marine biologists claim the area's coral reefs are some of the richest in Asia.

The east coast of **Sri Lanka** offers some spectacular dives. **Trincomalee** has become almost synonymous with blue, sperm and Bryde's whales and dolphins that are regularly spotted here by divers, who also encounter schools of barracuda, giant trevally and sharks. Further south, **Batticaloa** is the site of the *Hermes* wreck, a British aircraft carrier that was sunk by the Japanese in 1942 with the loss of over 300 men. Now lying in 60 metres of water, this dive is only

Martial Arts Getaway

Muay Thai (Thai Boxing) is the national sport of Thailand and is a martial art with origins in the ancient battlefield tactics of the Siamese army. If you and your lover have always dreamed of being able to punch, grapple and kick your way through a Muay Thai fight, the Suwit Muay Thai Training Camp (15 Moo 1, Choa Fa Rd, T. Chalong, A. Muang, Phuket, Thailand 83130; +66.76.374 313; www.muaythai-thailand.com) has been teaching the sport for over 20 years. Previously open only to professional boxers, the camp now welcomes guests from all over the world, regardless of their skill levels. Classes are held twice a day, and they include skipping, shadow boxing, bag work, pad work and clinching or sparring. Guests are welcome to sample Muay Thai on a one-off basis or sign up for courses that run between a week and a month in length. If you are skilled enough, you can also participate in matches. As an added bonus, Phuket offers a virtual cornucopia of romantic resorts to enjoy, including Banyan Tree, Six Senses and Amanpuri.

Action & Adventure

recommended for the very experienced. The sight of the huge, mangled warship, now teeming with sea life, is a truly memorable but eerie experience. The website (www.divesrilanka.com) is a veritable one-stop guide to diving off Trincomalee and other parts of Sri Lanka. It also includes a list of recommended dive operators.

Just a three-hour drive from Manila, the old US naval base at **Subic Bay** in **the Philippines** is also an amazing locale for wreck diving. Nineteen wrecks have been identified in the local waters, with some experts estimating there being another 60 or so lying around. Most of them, mainly from World War II, are in very calm water no more than 30 minutes from shore. Find out more from local dive operators like **Subic Bay Aqua Sports/Scuba Shack** (Bldg. 249, Waterfront Rd, Barrio Barretto, Subic Bay Freeport Zone, Zambales, Philippines; +63.47.252 3005 or +63.47.252 7343). In between scuba trips, couples can also enjoy a range of other water sports and activities in and around Subic Bay, from windsurfing and sea kayaking to sailing and fishing.

Wakeboarding & Kitesurfing

Surfing has been a popular pastime in Asia for at least 25 years and makes a great honeymoon activity for couples who love the sea. Asia's up-and-coming surf spots include Cherai in the south Indian state of Kerala, China Beach near Danang along the central coast of Vietnam, and Secret Point near Matara in Sri Lanka.

But **Indonesia** remains the most popular surfing destination. The variety is astounding: more than a hundred surf spots in seven different regions. The **Mentawai** islands are a wave-rich chain of about 70 islands and islets off the western coast of Sumatra. The biggest swells are found from June to September at breaks nicknamed Bank Vaults and Macaronis. Experienced surfers seeking the biggest thrills should try hanging ten at Uluwatu in **Bali** or Desert Point in **Lombok**, best accessed by boat, known among surfing circles to serve up the heaviest left hand barrels in the world.

Wakeboarding is an exhilarating sport in which you ride a single board while being pulled by a motorboat, sort of a combination of surfing and waterskiing. Jumps are performed by hitting the wake and launching into the air. The sport is perfect for the adrenaline junkie who has already mastered waterskiing. In **Singapore**, **Extreme Sports** (+65.6344 8813; www.extreme.com.sg or wakeboardsingapore.com) offers beginner courses at a private site with no other boats and they guarantee that you will be up on a board after four 30-minute lessons.

Thailand presents plenty of opportunities to learn and perfect wakeboarding, as there are wakeboarding schools located on private lakes or reservoirs around Bangkok, Phuket and Chang Rai, as well as wakeboarding parks in Pattaya and Ratchbburi. **Club Taco** (175/1, km 13 Bangna-Trad Rd, Moo 12, Tambon Bang Phli Yai, Samut Prakan

10540, Thailand; +66.2.316 7809), half an hour outside Bangkok, offers wakeboarding lessons using an overhead cable system.

With moderate yet consistent trade winds that blow between December and March, Bulabog Beach on **Boracay** island in **the Philippines** has ideal conditions for kitesurfing. The reef makes for safe kitesurfing in shallow, waist-deep waters within the 2.5-km expanse of the bay, while more experienced riders should head for the channels between the reefs where great rolling swells allow for higher jumps. **Isla Kite Surfing** (+63.36.288 5352; ww.slakitesurfing.com) on Bulabog Beach teaches courses that comply with the IKO (International Kite Organization) and VDWS (Verband deutscher Wassersport Schulen) standards. Kitesurfers certified with IKO level 2 can rent gear at any IKO centre worldwide. Isla caters to everyone, from novices to more experienced surfers. It also arranges multi-day kitesurfing safaris. There are not many luxury resorts on Boracay but the **Shangri-La's Boracay Resort & Spa** (Barangay Yapak, Boracay Island, Malay, Aklan 5608, Philippines; +63.36.288 4988; www.shangri-la.com) is a spectacular property, cascading down a hillside to a secluded, sparkling white-sand beach.

Vietnam is another destination that is becoming popular for kiteboarding, especially the beaches of **Mui Ne** about three hours from **Ho Chi Minh City**. The conditions here are bathwater warm sea,

moderate waves and strong sea breezes that blow between November and March, when the winter monsoon sweeps in from the north. As an added bonus, Mui Ne is less than an hour from **Bau Trang** (White Sand Dunes), where you can try your hand at a completely different adventure sport called sandboarding. ~ JC

Surviving More Than Your Honeymoon

Subic Bay is much more than a water sports centre. The surrounding region contains 10,000 hectares of virgin triple canopy rainforest and a jungle centre staffed by the local Aeta people who once taught survival techniques to American servicemen bound for Vietnam. The Jungle Environmental Survival Training School (www.clarksubicmarketing.com/sports_leisure/subic_bay_jest_camp.htm) now offers a range of experiences from brief demonstrations of basic techniques to full blown seven-day jungle survival courses. Skills taught during the courses include basic mountaineering, fire building, wildlife identification and other wilderness survival techniques. Couples opting for the more extensive programmes will be taken through the rainforest on an overnight adventure (without food or water) with an Aeta guide who will demonstrate how to retrieve water from various plant vines, and other important survival skills when you have nothing but a knife at your disposal. You and your companion will also be shown how to cook rice using green bamboo, as well as how to make insect repellent and soap from jungle plants.

THIS PAGE (FROM TOP): A wakeboarder enjoys the thrill on a single board while being pulled by a speedboat; kitesurfers employ the wind and their kite to propel them along the water and into the air at great speeds.

OPPOSITE (FROM TOP): Indonesia's secluded Mentawai Islands boast over a hundred surf spots, including Lance's Left; the 33-metre-long freighter Halaveli was intentionally sunk in 1991 to promote scuba diving around Ari Atoll in the Maldives.

Ocean & River Luxury Cruises

Privacy, pampering and exotic port calls make cruise ships one of the best ways for newlyweds to get away from it all and discover one another on the high seas in an atmosphere that's shipshape for romance.

The world didn't need Leonardo DiCaprio and Kate Winslet to show us that cruise ships are intrinsically romantic. For more than a century, lovers have taken to the high seas to enjoy time together in search of exotic lands. While the Caribbean and North Atlantic remain the prime sailing grounds, Asia is now firmly on the world's cruise map.

Asia's ocean cruise itineraries typically cover Southeast Asia, East Asia or the Indian Ocean in chic modern ships, some of them large and bustling, others small (under 100 passengers) and much more private. As a rule, the larger ones offer much more onboard entertainment and facilities (think five-star resorts on the sea), whereas smaller ships are able to take you to more remote ports of call.

Some of the more popular ocean-cruising routes in Asia include Singapore to Penang, Langkawi and Phuket; Hong Kong to Shanghai and Beijing (or Tianjin); Tokyo and Japan's Inland Sea; and the Indonesian archipelago between Bali and Timor.

Asia also offers the possibility of romantic river cruises along same fabled waterways – the Mekong, Yangtze, Irrawaddy and Ganges. River cruises generally offer a more intimate experience, allowing passengers to learn about the history and culture of a place while granting them "inland" access to regions and places that would otherwise be extremely difficult to reach.

The adventure cruise market has also taken off in Asia: journeys through the exotic eastern isles of Indonesia all the way to New Guinea and back; explorations of the secluded Kuril Islands and Kamchatka Peninsula on Russia's remote Pacific coast; and scuba diving and watersport-oriented voyages in Palau and Micronesia.

Big Ships: Party Around the Clock

The advantage of larger cruise ships is non-stop action and activities, a giant floating party that couples can join, or not, depending on their mood. Given their size, these ships tend to call at larger ports, including many of Asia's most fabled seaports. Economy of scale means that big ship cruises are often lower in price than their small ship cousins. The downside is that you and your lover will have plenty of company around the pool, at the buffet table and walking down the gangplank at port calls.

One of the world's most famous cruise lines, **Royal Caribbean International** (3 Anson Road, #13-02 Springleaf Tower; +65.6305 0033 in Singapore or +1.866.562 7625 in the USA; www.royalcaribbean.com; see pages 116–117) offers cruises from Singapore to Malaysia, Thailand and Indonesia, and from Hong Kong and Shanghai to Vietnam, Taiwan, Japan and South Korea on the 2,000-passenger *Legend of the Seas*.

On these voyages, Royal Caribbean Productions puts on a constantly changing array of Vegas-style revues, Broadway shows (*Hairspray*, *Chicago*, etc.), comedy routines, musical acts and even ice shows, performed by top-notch entertainers from around the world. Gaming, themed parties, bingo, karaoke, contests, the list is endless.

For the sports (or just fun)-minded, there is a rock wall, as well as swimming pools, scuba diving courses, sports deck with basketball, golf, running track and, of course, the fitness and wellness centre and spa.

Being the romantic spot that a Royal Caribbean vessel is, you can always arrange to get engaged, married or have a vow renewal ceremony onboard. They even offer an extreme wedding experience where you can get married, for example, on the ship's rock wall or in an especially romantic place at one of the destination ports. Themed weddings are also possible. The company offers a stress-free wedding, with their consultants doing all the work. The bride and groom only need to show up in their chosen attire.

As the largest European cruise operator, **Costa Cruises** (www.costacruisesasia.com) is able to offer one of the largest choices of itineraries and ships available today. Spa treatments, great food, wine tastings, stage shows, educational sessions and group games are all part of the Costa package. Their cruise menu in Asia spans from Thailand to Taiwan, Singapore to South Korea, India to Indonesia and everywhere else in between. The 15 ships in the Costa fleet vary in size, from large and packed full of facilities to smaller and more intimate vessels. All are modern and comfortable with distinct Italian styling, no less.

Star Cruises (1528 Ocean Centre, 5 Canton Rd, Tsimshatsui, Hong Kong; +852.2317 7711; www.starcruises.com) offers several pan-Asian itineraries on ships that carry more than 1,000 passengers, including voyages that call at ports in Malaysia, Thailand, Vietnam, Singapore, Japan, Taiwan and Hong Kong. Star's floating five-star resorts promise endless fun, entertainment and activities on itineraries from two to five nights. The non-stop action onboard includes mini-golfing, a golf driving range, swimming pools, gyms, basketball courts, table tennis, casinos, spas, multiple restaurants, lounges, top-rated cabarets and novelty acts, karaoke as well as luxury shopping.

Medium Ships: The Best of Both Worlds

Cruise ships that carry between 500 and 1,000 passengers may offer the best of both worlds: enough people to keep the party going until well into the night, but not so many that you feel overwhelmed by the crowd. While there are other couples to socialise with, there is plenty of space to play out your private love story on the high seas.

One of the few medium-sized ships that regularly sails Asian waters is the 694-passenger *Azamara Quest*. Operated by **Azamara Club Cruises** (3 Anson Road, #13-02 Springleaf Tower; +65.6305 0033; www.azamaraclubcruises.com; see pages 110–111), the ship ventures to many corners of the continent – from Beijing, Cambodia and Singapore to Hong Kong, Thailand and Japan, during an Asian season that runs roughly from December through April. The *Azamara Quest* is perfect for couples who prefer a boutique-

THIS PAGE (FROM TOP): *Large cruise ships such as Oasis of the Seas or Allure of the Seas have an AquaTheatre to provide live entertainment onboard; onboard gourmet restaurants are great places for couples to connect.*
OPPOSITE: *At the Shangri-La's Villingili resort in the Maldives, couples can cruise on the luxury yacht "Horizon" to a romantic lunch on the equator.*

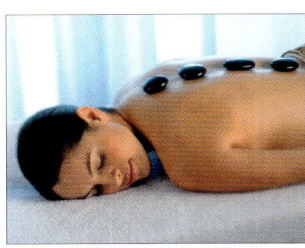

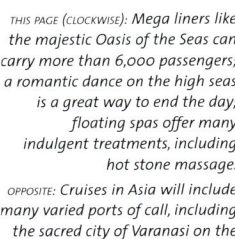

THIS PAGE (CLOCKWISE): Mega liners like the majestic Oasis of the Seas can carry more than 6,000 passengers; a romantic dance on the high seas is a great way to end the day; floating spas offer many indulgent treatments, including hot stone massage.

OPPOSITE: Cruises in Asia will include many varied ports of call, including the sacred city of Varanasi on the Ganges River in northern India.

hotel atmosphere without sacrificing amenities. It also comes minus the super luxury-class price tag. The cruise line's philosophy is to provide an in-depth experience at each destination so passengers won't feel like they are merely observing from afar. To this end, they call their land programmes "shore immersions" rather than shore excursions.

Onboard facilities include a European-style casino, showcase theatre and luxury spa, including in-cabin treatments and acupuncture. Among the spa offerings is a "Journey for Two" couple's treatment that includes a pampering combination of teeth-whitening, microdermabrasion and Swedish massage. *Azamara Quest* also features a well equipped aerobic and weight-training centre where you can work out on your own or with a personal trainer, or take yoga and Pilates lessons. Another indulgence is a soothing saltwater Thalassotherapy pool.

To keep your mind in shape, *Azamara Quest* offers a number of daily lectures on a wide range of "enrichment" topics, from culinary to photography and special informative sessions about specific ports of call in situ. There are also workshops on cyberspace and digital media to get passengers up to speed on the latest computer technology. The calendar also includes lots of fun activities – from dance lessons to trivia contests and an original onboard game show called "Star Struck". Luxury is assured through beautifully appointed cabins, butler service for every suite and gourmet dining. This is not all, the ship can create the wedding (or vow renewal) of your dreams at many of their destinations or onboard with the captain officiating the ceremony.

Small Ships: Intimate Adventures

"We get you closer" is the motto of **Spirit of Adventure** (Enbrook Park, Sandgate, Folkestone, Kent CT20 3SE, England; +0800.015 6984 in the UK; www.spiritofadventure.co.uk). Having a capacity of up to 348 passengers, the cruise ship calls on smaller, and often much more exotic ports that larger ships just can't get into. Despite its size, the ship does not lack in style or amenities. This is an informal ship with indoor and al fresco restaurants, cocktail bars and a library. Indoor and outdoor pools and exercise machines are amongst the onboard recreational options, and the ship carries a fleet of mountain bikes for passengers to use, free of charge, at certain ports of call. The main onboard entertainment is guest lecturers who give presentations on different topics. If weather permits, outdoor movies are shown on the top deck.

MV *Spirit of Adventure* makes three or four trips a year in Asian waters, including sailing from Port Kelang, Malaysia to Phuket, Thailand; Port Blair, Andaman Island; Trincomalee and Colombo, Sri Lanka as well as Mangalore and Mumbai, India. There are other routes available periodically: between Mauritius, Seychelles and the Maldives, India and Sri Lanka. Their Southeast Asian trips include stops in Vietnam, Hong Kong, China, Cambodia or Malaysia, Borneo, the

Philippines and Singapore, in various permutations. They also offer an itinerary with ten stops throughout Indonesia. In addition, MV *Spirit of Adventure* makes it easy to extend your honeymoon before or after the cruise through hotel stays at a particular destination with comprehensive overland tours. For instance, prior to embarking on the "Crossroads of Continents" cruise, couples can explore India's Golden Triangle

Kerala Houseboat Adventure

For couples who want to have a vessel all to themselves (besides a driver, chef and cabin assistant), a houseboat is the perfect mode of transportation to explore the inland waterways of Kerala with its interconnected system of canals, rivers, lagoons and lakes in southern India. You'll enjoy the beauty of paddy fields, temples, coconut groves and villages, where the inhabitants make their living from the coir found in coconut husks. The ecosystem here is fascinating, as it's a mixture of freshwater and seawater. The comfortable houseboats from Kerala Houseboats (www.keralahouseboat. org) range from 29 to 33 metres in length and have between one and five fully furnished bedrooms (with or without air conditioning). In addition, the company also offers a variety of packages of between two- and eight-night cruises, but also gives you the flexibility to design your own dream trip. The Kerala Department of Tourism (www.keralatourism.org) lists approved houseboat operators on its website.

(Delhi, Agra and Jaipur) on a 6-day extension arranged by the cruise line.

Many small ships specialise in a combination of luxury and high adventure, in particular the *Clipper Odyssey*, a 110-passenger expedition ship run by **Zegrahm Expeditions** (192 Nickerson St #200, Seattle, WA 98109 USA; +1.206.285 4000; ww.zeco.com). For more than 20 years, Zegrahm has specialised in creating exclusive and unusual cruises to the far corners of the globe. No matter where they go, each cruise comes with a palpable sense of discovery and exploration, a feeling that you might actually see or do something that few people have seen or done before. The mix also includes gourmet food, lavish

accommodation and possibly the best pool of guest lecturers in the business. Due to their small size and upscale nature, Zegrahm cruises have a reputation for attracting passengers who want something more than a hangover from their cruise each morning.

All cabins aboard *Clipper Odyssey* have an ocean view with sitting area and ensuite bathrooms complete with a small bathtub. Passengers can track the progress of their voyage on the Global Positioning System broadcast in each cabin. Onboard facilities include a lounge, a small library and gym, a gift shop and an outdoor pool.

Clipper Odyssey undertakes several voyages each year in and

around Asia, including a 21-day cruise around the Bay of Bengal and the Andaman Sea between Singapore and Chennai (Madras); a 15-day journey from Palau to Yap in the Micronesian islands just east of the Philippines; and an 18-day circumnavigation of Sumatra that starts and ends in Singapore. Among the destinations on the Sumatran cruise are Gunung Leuser National Park (famous for its orang-utan inhabitants), the remote Siberut and Nias Islands, and Krakatoa volcano. Along the way couples can explore unspoilt beaches and reefs, watch craft demonstrations and purchase *ikat* weavings and other local works of art.

THIS PAGE (FROM TOP): With its fabulous beaches and blue lagoons, Palau attracts cruises with an emphasis on sun, sea and scuba diving spots; shore excursions might include a trip to Sumatra's Gunung Leuser National Park to see the native orang-utans.

OPPOSITE: Sunset over Luang Prabang, southern terminus of riverboat cruises along the Mekong River between Laos and Thailand.

Cruising the Yangtze

As the world's third longest river, the **Yangtze** flows for 6,300 km on a meandering route from the Tibetan Plateau to the East China Sea near **Shanghai**. Several companies offer luxury trips down one of the world's great rivers in terms of both geography and cultural significance.

With a total fleet of eight ships, **Victoria Cruises** (Chongqing Dong Jiang Co., Ltd. #9 Shanxi Rd, 11th Floor, Building B, Jiliang Square, Yuzhong District, Chongqing, China; +86.23.6163 7688; victoriacruises.com) offers its Yangtze River Cruises throughout the year, including special winter sailings. All itineraries include passage through the locks adjacent to China's Three Gorges Dam and a sightseeing tour of this modern engineering marvel, spectacular views of centuries-old villages and pagodas along the way, as well as some combination of stops in Chongqing, Yichang and Shanghai.

The line's newest ship is the *Victoria Jenna* which can accommodate as many as 400 passengers in 200 staterooms. The sleek river cruiser offers four elevators, four separate full-service kitchens (two catering to customised dietary requests), and wireless Internet service, in addition to full-size bathtubs and high efficiency dual-flush toilets in each cabin. The ship's Executive Suite Decks has concierge service, a private lounge area and a private a la carte restaurant.

The *Victoria Jenna* also features a special room for historical and cultural lectures, tai chi and mahjong lessons, as well as a library and reading room, cocktail lounge, beauty parlour and mini-spa, observation deck, business centre and health clinic.

Expanding into Asia from its European home base, **Viking River Cruises** (5700 Canoga Ave, Suite 200, Woodland Hills, CA 91367, USA or 17/F Millennium City 6, 392 Kwun Tong Rd, Kwun Tong, Kowloon, Hong Kong; +852.2808 2828 or +1.818.227 1234; www.vikingrivercruises.com) also sails the Yangtze. Viking's "China Cultural Delights" experience explores China's cradle of civilisation with an epic 11-day river journey between Chongqing and Nanjing, plus land tours of Beijing, Xi'an, Shanghai and Suzhou on either end. Among the historical icons along the way are the Great Wall, the Forbidden City, the terracotta army in Xi'an, the city of Jingdezhen (birthplace of Chinese porcelain), the remote Buddhist temple on Mount Jiu Hua and the elegant classical gardens of Suzhou.

Plying this route from 2011 is the *Viking Emerald*, the newest and, in many respects, the most luxurious ship sailing the Yangtze on a regular basis. Every stateroom and suite features sliding glass doors that open onto a private balcony on the outside of the ship. Couples can splurge on one of the 78-sq-metre presidential suites that come complete with king-size bed, separate sitting room and private wraparound balcony.

Kipling's Fabled River: The Irrawaddy

For thousands of years, the **Irrawaddy** (Ayeyarwady) **River** has served as the main "highway" between southern and northern **Burma** (Myanmar), the watery route by which civilisation and conquering armies spread up and down the vast Southeast Asian nation. But it wasn't until the late 19th century that the mighty river earned global fame, thanks to British author Rudyard Kipling and a romantic poem "Mandalay", about love found and then lost along the banks of the Irrawaddy. Being the largest of the mainland Southeast Asian countries, Burma offers a great variety of scenery. River life still dominates much of this country's inland areas, so there is lots of action on the Irrawaddy as well as monuments, temples and scenery to enjoy enroute.

Inspired by both the classic verse and Burma's exotic landscapes, **Orient-Express** (100 Beach Rd, #32-01/03 Shaw Tower, Singapore 189702 or 20 Upper Ground, London SE1 9PF England; +65 6395 0678 or +44.20.7921 4000; www.orient-express.com; see pages 114–115) created a modern river cruiser called *Road to Mandalay* that sails for three to eleven nights on the Irrawaddy. The highlight of each voyage is a chance to explore the riverside ruins of **Pagan** (Bagan), a UNESCO World Heritage Site with thousands of temples and pagodas, each one different from the other. But there are plenty of other stops along the way. **Bhamo**, a trading post close to the Chinese border, hosts colourful daily markets attended by nearby ethnic minorities including the Kachin, Shan, Lisu and Palaung. **Mandalay**, the country's last royal capital and second largest city, is Burma's cultural hub. Not to be missed are the remains of Mandalay Palace, Shwenandaw Monastery and numerous other religious shrines, including the highly venerated Mahamuni Buddha.

With space for no more than 82 passengers, *Road to Mandalay* is an intimate ship with lots of privacy. Facilities are spread across four decks, including a swimming pool, fitness room and spa, doctor's office, restaurant and piano bar. The spacious State Cabins feature a double bed, sitting area and bathroom with shower big enough for two. The entire ship can be chartered for a wedding or honeymoon cruise during which Orient-Express can make all sorts of

Ocean & River Luxury Cruises

special arrangements like flowers, champagne, traditional dancers and even a procession of local Buddhist monks to bless your embarkation.

Other steamship lines offer slightly less luxurious but no less fascinating voyages along the Irrawaddy. Singapore-based **Pandaw River Cruises** (7 Mohamed Sultan Rd, Singapore 238971; +65.6238 7863; www.pandaw.com) offers seven itineraries, the longest of which is the 20-night "Burma: Land of Great Rivers" aboard the 48-passenger *Pandaw II*. Hand finished in brass and teak by traditional craftsmen and modelled after the British colonial steamers of old, the

55-metre vessel fits right into the Irrawaddy landscape. The ultra-shallow draft allows the ship to slip into remote riverside areas unreachable by larger vessels, let alone overland. An extra incentive for sailing with Pandaw is the fact that the company supports a number of charity projects along the river – building schools and medical clinics, and running a small hospital ship that travels from village to village.

The Mighty Mekong

As the longest river (totalling 4,350 km) in Southeast Asia, the **Mekong** traverses six countries – China, Burma, Laos, Thailand,

Cambodia and Vietnam – on its journey from the Himalayan foothills to the South China Sea. However, due to rapids and other barriers, only certain stretches are navigable. The most popular sections for cruising are the lower Mekong between **Phnom Penh** (Cambodia) and **Ho Chi Minh City** (Vietnam), and the middle stretch of the river between Thailand and Laos.

French-managed **Mekong Cruises** (50/4 Sakkarine Rd, Ban Vat Sene, Luang Prabang, Laos; +856.71.252 553; mekong-cruises.com) has two teakwood riverboats, restored from old ferries, cruising the Mekong in northern Laos. The 18-metre-long

Luang Say offers two- and three-day trips from **Houei Sai** to **Luang Prabang** and, in the other direction, from Luang Prabang to Houei Sai, with nights spent in a riverside eco-lodge consisting of bungalows and luxury tented rooms. The vessel makes stops along the way at several hilltribe villages as well as the famed Pak Ou caves. Its sister ship, the *Vat Phou*, has a three-day, two-night cruise on the southern part of the Mekong which starts and finishes in Pakse, Laos. During the overland tours, passengers stay onboard overnight in 12 comfortable cabins. Visitors get to explore the Vat Phou ruins at Champassak, the Oum Muong ruins at Huei Thamo, the area known as the 4,000 Islands, as well as the Pha Peng waterfall near the Cambodian border.

Viking River Cruises (see page 64) also offers one of the more comfortable ways to explore the lower end of the Mekong. Many of the cruises include a significant land tour portion to visit cities and sites away from the river.

An example is the 15-day "Magnificent Mekong" cruise-tour that includes visiting the cities of Ho Chi Minh City and Hanoi in Vietnam, and laid-back Phnom Penh, capital of Cambodia, besides cruising down the Mekong. Along the way, couples have plenty of time to appreciate the ancient monuments, archaeological sites, floating markets, tribal villages, amazing scenery and the region's rich history. The cruise takes place on the RV *Tonle*, a handcrafted ship that's able to navigate tight spots and remote areas of the Mekong. With 33 cabins, it accommodates no more than 66 passengers and offers a series of onboard multimedia talks on the history and culture of the places you visit.

Navigating the Indonesian Archipelago

With more than 17,000 islands, the vast Indonesian archipelago is an ideal place for cruising. Many of the big ships call at Indonesian ports as part of the multi-country itineraries. But **Indonesia** is also blessed with small, indigenous cruise lines that add local flavour to a seafaring honeymoon or getaway. **Sea Safaris of Indonesia** (Jalan Dermaga II, Pelabuhan Benoa, Denpasar, Bali, Indonesia; +62 361.721 212; www.seasafaricruises.com) organises trips to out-of-the-way islands east of **Bali** in four magnificent teak sailing ships built with all the creature

Bygone Romance: Indochine Junks

Get a taste of the opulence and grandeur of old Asia on the five-star junks operated by Halong Cruises (www.luxuryhalongcruises.com) in Vietnam. Their newest offering – the *Halong Violet* – is fitted out in romantic 1930s Indochine style with six themed cabins. In addition to private balconies, the cabins feature marble bathrooms with Jacuzzis easily big enough for two. Other features onboard include a library and lounge, spa and gym, boutique dining room with gourmet meals comprising fresh seafood and Vietnamese fusion cuisine. Its three-day Halong Bay itineraries include side trips to secluded beaches and fishing villages.

comforts. Ports of call include Komodo National Park and its celebrated giant lizards, the little-visited **Raja Ampat** and **Lembongan** group of islands, and culturally rich **Sumbawa**. Under billowing sails, trips run from a short three days and two nights to a lengthy 15 days and 14 nights. Pink sand beaches, Komodo dragons, *ikat* weavers, villages where time seems to have stood still, historic Dutch and Portuguese forts and pristine coral reefs are all part of the experience of these cruises.

Each ship has a crew of 15 to take care of all your needs; passenger numbers range between 20 and 30, depending on the vessel. Cabins are air-conditioned with ensuite bathrooms. Diving and snorkelling gear, jet skis and other equipment are available for passengers to use. Sea Safaris also has other vessels available for scuba diving trips or charters, which would allow you to plan a private trip that includes a stop at the annual Asmat Art Auction (usually in October) in Indonesia's Irian Jaya region. The art comprises mainly stylised woodcarvings that are world renowned.

Another chartering possibility is **Silolana Sojourns** (Jalan Pengembak 15A, Sanur, Bali, Indonesia; +62.361.287 326; www.silolona.com). in a traditional wooden vessel that carries 10 passengers. As the trip is yours to plan, you can ask for diving, waterskiing, kayaking, sport fishing, windsurfing, wakeboarding and snorkelling equipment, or even a masseuse or personal trainer to be onboard at your beck and call. ~ JC

THIS PAGE (FROM TOP): The exotic island of Bali is just one of the many ports of call in Indonesia; Komodo dragons, the world's largest and most dangerous lizard, intrigue cruise-ship passengers at Komodo National Park in eastern Indonesia.

OPPOSITE: Traditional junks in Vietnam's Halong Bay conjure up an era of bygone luxury.

Romantic Train Journeys

Discover old-world elegance on Asia's luxury trains, replete with five-star amenities such as air-conditioned cabins with ensuite bathrooms, as well as butler service, evening entertainment and gourmet meals accompanied by fine wines.

After years of turning their noses up at trains as something more fitting for backpackers, jet-setters suddenly rediscovered the romance of rail in the 1980s when a luxury version of the fabled *Orient-Express* was launched in Europe. When trains first appeared in the early 19th century, they were considered a blight on the pastoral landscapes through which they chugged – "iron horses" that spewed smoke and spooked the cows. By the end of the century they were interwoven with the fabric of modern life, the primary means by which passengers and freight crossed whole continents. It took the invention of motion pictures to romanticise what had basically been a utilitarian machine.

From very early days, film directors realised that trains were perfect venues for boy-meets-girl love stories and romantic comedies. Broadway producer John Barrymore tries to recapture the heart of former girlfriend Carole Lombard while travelling on the *Twentieth Century* (1934). Gold-digger Ingrid Bergman and gambler Gary Cooper battle for control of a railroad and fall in love in *Saratoga Trunk* (1945). At the peak of her sex appeal, Marilyn Monroe frolics with Tony Curtis and Jack Lemmon (who were disguised as women) in the famous sleeper car from *Some Like It Hot* (1959). In one of the earliest James Bond movies – *From Russia With Love* (1963) – Sean Connery and Daniela Bianchi fight off a deadly assassin on a speeding express train. Movies have stoked our imagination, created an aura that spies, stars and sex symbols ride trains, not just ordinary folk.

Yet even without all the movie hype, there is something special about riding the rails. Start with the gentle rumble of the wheels, a rhythmic clickety-clack that eventually sets you at ease no matter what the surroundings. Add the view outside your window, the continuously changing scenery, a hypnotic journey through landscapes that are often exotic, alien or incredibly picturesque. Round it off with the fact that (unlike so many other modes of transport) you can enjoy a proper sit-down meal, a couple of drinks at a genuine bar and then slip away for a romantic encounter in your private sleeper compartment. You can write your own script on any overnight train.

Of course, some trains are more conducive to romance than others. The Eastern & Oriental train service through Singapore, Malaysia and Thailand, and more recently Laos, set the stage for a wave of private luxury trains in Asia, particularly in India and China. While conjuring romantic images of the past, these trains are also outfitted with modern conveniences and five-star amenities, from air-conditioned cabins and hot-water showers to butler service and gourmet meals paired with fine wines.

Rumbling through Southeast Asia

Cocktails in hand and a warm breeze blowing through your hair, you and your lover stand on the open deck at the back of a railway car as Southeast Asia rolls by, an ever-changing panorama that at any given time might include a shimmering golden stupa, monkeys frolicking through jungle trees, a gorgeous white-sand beach or some of the world's most stunning modern architecture. But the real attraction is the train itself. The train in question is the **Eastern & Oriental Express** (100 Beach Road, #32-01/03 Shaw Tower, Singapore 189702; +65.6395 0678 or 1800.8392 3500; www.orient-express. com; see pages 112–113). As a fully fledged offspring of the famed *Orient-Express* in Europe, the E&O delivers a standard of railway comfort and luxury that was previously unknown in Southeast Asia, even during the heyday of the British Empire.

The entire operation is something of a transportation miracle. A major act of diplomacy on the part of E&O's backers – who spent several years persuading local railway authorities to break with tradition and their coveted government monopolies – and the culmination of a worldwide "hardware" search for rolling stock. Originally built for service on the Silver Star and Silver Fern trains in New Zealand, the carriages feature sumptuous 1930s décor with wood panelling and plush upholstery.

Yet, behind the Art Deco façades lurk modern electrical and plumbing fixtures, including a complete toilet and shower in every cabin – something rarely seen on rails before – not even on the legendary *Orient-Express*. The full train comprises 22 cars including two restaurant cars, a piano bar, a saloon car and an observation car with a unique open-air deck where the Asian jungle, plantations and rice paddies can be

THIS PAGE: *Romance comes in many different forms on the E&O Express, including an open-air observation deck, incredible landscapes and shopping at trackside markets.*

OPPOSITE: *Another E&O trump card is gourmet dining that blends the best of Eastern and Western cuisines.*

Romantic Train Journeys

viewed at close range. Lodging ranges from double sleepers to huge presidential suites that stretch over half a carriage.

Menus in the dining car appeal to both Asian and European palates, with an extensive wine list and custom-made table settings. Dishes range from a curry tiffin lunch to spicy *tom yum* soup at dinner, but you can also order smoked salmon and beluga caviar if your tastes happen to run in that direction. Your fellow passengers are just as eclectic. Kings and queens, presidents and prime ministers, movie actors and corporate taipans have already ventured on the E&O Express, making it not just a train trip, but a rolling chronicle of modern history.

Wedding, honeymoon or anniversary parties comprising 12 or more people can privately hire the

E&O for the full journey between Singapore and Bangkok, or for any shorter route. This allows for special arrangements or activities onboard the train or stops along the way. The possibilities range from champagne, cocktails or flowers to a Gurkha piper band, string quartet, murder mystery entertainment, Malay or Thai classical dancers or even a Chinese opera.

Another romantic train journey is the service between Jakarta and Yogyakarta across the heart of Java. The scenery quickly evolves from urban jungle into the real deal, a lush landscape of rice terraces, thatched-roof villages and smouldering volcanoes that seem little changed in modern times. You can break the journey at the highland university town of **Bandung** or travel all the way through in a single day. The trip takes anywhere from 8 to 12 hours

depending on the level of service, with the express "Gajayana" trains being the fastest. Tickets can be purchased online at the official website of **Indonesian Railways** (www.kereta-api.co.id).

India & Sri Lanka

India has a long love affair with rails, a romance that stretches back more than a hundred years when trains were the primary means of travelling around the subcontinent. India's stations continue to swirl with a boundless spirit, a feast for the eyes, ears and nose that blends South Asian market, mores and machines. Moving through the mob on your way to the train, it's hard not to get swept up in the energy that pulsates through every big-city depot, an urge to spontaneously burst into the song *Jai Ho* and dance your way down the platform.

India's trains are also something to shout about. The sumptuous **Palace on Wheels** (20 Wall Street, Princeton, New Jersey, USA 08540; +1.609.683 5018; www.palaceonwheels.net) resurrects the lavish lifestyles of the former maharajahs. The route is a seven-day round trip from **Delhi** that includes stops in the magical desert city of **Jaipur** and riverside **Agra** to see the Taj Mahal. The 14-passenger coaches are named after bygone princely states and decorated with colourful motifs that reflect their namesakes. Each car contains a pantry, lounge and four private cabins with twin beds, furnished in Rajasthani style and modern touches like wall-to-wall carpeting and adjacent bathrooms with hot-water showers. A new all-suite version called the **Royal Rajasthan on Wheels** (www.royalpalaceonwheels.com) commenced in 2009 with a similar timetable and itinerary.

Another private luxury train called the **Golden Chariot** (Ground Floor, Chandralok Bldg, 36 Janpath, New Delhi, India 110 001; +91.11.4686 8686; www.goldenchariottrain.com) roams several routes in southern India from its home base in high-tech **Bangalore**. One itinerary covers historic towns and wildlife reserves in Karnataka state as well as the beach resort city of Goa; the other rambles along the Tamil Nadu and Kerala coasts before swinging back to Bangalore. Like its well-heeled predecessor, the Golden Chariot features private sleeping chambers for two, including some with double beds. In addition to two dining cars and an opulent bar car, the train also boasts a small gymnasium, a business centre where you can keep in touch with the world, and a mini spa with Ayurvedic massage and other treatments.

The royal blue **Deccan Odyssey** (+91.11.2568 686; www.deccan-odyssey-india.com) explores a completely different part of India than the other two – the forts, palaces and temples of Maharashtra state and the Deccan Plateau (with a brief stop in Goa for a little sea, sun and sand). Among the journey highlights are the cave temples and monasteries of Ellora, where three different religions created shrines over a 600-year span; the Bengal tigers of Tadoba Wildlife Sanctuary; and the majestic Daulatabad Fort, once home to the region's powerful Yadava rulers. One-week journeys

start and end in modern **Mumbai**. In addition to twin beds, the train's air-conditioned private compartments are equipped with CD and MP3 players, hot-water showers and ensuite toilets.

Trains still rumble across much of **Sri Lanka** including a coastal line from Colombo to Galle on the south coast and a winding hill-country route from Colombo to Kandy, Nuwara Eliya and Badulla. There are three types of first class: reserved seats in the observation car, reserved seats in an air-conditioned carriage, and private sleeping berths (overnight routes only) with lockable doors, fresh bedding and separate toilet and washbasin. The journeys are long and languid, great ways to see the countryside and very evocative of bygone days when trains ruled the world. **Red Dot Tours** (+94.11.7895 810; www.reddottours.com) books train tickets, as well as hotels, guides and other services at Sri Lanka's major rail destinations.

China's Himalayan Tracks

Couples looking for something slightly more adventurous in terms of accommodation, cuisine and ambience might want to consider a luxury train trip through **China**. The new *Llasa Express* runs daily between **Beijing** and the Tibetan metropolis, starting off on the fertile plains of eastern China, making a whistle-stop in the historic city of Xi'an and then gradually climbing onto the Tibetan Plateau.

Completed in 2006, the 1,956-km-long Tibetan portion (the Qingzang Railway) is the world's highest

THIS PAGE (FROM TOP): Sri Lanka's mosaic of railway lines includes the lush tea country around Nuwara Eliya; the luxury Deccan Odyssey train meanders through southern India; a private cabin on the aptly named Palace on Wheels.

OPPOSITE: In addition to its regular route between Singapore and Bangkok, the E&O makes side trips to various parts of Thailand.

Romantic Train Journeys

THIS PAGE (FROM TOP): Potala Palace lies at the end of the new railway line between Beijing and Llasa; traditional Tibetan yurts are just one of the sights along the high-altitude railway line; elevated tracks help the Llasa Express cross permafrost.

OPPOSITE: A couple of Japanese Shinkansen (bullet trains) cross at warp speeds beneath the majestic Mt Fuji.

railway line and counts among the modern wonders of engineering. Over 80 percent of the route is above 4,000 metres and more than half runs across permafrost on elevated tracks with special cooling systems that keep the rail-bed frozen throughout the summer. Built especially for this line, the passenger cars are pressurised like an aeroplane, framed by tinted, ultraviolet ray-reflecting windows, and equipped with extra oxygen to prevent high-altitude-related maladies.

Total travel time between Beijing and **Llasa** is roughly 48 hours, including two overnights. Upper class compartments feature four soft sleeper bunks, but the passage is reasonable enough to entice couples into buying out the whole compartment to cater to their privacy. Each cabin is equipped with a flat-screen TV, headphones, bed linen, oxygen canisters and a hot-water thermos. Shared toilets are down the hall. Meals are enjoyed in a dining car with panoramic windows, a menu that includes a la carte items and a Chinese buffet.

The highlight of the journey is obviously the scenery, a chance to get up close and personal with one of the world's most remote landscapes, the windswept and snow-covered Tibetan highlands, with the legendary city of Llasa at the end of the line. A super-luxury version of the train called the *Tanggula Express* is planned for the near future. Passengers can book their seats on the *Llasa Express* at Beijing Station, or purchase tickets ahead of time online through several

agencies including the **Tibet Train Travel** (8 Zhishan Road, Guilin, China 541002; +86.77.3381 0138; www.tibettraintravel.com).

Various international travel agencies charter private trains in China for guided rail journeys that include several destinations. The *Shangri-La Express* is one such train which makes a trip along the old Silk Road between Beijing and **Urumqi** in western China that includes stops in Xi'an, Lanzhou, Dunhuang and Turpan. **Xi'an** is home to the Terracotta Army, with its hundreds of royal tombs and other architectural icons like the Giant Wild Goose Pagoda. Set along the banks of the Yellow River, **Lanzhou** is home to an excellent provincial museum that revolves around the Silk Road. **Dunhuang** is where it finally starts to feel more like arid central Asia than the rest of China, an oasis town with a crescent lake and sand dunes. By the time the train reaches **Turpan** the transition is complete: a desert city with a largely Muslim population of Uyghur ethnic minority people.

The train's luxury twin-bed "Heritage Class" compartments feature mahogany furnishings, wool carpets, air conditioning, provide daily cleaning and 24-hour butler service, as well as VIP station privileges including express boarding. Each cabin has an adjacent washroom, while bathing is down the hall in a shower car with private stalls and changing area. The dining car features Western breakfast and Chinese specialities for lunch and dinner.

Hotel stays in major cities break up the two-to-three-week train journey. **Mir Corporation** (85 South Washington St, Suite 210 Seattle, WA, USA 98104; +1.206.624 7289; www. mircorp.com) is one of several agencies that book luxury rail tours which include passage on the *Shangri-La Express*. Whether for a honeymoon, anniversary or couples getaway, Mir can handcraft the itinerary to suit your personal travel style and needs, including romantic hotels at both ends of the line. The amount of guided touring and the pace are up to the two of you, letting you enjoy the whistle-stop destinations along the route in your own unique way. The company can also arrange all of your land tour needs in China, including meeting

you on arrival at the airport and seeing you off at the end of your trip.

Japanese Rail Adventures

Japan's aptly named bullet trains (Shinkansen) are among the fastest in the world, so fast that sleepers and private cabins aren't necessary because very few rail journeys are long enough to have to spend the night on the train. What makes them "sexy" is the speed you are travelling – upwards of 300 km per hour – as you zip through the Japanese countryside, as well as the dozens of romantic locations where you can hop off. **Tokyo** is a natural starting point for a week-long rail vacation that might include the historic cities of Kyoto and Nara, Japanese pop culture theme parks like the Hello

Kitty-inspired Sanrio Puroland, a trek to the top of Mount Fuji and the rural tranquillity of a hot spring resort of Nikko National Park.

Japan Rail Passes (www. japanrailpass.net) must be purchased prior to arrival in Japan. They cost anywhere from US$346 for a seven-day ordinary pass to US$974 for a 21-day first class (Green Car) pass. The actual cost (in local currency) is calculated upon purchase depending on the exchange rate of the day. Japan Rail posts all of their bullet train schedules online (in English). It's best to make seat reservations the day before each leg, especially on popular routes like Tokyo to Kyoto. Once you have your JR Pass in hand, the Japanese islands are your oyster. ~ JY

Asian Train Romance On-screen

Slumdog Millionaire (2008), in the scene at the end when boy-finally-gets-girl and the movie's uplifting *Jai Ho* dance number on the platform at Mumbai's old Victoria Station (Chhatrapati Shivaji Terminus), is the latest in a long line of Asian films that flaunt the romance of trains and rail travel.

One of the earliest Asian train movies was *Shanghai Express* (1932), starring a sultry Marlene Dietrich as "Shanghai Lil" and Donald Harvey as the British army doctor who once loved her – and would gladly court her again – if their train ever makes it through wartime China to safety on the coast.

Others are much more recent. In the quirky comedy *The Darjeeling Limited* (2007), three American brothers set off on a train voyage across India on a spiritual quest that eventually runs off the tracks as the brothers get waylaid by a beautiful train hostess, a man-eating tiger and various other subcontinental distractions. A high point of the film is the gorgeous Indian scenery the trains run through.

Asia's best-known train book is probably *Train Man* by Hitori Nakano, a classic manga (comic book) that inspired a hit TV series and feature film of the same name. It's a love story between a nerdy guy and a young woman who meet on a Japanese train.

Another offbeat Asian train story is *Transsiberian* (2008) in which an American honeymoon couple travelling from Beijing to Moscow during the depths of winter get sidetracked by a couple of sexy smugglers. Like Agatha Christie's famed train book, murder becomes the mystery on this express.

Spas & Wellness Retreats

Spas have evolved from bastions of solitude into bona fide couple escapes, places where couples can indulge in pure sensual pampering in serene and luxurious settings – away from the daily grind.

Even though the modern spa movement started in Europe and North America during Victorian times, the latest wave was largely generated in Asia, where centuries-old traditions of healing arts were meshed with exotic locations and impeccable service to spark the worldwide spa craze of today.

These havens of health are the New Age way for people to de-stress and recharge. Spa treatments run the gamut, from simple massages and facials to a wide array of exotic treatments from all around the globe. Couple add-ons might include guided pre-treatment relaxation techniques, private bathing or steaming, and cosying up afterwards in plush relaxation rooms while enjoying wine, champagne or tea, or even oysters. Couple spas offer a place to experience pampering with your amour. Prior to going into your very first couple spa treatment, it might be a good idea to discuss the type of experience each of you would like, and small details such as whether you want to converse during treatment or prefer to sleep.

Most countries in Asia have their own "indigenous" spa treatments, with roots in centuries-old traditional medicine. But most modern spas in the region now offer a combination of pan Eastern and Western treatments with only a few specialising in one type of treatment.

Native to India, Ayurvedic treatments are revitalising and therapeutic, aiming to keep one's mind and body balanced. According to Ayurvedic theory, all the ailments and sufferings that one endures are due to a disequilibrium and disharmony of the body's *dosha* (subtle energies). The main aim of

Ayurvedic therapies is to rebalance the *dosha* and eliminate toxins, increase immunity and soothe the senses, as part of a comprehensive effort to enhance physical and mental well-being. Thai massage involves deep pressure without oils and usually includes stretching. Traditional Chinese medicine (TCM), on the other hand, aims for a balance between the yin and yang, through various techniques including acupuncture and foot reflexology.

Although the word Shiatsu means "finger pressure" in Japanese, a Shiatsu treatment also includes the use of palms, knees, forearms, elbows and feet to apply pressure to energy lines to stimulate the body's *qi* or energy flow. Traditional Indonesian spa treatments include *mandi susu*, originally a milk bath, which is seen as the elixir of youth; *mandi lulur*, which exfoliates and polishes the body; and a traditional massage which involves medium pressure using coconut oil. Also prevalent in Asian spas are Swedish massages, consisting of a variety of techniques, all designed to relax muscles by applying pressure to them and rubbing in the same direction as the flow of blood to the heart.

Signature Treatments

To set themselves apart from the competition, many top spas offer a signature ritual or treatment. At the **Chi Spa** in Shangri-La Hotel, Bangkok (89 Soi Wat Suan Plu, New Rd, Bangrak, Bangkok 10500, Thailand; +66.2.236 7777; www.shangri-la.com), the signature "Chi Balance Massage"

THIS PAGE (CLOCKWISE FROM TOP): *The Spa Pool Villa at Banyan Tree Phuket allows couples to enjoy private treatments while "floating" in the middle of a lily pond; the natural, indigenous ingredients used the CHI Spa at Shangri-La Hotel Bangkok; and the spa incorporates ancient massage techniques in their treatments.*

OPPOSITE: *After their spa treatment, couples at the Coco Spa in Coco Palm Bodu Hithi can relax in a petal-strewn soaking tub.*

is based on the guest's personal configuration of the five elements: metal, water, wood, fire and earth.

Every spa visit at the **Pangkor Laut Resort** (Pangkor Laut Island; +603.2783 1000; www.pangkorlautresort.com) in Malaysia begins with a ritual representing the bathing traditions from around Asia. This includes Chinese foot pounding; Malay circulating bath; Japanese *goshi-goshi* cleansing; Shanghai scrub, and ends with a cup of tea, before you begin your chosen spa treatment.

The hip **Banyan Tree Resorts** (www.banyantree.com) on Phuket in **Thailand** and Hangzhou, Lijiang and Sanya in **China**, initiated a "Retreat for the Senses" campaign that promises to take the spa experience to an even more luxuriant level. "This all-inclusive programme is designed to provide guests with a holistic experience of rejuvenation, wellness and discovery with a thoughtful selection of signature spa treatments and cultural activities that suits the guest's lifestyle and personal preferences," says Arthur Kiong, managing director of sales and marketing for the group.

Depending on the need, the spa package can include a consultation with TCM specialists, yoga or tai chi lessons, and even cookery classes. All the options include Banyan Tree's signature "Night of Bliss" during which the guests' villa is set aglow with soft candlelight and infused with aromatic oils. In addition, the outdoor sunken bath is strewn with fragrant flowers, and soothing music is played, setting the final stage for intimate bliss.

Thailand: Global Spa Mecca

A full two percent of all spas in the world are in Thailand, employing over 11,000 people. It's no wonder that the competition among Thai spas is so intense and the range of services so broad.

Located in northern Thailand, the **Anantara Golden Triangle Resort & Spa** (229 Moo 1, Chiang Saen, Chiang Rai 57150, Thailand; +665.378 4084; spa.anantara.com/goldentriangle) near Chiang Rai recently launched a unique Jungle Yoga, Elephant & Spa Experience. Guests get to ride an elephant through bamboo forest beside the Mekong River to and from an outdoor yoga studio to work on *asana* postures and breathing techniques. Once back at the hotel, guests get a tension-relief massage in the main spa.

Four Seasons hotels encourage guests to "sample" their spas and experience the differences by staying in more than one of their Thailand hotels. A suggestion may include a rural and urban combo at **Four Seasons Resort Chiang Mai** (Mae Rim-Samoeng Old Rd, Mae Rim, Chiang Mai 50180, Thailand; +665.3298 181; www.fourseasons.com; see pages 182–183) and the famed **Four Seasons Bangkok** (155 Rajadamri Rd, Bangkok 10330, Thailand, +662.1268 866; www.fourseasons.com).

Couples who need utmost privacy – or perhaps a bit of Hollywood fantasy on their honeymoon – might want to try **S Medical Spa** (2/2 Bhakdi Building, Wireless Rd, Lumpini, Bangkok 10330 Thailand; +662.253 1010; www.smedspa.com). Designed with

celebrities in mind, the facility includes underground car parks and waiting rooms for bodyguards. Slimming, sculpting and anti-aging procedures, and laser hair removal as well as detoxification, executive check-ups and spa services are rendered in indulgent surroundings far from prying eyes and paparazzi.

High Times at Himalayan Spas

Situated at an elevation of over 2,438 metres, the **Wildflower Hall, Shimla in the Himalayas – An Oberoi Resort** (Shimla 171 012, Himachal Pradesh, India; +91.177.264 8585;

www.oberoihotels.com) in the Indian hill station of **Shimla** oozes old-world charm. The tranquil sanctuary is set in 22 acres of virgin pine and cedar woods. The former residence of Lord Kitchener, the resort boasts teakwood floors, hand-knotted rugs and rich furnishings complemented by spectacular views of the surrounding snowy peaks. The resort also features an Oberoi spa with holistic treatments based on Ayurvedic, Oriental and Western traditions. Once the treatment is complete, guests can relish in the high-altitude environment in the outdoor Jacuzzi

and swimming pool, or take a romantic walk on one of the many trails through the lush property.

The primary aim of the **Ayurveda Health Home** (Tilingatar, Dhapasi-7, Kathmandu, Nepal; +977.1435 8761; www.ayurveda.com. np) in **Kathmandu** is to awaken the individual's natural healing source and restore inner harmony, balance and rhythm. The spa offers a wide range of Ayurvedic therapy, based on ancient scriptures, including Shirodhara oil dripping on the "third eye" as well as relaxing, cleansing or herbal Abhyanga massages.

THIS PAGE: What better way to relax than lazing beside a whirlpool, taking in the dramatic Himalayas after a spa treatment at Wildflower Hall, Shimla in the Himalaysas – An Oberoi Resort in northern India?

OPPOSITE (FROM TOP): The swanky Four Seasons Resort Chiang Mai in northern Thailand offers serene meditation and yoga pavilions; soak and relax in a scented floral bath big enough for two after the treatment.

Spas & Wellness Retreats

THIS PAGE (CLOCKWISE FROM TOP): *The Cowrie Shell Massage at Shangri-La's Villingili Resort & Spa in the Maldives draws its essential energy from the ocean; the Beach Spa, under billowing white fabric, at the Coco Spa, Coco Palm Dhuni Kolhu in the Maldives; native to nearby India, Ayurvedic spa treatments at Villingili balance the body's subtle energies.*

OPPOSITE: *Couples are transported in a traditional dhoni to the Island Spa at the Four Seasons Kuda Huraa in the Maldives.*

For a much more modern take on Nepalese spa services, the contemporary **Hyatt Regency Kathmandu** (Taragaon, Boudha, Kathmandu, Nepal; +977.1449 1234; www.kathmandu.regency.hyatt.com) offers the swanky Club Oasis. A combination high-tech gym and spa, with separate areas for men and women, the club includes a steam bath, sauna and Jacuzzi. Among the four treatment rooms, one is reserved for couples and one expressly used for Ayurvedic treatments. Yoga and meditation sessions are complemented by 37 acres of landscaped grounds, including a 1,600-metre jogging track.

Nouvelle Spa Retreat: The Maldives

The **Maldives**, a chain of coral atolls in the Indian Ocean south of Sri Lanka, has come into its own in recent years as an oasis of health, beauty and pampering. The spas are usually attached to luxury private island resorts that can only be reached by boat or seaplane. Many give guests the option of treatments indoors, al fresco or in the privacy of their own over-water bungalows.

The first resort in the Maldives to achieve the international Green Globe "Building, Planning and Design Standard" certification, **Alila Villas Hadahaa** (North Huvahoo Atoll, Maldives; +960.682 8888; www.alilahotels.com) achieves that fine balance in environmental responsibility while maintaining its chic appeal. Continuing the green theme, the resort's **Spa by Mandara** was named

2009 Eco Spa of the Year by *AsiaSpa* and included in Hot List Spas 2010 by *Condé Nast Traveler*.

Tucked into a quiet corner of the resort with its own tranquillity pool, Spa by Mandara features five spa villas designed specifically for couples, each with an oversized bathtub and shower, plus an outdoor lounging area for post-treatment relaxation. Products are made with natural ingredients and many are exclusive, such as the White Hadahaa Tea blend consisting of coriander, peppermint and ginger served to guests before their treatments. The spa's signature treatment is the 80-minute "Island Rhythm Massage" which begins with a 15-minute foot ritual and ends with a head massage.

Another over-the-top spa experience awaits at **Four Seasons Resort Kuda Huraa** (North Malé Atoll; Maldives; +960.6644 888; www.fourseasons.com). In order to reach the aptly named **Island Spa**, guests must take a short boat ride aboard a traditional Maldivian dhoni sailing craft to a small sandy "island of pampering" with private over-water spa pavilions. Glass floors in the treatment room let guests watch tropical fish dart through the crystal-clear water below while the therapist performs the signature treatment – a mixture of massage techniques from Thailand, Bali and the Philippines.

Designer Spas & Fantasy Worlds

Le Spa du Metropole at the Sofitel Legend Metropole Hanoi (1 Thanh Nien Rd, Ba Dinh District, 10000 Hanoi, Vietnam; +84.4.3823 8888;

www.sofitel.com) is all about recapturing old world elegance. Rich textiles, objets d'art, ceiling fans and gilt-framed mirrors are all part of the décor at this oasis of pleasure in the Vietnamese capital. Less is certainly not considered more here. The spa's 400 sq metres comprise two treatment rooms, two themed couple's spa suites, and three themed individual suites: the Vietnam Suite, Retro Suite and Thailand Suite. There is also a reflexology treatment room.

In **Tokyo**, one of the world's most exciting fashion houses offers **Ginza Armani Spa** (5-5-4 Ginza, Chuo-Ku, Tokyo, Japan; +81.3.6274 7000; www.armaniginzatower.com) on the fifth floor of the Armani flagship store in the famous Ginza district. The black décor, with touches of glowing amber, bronze and fresh

Spa Extravaganza

Even in the world of luxury spas, some are more opulent than others. An organic green tea sea salt exfoliation and seaweed and algae mask are among various elements of the five-hour "Exceptional Ritual" at the Talise Spa in the Madinat Jumeirah resort in Dubai (US$600). The "Bulgari Royal Lulur For Two" – a sumptuous three-hour couples treatment at the Bulgari Resort in Bali – comes in at US$975. But the coup de grace? Spa V at the Hotel Victor in Miami's swish South Beach neighbourhood can arrange an "Evian Bath" filled with 1,000 litres of the pricey French water, the tub ringed in flowers, caviar and gourmet chocolates within an arm's reach. The price for that? A cool US$5,000.

THIS PAGE (FROM TOP): Le Spa du Metropole at the Sofitel Legend Metropole hotel in Hanoi is an oasis of old-world elegance and calm in the midst of the bustling city; Chi The Spa at the Shangri-La's Tanjung Aru Resort comprises a "spa village" made up of eight villas.

OPPOSITE: The ultra-modern Altira Spa in Macau features sophisticated water treatments and facilities including swimming and vitality pools, crystal steam rooms, saunas, rasul and experience showers.

neutrals, counters the bright white one finds in so many spas. The circular, dome-shaped treatment rooms feel almost like a cocoon. The signature offering here is "The Ceremony" – a personalised ritual that commences with an analysis by a Spa Master. This is followed by a three-zone journey, moving from room to room, that combines healing and revitalising pamperings complete with skin treatments.

Rock Spa at the new Hard Rock Hotel (City of Dreams, Estrada do Istmo, Cotai, Macau; +853.8868 3338; www.hardrockhotelmacau.com) in **Macau** affords a brief glimpse of what life must be like as a rock star – constantly being preened and pampered. The hushed tranquillity one finds at so many spas is replaced with soft rock playing in the background, and the therapists are friendly and upbeat rather than quiet. Couples can laze away an entire day on "Love Potion No. 9" – a six-hour treatment that includes dual massage and facials, exfoliation and wraps, poolside lunch, a private session during which the lovebirds apply "love potion" to one another, and a champagne ceremony with fresh berries and chocolate.

Another designer-savvy Macau escape is the sprawling 6,000-sq-metre spa at the five-star **Altira Macau** (Avenida de Kwong Tung, Taipa, Macau; +853.2886 8886; www.altiramacau.com). The futuristic facility, designed by California hotel, restaurant and spa maestro Peter Remedios, spans two storeys, with stunning views of the Macau waterfront beyond the infinity pool with underwater music. **Altira Spa** has been awarded with five star ratings for the second consecutive year by the 2011 *Forbes Travel Guide*.

Hong Kong's Urban Spas

Hong Kong is one of Asia's most hectic cities, which makes it both fun and stressful, but there are many luxury spas just waiting to get those knots out of your shoulders and restore the ultimate in inner calm. Despite being

right in the middle of Hong Kong's main financial and business district, **Farm, The Organic Spa** (5/F, Baskerville House, 13 Duddell St, Central, Hong Kong; +852.2866 8238; www.farmtheorganicspa.com) features a pebble-strewn outdoor terrace with a wonderful view over the city's Botanical Gardens. Treatments are all devoted to rejuvenation and only certified organic products are used. The popular deluxe rejuvenating firming facial takes a full 90 minutes and features a combination of 21 Amala products including clay, serum and eye cream. Their two-hour "Detox and Cellulite Treatment" promises to rid the body of the harmful effects of lunches on the run, heavy business dinners and too much coffee. It comprises a blend of cleansing citrus oils known for their diuretic properties, which help the body quickly rid itself of toxins and restore its optimal metabolic balance. The immune system is also boosted with a blend of tea tree and eucalyptus oils, which are renowned for their natural anti-viral and anti-bacterial powers.

With two outlets in **Hong Kong** (Causeway Bay and Lantau), as well as Beijing and Shanghai in China proper, the stylish **Spas by MTM** (www.spamtm.com) are a breath of fresh air in the busy city. Their spa products are all custom-blended on the spot, formulated from a therapist's diagnosis of your physical and spiritual needs. The three-hour "Bridal Treatment" includes a hydrating and moisturising Indo Exfo Scrub to exfoliate the skin's dead cells, while restoring the body's natural glow and radiance, followed by a honey-milk wrap to ensure supple skin and an aromatherapy massage to relieve tension and reduce stress. The treatment finishes with a red wine bath to stimulate the skin's natural collagen and reduce swelling. The ingredients also boast antioxidant effects.

The **Victorian Spa** in Hong Kong Disneyland (+852.1830 830; park. hongkongdisneyland.com) on Lantau Island gives couples an added reason to visit the happiest place on earth. Mickey's suite of 10 treatment rooms includes three doubles where couples can cast aside their mouse ears for treatments like the Timeless Victorian which starts with a foot ritual, moves through a massage, facial, manicure, and ends with a hair cleanse and finish in the salon.

Spa Escape in Sabah

Situated on a peninsula with fabulous sea views, **CHI The Spa** at Shangri-La's Tanjung Aru Resort (20 Jalan Aru, Tanjung Aru 88100 Kota Kinabalu, Sabah, Malaysia; +60.88.792 888; www.shangri-la.com) features eight island villas with private treatment rooms, lounging areas, steam rooms, outdoor gardens and bathing facilities. Three of the villas, complete with a private garden and outdoor showers, are designed especially for couples. The spa also features a yoga pavilion. The extensive menu offers signature therapies like "Borneo Therapy", inspired by the traditions of the *bobohizan*, the island's native healers. The treatment employs local herbs like nutmeg, red ginger and betel leaf to remove negative energy. **~ JC**

Eco Chic Escapes

"Eco" honeymoons can take various forms – from scuba diving among incredible coral reefs and wildlife safaris on elephant back, to helping to construct a village school or volunteering to plant trees. But going green doesn't mean you have to sacrifice comfort or romance.

Awareness of the environment and social responsibility are driving more and more enlightened couples, who want to minimise their carbon footprint, to seek out honeymoons and romantic getaways that tread gently on the earth. They want to show that they care about the local communities and cultures they visit. Increasingly, eco-friendly (but still chic) resorts that recycle waste materials, use renewable energy sources, grow their own organic produce on site and provide employment for the local community are gaining popularity and recognition.

Some of the world's most sustainable hotels and resorts are located in Asia. They minimise their impact on the environment through various good practices, including generating power from solar energy, as well as through water and other ecologically sound sources. They also create restaurant menus with dishes made from organic produce purchased from local farmers, and recycle plastic, water, paper and anything else that can be reused. In addition, they work with local villagers to create job opportunities and ensure a shared sense of responsibility in protecting Mother Earth and the future of tourism in the area.

The guest experience at eco resorts runs a broad gamut from passive pastimes such as birdwatching from the comfort of their private deck, or luxuriating in bathwater heated by solar panels to active pursuits like nature walks, scuba diving, helping to build a village school or replanting trees.

Preserving Asia's Underwater Treasures

Laid-back is the best way to describe the **El Nido Resorts** (Taytay, Palawan; +63.2.894 5644; www.elnidoresorts.com) in the **Palawan** region of the Philippines, 430 km southwest of Manila. The Lagen and Miniloc properties both offer scenic tropical landscapes, crystal clear waters and relative isolation. Couples can choose from a wide range of activities including sea kayaking, sailing and stargazing. From sea slugs to whale sharks, the surrounding waters teem with marine life. The area is also a nesting ground of three species of endangered sea turtles and a feeding ground of the elusive dugong (sea cow) as well as whales and dolphins.

The uninitiated in diving can get certified at the El Nido scuba school, and couples will then be ready to take their first dive together in the warm Sulu Sea. If terrestrial activities are preferred, take a long walk through the surrounding jungle. Among the strange mammals one might come across are the Palawan Bear Cat, Palawan Stink Badger and Palawan Tree Shrew. The resorts can also arrange to drop guests off at more than a hundred private beaches in the area for a day of seclusion.

Both hotels were designed to have minimal impact on the natural surroundings. At the Lagen Island Resort, for instance, the pool is only 1.2 metres deep so as not to disturb the tree roots underneath. All cottages, rooms and suites have antique wood floors as well as furniture fashioned from wood

reclaimed from old Filipino houses. El Nido works closely with local communities on a range of issues, including discouraging illegal fishing, watershed rehabilitation, coastal clean-ups, environmental education, installation and maintenance of mooring buoys (to protect coral reefs) and the development of coastal resource management plans.

Off the northwest coast of Borneo at the edge of Tunku Abdul Rahman Marine Park in **Sabah** is an island retreat called **Gayana Eco Resort** (Gaya Island, Kota Kinabalu, Sabah, Malaysia; +60.88.442 233; www.gayana-eco-resort.com). Being "eco" doesn't mean any modern comforts have been sacrificed. The 44 overwater bungalows feature contemporary amenities like beds

with Frette linen, wireless Internet service, rainwater showers, organic Harnn bath products from Thailand and stylish rattan and wooden furniture. All the rooms boast stunning jungle, lagoon, mangrove or ocean views.

Taking rustic comfort to an even higher level, the 153-sq-metre Palm Villa features glass floors in the living room for watching the tropical fish frolic beneath the bungalow. Other amenities include a private plunge pool, a two-person bathtub with sea views and a sanctuary room for couple's spa treatments. The resort restaurants are nothing short of gourmet, with the freshest seafood supplied by Gayana's own fish farm.

Eco friendly activities comprise hiking, kayaking, diving, snorkelling,

THIS PAGE (FROM TOP): The eco-chic Lagen water cottages at the El Nido Resorts offer couples a romantic back-to-nature holiday; Guests kayaking around limestone cliffs in a crystal clear lagoon near the El Nido Resorts.

OPPOSITE: Elephant trekking in Thailand's Golden Triangle through bamboo forests and river flood plains is an ideal way to discover the region's flora and fauna.

fish feeding, catch-and-release fishing as well as island-hopping trips. In keeping with the resort's "save the planet" ethos, there are no motorised sports. Be mesmerised by the exotic and amazingly varied sea life at night when the resort turns on the floodlights underwater.

Gayana also has its own Marine Ecology Research Centre (MERC), which recently announced success in spawning all seven species of endangered giant clams found in Malaysian waters. The resort chose clams for their project due to the crustaceans' contribution to the marine ecosystem. Described as the "kidneys of the waters", clams have the ability to filter harmful waste nutrients in seawater. Gayana also has a reef-regenerating programme where guests can help replant coral on nearby reefs, a turtle care centre, as well as holding tanks and educational exhibits.

Rural Settings in China & Vietnam

Designed to resemble a bygone rural community, **Pilgrimage Village** (130 Minh Mang Rd, Hue City, Vietnam; +84.54.388 5461; www. pilgrimagevillage.com) is a boutique resort located on the wooded outskirts of **Hue**, the ancient royal capital of Vietnam. The charm of this unique Vietnamese property is two-fold: an overwhelming sense of tranquillity combined with a rustic village setting of thatched-roof stone or wooden bungalows connected by bridges and garden paths.

Balancing its natural environment and the preservation of local culture with modern conveniences, Pilgrimage Village offers a total of 99 rooms, including 15 honeymoon bungalows and five honeymoon pool huts. The resort's **Vedana Spa** specialises in very unique, traditional Vietnamese treatments,

like an ancient royal hairwash done with *bo ket* (black bean soap) and a flower bath strewn with petals, and suffused with essential oils made from local ingredients. The resort also provides venues for local artisans to create embroidery, ceramics and woodcarvings, which guests can purchase.

Nature-loving newlyweds will also enjoy **Crosswaters Eco Lodge & Spa** (Nankun Mountain National Forest Park, Longmen District, Huizhou 516876, China; +86.752.769 3666; www.crosswaters. net.cn), tucked in the mountains of southern China in **Huizhou** at the confluence of two rivers. To appreciate the true romance of this resort, couples should visit the Star Gazing Tower at night and the river Viewing Tower by day. The 53 villas were designed to blend with the remote scenery, with lots of creature comforts but also ecological features

like recycled roof tiles, rammed-earth walls and all-natural materials. And of course, the whole resort was planned in consultation with a feng shui master. The Presidential Suite offers views of the river and forest, while the Deluxe Honeymoon Spa Villa features private steam and sauna facilities as well as its own garden and views of the surroundings.

The **Crossroads Forest Spa** only uses treatment ingredients found within Nankunshan Park, including bamboo, honey, nectar and alkaline-free cocoa tea. The treatments are customised to suit your skin's needs and cater to different weather conditions. The open-sided restaurant serves Hakka dishes, many of which use ingredients harvested from the resort's own orchard, farm and lotus ponds. Other amenities include a swimming pool, a yoga pavilion, badminton courts and an education centre, where you can take classes in, for example, regional wine-making techniques.

Bali Goes Organic

Hidden high up in the jungle overlooking Bali's north shore, **Damai Lovina Villas** (Jalan Damai, Kayuputih, Lovina, Bali, Indonesia; +623.6241 008; www.damai.com) features 14 opulent villas set in a lush tropical paradise beside terraced rice fields. In 2009, the resort was chosen by the local government as a role model for other properties to emulate in the areas of waste management, water and energy conservation and organic resort operation. The resort also serves as a field laboratory for sustainable tourism. In addition to the environmentally friendly surroundings, it is a great place to experience the Seduce Your Senses programme. It encourages couples to embark on a journey of mutual exploration through the resort's Damai Lovina's signature cuisine and spa treatments.

Decorated in Bali's inimitable style with local Indonesian antiques, the villas include features such as outdoor bathrooms, private pools and large verandahs. The lavish Umah Raja Villa even has its own large library, cinema and two private pools. The award-winning resort restaurant serves organic vegetables and meats from Damai Lovina's own farm, together with fish freshly caught from a nearby river. The establishment raises pigs, rabbits, ducks, frogs and snails, as well as lobsters bred in saltwater basins in a neighbouring valley. Spa treatments – offered inside the villa or one of the spa pavilions – utilise

THIS PAGE (CLOCKWISE FROM TOP): A romantic experience awaits – the master pool and bale pavillion at the Damai Lovina Villas; The bed in the Master Bedroom at Umah Raja is fit for a king.

OPPOSITE (FROM LEFT): Fountains dance at the pool's edge in the evening light at the Gayana Eco Resort; A diver gets up close to a giant clam in the waters surrounding the Gayana Eco Resort.

Eco Chic Escapes

THIS PAGE: *Perched on top of a cliff on Bali's southern coast, Alila Villas Uluwatu is a contemporary masterpiece.*

OPPOSITE (FROM TOP): *Nihiwatu resort on the Indonesian island of Sumba is surrounded by ultra-remote tropical forest, grassland and amazing beaches; the barefoot chic restaurant at Nihiwatu features a sand floor.*

traditional Balinese techniques mixed with methods from the rest of Asia as well as Western countries, and use only natural and organic products. The resort claims that all their spa products are based on ancient recipes once used in the royal palace in Solo, originally meant only for the royal family.

Alila has a reputation for creating resorts that are serene, sensual and surprisingly different, and the **Alila Villas Uluwatu** (Jalan Belimbing Sari, Banjar Tambiyak, Desa Pecatu 80364, Bali, Indonesia; +62.361.848 2166; www.alilahotels.com/uluwatu) certainly fits in with this goal. Perched along high cliffs on the island's rugged southern coast, this contemporary masterpiece offers almost everything a couple could want in a romantic getaway – lush surroundings, personal butler, fine dining and spa.

The resort combines contemporary décor and Balinese accents, and has stylish open-plan villas with private pools and cabanas overlooking the Indian Ocean. Guests can laze away an afternoon in style on spacious daybeds. Behind its modern façade, the resort is also very eco friendly, the first in Bali to earn the highest possible certification in Environmentally Sustainable Design (ESD). All building materials have been locally sourced, recycled and are therefore sustainable. In order to conserve water, methods employed include trapping rainwater in gardens, as well as grey water recycling. The resort's vegetation system is based on the Balinese savannah ecosystem – one that encourages the colonisation of local birds.

Saving Mankind & the Planet

Located in the cultural triangle of northern **Sri Lanka**, **Jetwing Vil Uyana** (Sigiriya, Sri Lanka; +94.66.492 3584; www.jetwinghotels.com/jetwingviluyana) exemplifies how a hotel can save the planet from mankind's abuse. To create the resort, the developers transformed rundown agricultural land into habitat-rich wetlands where birds, fish and other wildlife can thrive. The wetlands provide a setting for Sri Lanka's only over-water bungalows. A bicycle path was also created so that guests can cycle to bird-watching perches. There is a Buddhist meditation centre only half a kilometre from the resort for couples who want to revel in its totally serene atmosphere.

Vil Uyana practises energy and water conservation, air quality management, pollution reduction, uses environmentally friendly resources, recycles a variety of different items and conducts regular awareness programmes for guests, staff and the local community. Two of the property's ten hectares are being used to redevelop paddy fields using traditional organic harvesting methods. Another hectare is being reforested using native plants. The owners have also established an award-winning youth training programme that teaches teenagers and young adults from three local hamlets about the hospitality industry and prepares them for jobs as cooks, customer care and front office staff and nature guides.

The resort's 25 *avasas* (guest dwellings) are set in four habitats: three Water Villas; six Paddy Field Villas, six Marsh Dwellings and ten Forest Villas each with private dining decks and swimming pools. All villas have teak floors, and offer air conditioning, Internet access and cable TV with Bose entertainment system. Hotel facilities include a spa which blends Western methods with naturopathy and Ayurvedic approaches. There are two in-house restaurants and a bar to visit, or you can opt for a romantic dinner in your villa or dine al fresco under the stars in the night sky. Visitors can explore the grounds in search of rare birds and wildlife via wooden walkways or boat.

Nihiwatu (Nihiwatu beach, Sumba, Indonesia 80361 Bali;

+62.361.757 149 (reservations office in Bali); www.nihiwatu.com) on Indonesia's **Sumba Island** is a barefoot-chic locale suitable for fishing, surfing and diving. The vibe is thoroughly "unplugged" – think restaurants with sand floors and reading a book in a hammock strung between coconut palms rather than loud music and flat-screen TVs. The place is rather remote – perfect for a sunset walk along the beach where t seems like you're the only couple in the world – accessible only by the resort's weekly charter plane.

Set on an area of more than 162 hectares of tropical forest, grassland, rice terraces and unspoilt beach, the accommodation for 30 comprises seven stylish thatched-roof bungalows and three two-bedroom villas, built by native craftsmen using local materials. Glass walls are used so that guests can take in the spectacular views.

Despite its end-of-the-earth location, Nihiwatu has also become a model for sustainability. The hotel was instrumental in founding the Sumba Foundation, dedicated to lessening the consequences of poverty on the island. Guests can volunteer time helping out with the local community. Nihiwatu is also one of nine founding members (the only one in Asia) of Global Ecosphere Retreats – resorts that have been selected for their commitment to fostering long-term change through sustainable ecosystem management to deliver balance between conservation and commerce, while preserving the cultural and other needs of local communities. **~JC**

Winter Vacations

Asia may not seem like the most obvious place for a winter vacation. But with copious amounts of snow in the northern parts of Japan, China and Korea, and the world's greatest mountain range stretching across the north of India, there is plenty of scope for skiing, snowboarding and other cold-weather adventures that stoke the fires of winter romance.

Many of the trimmings of winter romance come from Western culture – chestnuts roasting on an open fire; riding in a one-horse open sleigh and smooching beneath the mistletoe. It is no longer uniquely so; now it's possible to plan a cool white getaway in Asia. Like a winter storm bearing down from Siberia, snow culture has swept across the region. The result: a blizzard of cold-weather resorts with world-class skiing and snowboarding amenities, eclectic eating and après-ski life, and rooms with roaring fireplaces, hot tubs and goose down comforters. From Japan to China, and Mongolia to India, avid travellers pack their woollies, get togged up in designer winter gear and ski or snowboard down the powdery snow-capped mountain slopes at Asia's top winter resorts from December through March.

Asia boasts the world's largest and highest mountain range in the mighty Himalayas. In addition to huge amounts of snow – and the planet's largest collection of snow-capped peaks – the range claims more glaciers than anywhere outside the polar regions. Sapporo in northern Japan lies on the same latitude as Sun Valley, Idaho. China's Yabuli ski resort is around the same latitude as the renowned winter resorts of Grenoble in France and Zermatt, Switzerland. Korea's winter resorts are at about the same latitude as California's Mammoth Mountain and Aspen, Colorado.

Anyone who thinks the Asian slopes aren't up to scratch should consider the fact that countries in the region have hosted two Winter

Olympics. Several resorts are regular stops on the world professional skiing and snowboard circuits. Contrary to common belief, holidaymakers don't have to be pros to enjoy Asian winters. All the top resorts offer schools for those who want to learn the basics. For those who don't, there are plenty of other cold-weather activities: sledding and snowball fights, hot springs and soothing spas, winter wildlife watching and stargazing, shopping and nightlife. These, plus some of the best food one comes across anywhere in the snow sports world, will certainly make it a memorable escapade.

Japan: Blessed with Snow & Hot Springs

With a long tradition of winter revelry, **Japan** offers more cold-weather recreation options than any other Asian nation. **Sapporo** and **Nagano** have both hosted the Winter Olympics and remain bustling hubs of cold-weather sports and après snow action. Winter resorts like **Niseko** and **Furano** are found up and down the length of the rugged Japanese Alps, some of them are very accessible from major cities and convenient for daytrips while others require overnight stays and are more remote. At these resorts, outdoor winter spas and hot springs are also popular, and provide different levels of comfort, some rustic yet chic.

"Blessed by Snow" is Sapporo's motto, and indeed the northern metropolis has a longer, harder winter than any other major Japanese city. The capital of Hokkaido Island placed itself squarely on the world snow sports map in 1972 when it staged the first Winter Games ever held outside Europe or North America.

Mount Teine, a one-hour drive northwest of the city, is where the Olympic slalom and giant slalom were contested. It's actually two separate areas (Highland and Olympia) that operate as one resort with interchangeable lift tickets. Teine's varied terrain makes it ideal for both novices and experienced skiers and snowboarders. Six lifts, including a new express quad chair, whisk couples to the top of seven marked runs and a huge off-piste backcountry area with fresh powder throughout the winter. Even if you and your partner aren't into perfecting your downhill, the views from the top are breathtaking, providing gorgeous panoramas of an endless snow-covered Hokkaido. The action doesn't stop at sundown: Teine offers night skiing, followed by après-ski revelry in Sapporo's rowdy Susukino nightlife district.

Sapporo's other claim to winter fame is the annual Snow Festival held in February. More than two million people flock to this week-long winter wonderland of concerts, beauty pageants, snow sports and around 400 outdoor snow statues and ice sculptures. The climax of the festival is an international ice sculpture competition in Odori Park, that draws teams from more than a dozen nations.

Onsen (communal baths and hot springs) are a long and honoured Japanese tradition. They vary in size from large natural pools where dozens of people can soak, to intimate private bathing for two.

THIS PAGE (FROM TOP): Ice climbing is one of the newer (and more challenging) winter sports; South Korea is Asia's hotbed for snowmobiling; snow monkeys soak in the hot springs of Japan's Jigokudani Yaenkoen Park.

OPPOSITE: Asia offers a surprisingly large and varied selection of places for snow play and cold-weather fun.

Winter Vacations

THIS PAGE (FROM TOP): Asia's ski resorts have added dozens of new lifts and gondolas over the past decade; a couple snowboarding on the slopes, enjoying each other's company; India's Himalayan region has discovered heli-skiing.

OPPOSITE: The snow-covered Great Wall is located near the popular Nanshan Ski Resort, just outside of Beijing in northern China.

Some of the most romantic are found at *ryokan* (traditional inns) in snow-covered mountain and forest locales. Several villages in the Japanese Alps combine hot springs and ski slopes, including **Zao Onsen** (999-2301, Yamagata-ken, Yamagata-shii, Zao Onsen 708-1; +81.23.694 9328; www.zao-spa.or.jp/english/index.html) in **Yamagata** Prefecture and **Nozawa Onsen** (www.nozawaski.com/winter/en) in **Nagano** Prefecture.

Humans aren't the only creatures who flock to *onsen* in winter. Japan's famous snow monkeys soak in the hot springs at **Jigokudani Yaenkoen Park** near Nagano. Visitors are not allowed into the water with the animals, but you can get quite close for photographs. The park website (www.jigokudani-yaenkoen.co.jp) includes a live webcam that shows the snow monkeys at play.

South Korea: Skiing Down the "Silk Road"

South Korea may not be the first place that comes to mind when you consider a snow vacation, but with around 70 percent of the peninsula covered with mountains, it offers a surprisingly wide selection of winter resorts to suit most tastes and levels. The nation boasts more than a dozen winter sports resorts, including four within an hour's drive of Seoul. Facilities are generally world-class, with superbly groomed slopes, speedy lifts and a good selection of rental equipment, as well as ski schools for all ages.

With the peninsula's steepest and longest runs – including a 6-km track called the "Silk Road" – **Muju**

Resort (San 43-15, Simgok-ri, Solchun-myeon, Muju-kun, Jeonbak, Korea; +82.63.322 900; www.mujuresort.com) is the nation's most challenging ski area. Temperatures rarely stray above freezing between November and April, and with more than a hundred days of snowfall each year, powder (soft new snow that looks and feels like cold white powder – what skiers always wish for) is rarely in short supply. Other outdoor activities available at this resort include sledding, heated pool swimming and snowmobiling on marked trails through thickly wooded backcountry. This sprawling property also features a Korean cultural theme park and artisan village. Located in Mount Deogyo National Park, plenty of winter photo opportunities await. Of the resort's three hotels, the Austrian-style Tyrol is the most romantic, especially the Alpine Suites with their four-poster beds, roaring fireplaces, big-enough-for-two bathtubs and private steam rooms.

Korea's other top-notch snow resort is **Yong Pyong Resort** (Gangwon-do, Pyungchang-gun, Doam-myeon, Yongsan-ri 130; +82.33.335 5757; www.yongpyong.co.kr), which bid for the 2010 and 2014 Winter Games. Snowboarders flock to the mountain to challenge the terrain park and oversized halfpipe, which are among the best in Asia. But Yong Pyong also draws more than its fair share of non-athletes. Much of the hit miniseries *Winter Sonata* was filmed on location here, and one of the more popular resort pastimes is re-enacting romantic scenes from the show: eating at the Café Chuh-Eum and the

restaurant on the first floor of the Dragon Valley Hotel; snuggling on a bench near the bottom of the main piste; making a snowman together on the crest of Mount Balwang; or stealing a kiss on the gondola that rises up to Dragon Peak.

China: Snowboarding & Ice Sculptures

Located about an hour outside the Chinese national capital, **Beijing Nanshan Ski Resort** (Shengshuitou Village, Miyun County, Beijing 101500; +86.10.8909 1909; www.nanshanski.com;) is the country's largest winter resort and one of the best places to snowboard in all of Asia. The resort's sprawling Quicksilver Mellow snowboard terrain park is packed with features like a mini kicker, a down rail, wallrides and a 800-metre-long halfpipe. The resort's annual Red Bull Nanshan Open is one of the top spots on the world snowboard tour, but the park offers enough variety for both neophytes and seasoned pros.

Advanced skiers can ride the double chairlift to the top of **Nanshan** and test their luck on a steep, advanced mogul slope. For those who haven't mastered the board sports, despair not. There are several sled and toboggan runs, a large snow play area that begs you to build a snowman, or the mountaintop Lavender Tea House with its panoramic views of snowy northern China.

With limited accommodation in Nanshan, it may be better to base your snow vacation in Beijing, in particular north city hotels like the new **InterContinental Beijing Beichen** (8 Beichen West Rd, Chaoyang District, Beijing 100105, China; +86.10.8437 1188; www.ichotelsgroup.com). Built for the 2008 Summer Olympics, the hotel overlooks the famous "Bird's Nest" national stadium and lies within easy reach of the expressway leading to Nanshan. The northerly location also gives travellers the triple option of visiting the snowfields, Great Wall and central Beijing. Pamper your ski-weary body with a three-hour Asian Rejuvenation at the InterCon Spa or a dip in the heated indoor pool.

China's best winter resort is in **Yabuli** in the fabled Manchurian region north of Beijing. The village has hosted winter versions of both the Asian Games and World University Games, and is home-base of China's national ski team. Yabuli boasts three different ski areas, including one dedicated to beginners. Veteran skiers can ride heated, high-speed gondolas to the top of Sun Mountain, where three black diamond runs take on all challengers. Combine a snow sports vacation in Yabuli with a visit to the International Snow & Ice Sculpture Festival in

nearby Harbin, a month-long extravaganza showcasing Chinese cold-weather culture and giant frozen sculptures that are magically illuminated each night.

A recommended luxury abode at Yabuli is the all-suite **Sun Mountain Lodge** (Sun Mountain, Yabuli, Heilongjiang, China; +86.451.5345 8888; www.slh.com/sunmountain), a 24-room boutique hotel with lavish modern rooms designed for cold-weather romance – sunken tub and blazing fireplace adjacent to a king-size bed, in addition to views of the snow country over the top of your toes.

India: Heli-skiing in the Himalayas

Gulmarg ski resort (www.gulmargski.org) in **India** boasts the world's highest lift and the novelty of skiing or snowboarding the mighty Himalayas. The village looks out over the endless snow-capped peaks of **Kashmir** and is about one hour by road from the regional airport in **Srinagar**. The lofty retreat (the name means "Meadow of Flowers") has been a summer destination since the early 17th century when the Mughal emperor Jahangir was known to frequent Gulmarg, but its status as a cold weather destination dates from 1927 when a couple of British Army officers founded the first local ski club.

A French-built gondola takes skiers to the summit of Mount Apharwat at 4,000 metres above sea level, high enough to see Nanga Parbat (the world's eighth highest mountain) hovering in the distance.

From there it's all down hill via snow bowls, ridges and pistes flanked by virgin pine forest. Guided helicopter skiing is the latest craze, a chance to ski or snowboard ultra-fresh powder in the secluded Pir Panjal Wilderness Reserve. The British adventure travel company **Mountain Tracks** (250 York Rd, London SW11 3SJ, England; +44.20.8123 2978; www.mountaintracks.co.uk) offers a number of fully inclusive and guided Gulmarg trips each winter, including one exclusively for snowboarders.

With green A-frame bungalows scattered amongst the pines and a strategic location near the bottom of the slopes, **Highlands Park** (Gulmarg 193 403, Jammu & Kashmir; +91.1954.254 430; www.hotelhighlandspark.com) is the best place to stay at **Gulmarg**. The cosy wood-panelled rooms feature wood-burning stoves, satellite TV and room service. For couples who wish to mingle, there's a discotheque and restaurant with Indian, Chinese, European and Kashmiri cuisine.

India's other big winter playground is the Kullu-Manali region in **Himachal Pradesh** state. Surrounded by snow-capped peaks and thick forest, the Kullu Valley cuts a north-south path through the western Himalayas. Manali is the main town and resort area, one of India's favourite honeymoon spots and host of a fabulous Winter Carnival that blends Bollywood and outdoor sports. The "Winter Queen" beauty pageant and ski races, folk dancing and comedy shows are all part of the fun at this February event. Manali also provides an excellent base for helicopter skiing with **Himalayan Heli Adventures** (+91.981.602 5899; www.himachal.com). A private guide and helicopter for two can be reserved in addition to a package that also includes seven nights lodging in Manali.

Mongolia: Fresh Powder & New Resorts

Mongolia's first ski area – developed by a Swiss expatriate – opened on a mountainside just outside the capital **Ulan Bator** in 2009. **Sky Resort** (Bogd Khan Uul, Ulan Bator, Mongolia; +976.11.320 345; www.skyresort.mn) is quite modest by global standards. But then again, saying that you slipped away for a romantic week of skiing in **Mongolia** is likely to trump just about any dinner table conversation back home. Located just outside of Ulan Bator, the mountain features eight runs, two chairlifts and floodlights for night skiing, as well as a ski house with rental equipment, ski school and snacks. Despite Mongolia's notoriously harsh winters, most of the snow is artificially generated because of the region's super arid climate.

If skiing is not your cup of tea, Mongolia has some incredibly snug places for two to while away a cold winter night. Located less than an hour's drive from Sky Resort, the **HS Khaan Resort** (Khui doloon hudag, Argalant soum, Tov aimag, Ulan Bator, Mongolia; +976.9908 8102; hs-khaan-resort.com) is comprised entirely of luxury *gers* – traditional Mongolian tents that are really more like small houses. The décor is a blend of chic

Western and traditional Mongolian, including four-poster beds, iPod docks, Internet service, sitting areas that look out onto the endless plains, and whirlpool bathtubs easily large enough for two. Couples can also enjoy a full body oil massage in the resort spa, grab a cocktail (or two) in the intimate Bar Od, or feast on Mongolian dishes in Ger Restaurant Uuls. Depending on the weather, HS Khaan Resort also offers afternoon tea, horseback riding, birdwatching on the plains or a campfire under the stars. ~ JY

Asia at the Winter Olympics

One mark of how snow and ice sports have taken off in Asia is the region's success at the Winter Olympics. Japan has been a winter player since 1956, when skier Chiharu Igaya captured a silver medal in the slalom at Cortina d'Ampezzo in Italy. Since then, Japan has racked up an impressive 9 golds and a total of 37 medals in a wide range of winter disciplines from ski jumping and Nordic combined to figure skating and freestyle skiing. No other Asian nation won any medals at the Winter Games until 1992 at Albertville, France, when China and South Korea broke into the scene for the first time. Since then, both nations have become cold-sport powerhouses, with China amassing 44 medals (9 golds) and South Korea 45 medals (23 golds). Asia's all-time medal leaders are Chinese short-track speedskater Wang Meng (4 golds, 6 wins overall) and South Korean short-track star Chun Lee-Kyung (4 golds, 5 medals overall).

THIS PAGE (FROM TOP): Mongolia's winter offers a rare chance to cosy up in a romantic snow-covered ger; winter resorts in the Japanese Alps are every bit as sophisticated as their counterparts in Europe and North America.

OPPOSITE: The Himalayas in India and Nepal are evolving into a cutting-edge winter holiday destination.

High-altitude Holidays

From the legendary Himalayas to the jungle giant called Kinabalu, from the smouldering volcanic cones of Java to the tranquil tea country of the Indian subcontinent, Asia's highlands come in all shapes and sizes. So do the region's high-altitude holidays.

Asia's high-altitude holidays come in three degrees of physical difficulty – mountaineering, trekking and low-impact adventure with a high degree of relaxation. Veteran mountaineers can launch into technical climbs of legendary peaks like Everest, Annapurna and K-2 scattered across the crest of the Himalayas between Bhutan and northern Pakistan. Many of the highest peaks share a border between Nepal and China, meaning they can be tackled from either side. These journeys, however, are not for the faint of heart or inexperienced. As full-fledged expeditions, they require local guides, months of training and extreme safety precautions.

Most people opt for trekking holidays with views of these famous peaks. This type of vacation can last from several days to several weeks, and while participants need a certain level of fitness to undertake the treks, no technical climbing experience is necessary. Trekking can be done with or without guides, depending on one's knowledge of the terrain and skill using a map, compass and a Global Positioning System (GPS). The comfort level can vary greatly, with overnights anywhere from tents to luxury lodges. On basic long-distance walks, everyone carries their own gear, sleeps in two-person tents and mucks in with everyone else to prepare meals. At the opposite end of the trekking spectrum you can expect to have porters carry all of the equipment and supplies, a team of cooks to prepare gourmet meals in the wilderness, and an elevated level of comfort that might include luxury tents or plush mountainside lodges.

While the focus of trekking activities in Asia may be centred in the Himalayas, they are certainly not the only ranges to offer climbers some spectacular mountain scenery. The Japanese Alps, Southeast Asia's highlands, and the larger (and less active) Indonesian volcanoes also lend themselves to walking holidays.

The third and final high-altitude option requires the least energy: highland resorts with a wide variety of recreational activities, from day hikes, horseback riding and mountain biking to more cultivated pursuits such as golf, tennis and lounging around a swimming pool. The British laid the groundwork for many of Asia's best highland escapes when they established "hill stations" in many of their colonies. The original idea behind these lofty oases was for escaping the blistering heat of places like India, Burma and Malaysia. But in modern times they have morphed into relaxation, romantic and adventure destinations with a wide variety of accommodation and pursuits.

In recent years, almost all of the upcountry hot spots have evolved into very active adventure sports and outdoor hubs. Activities range from trekking and mountain biking to horseback riding, ATV tours, white-water rafting and plantation tours. Given their colonial heritage, many also offer opportunities for traditional afternoon tea, pub crawls and other bygone British Raj activities.

Himalayan Treks & Treats

With some of the world's most famous mountains and hundreds of different trekking options, **Nepal** is all about active highland holidays. The classic trek is up to Everest Base Camp at 5,350 metres – one of the highest places one can reach on the planet by simply walking – or a circuit around Annapurna. Neither is easy: the journeys normally take three weeks, moderate to strenuous walking for five to seven hours each day. The rewards are many, a gradual progression from the farmland and forest of Nepal's central valleys to the rocky, wind-blown and glacial terrain that skirts the base of the Himalayas. Nepal's trekking seasons are spring (March to May) and autumn (September to October).

Scores of companies organise guided treks on both routes including global outfitter **Mountain Travel Sobek** (1266, 66th Street, Suite 4 Emeryville, CA 94608; +1510.594 6000; www.mtsobek.com) and local agencies like **Himalaya Journey** (PO Box 21235, Thamel, Kathmandu, Nepal; +977.1438 3184; www. himalayajourneys.com). The latter offers an 11-day honeymoon adventure with stops in Kathmandu, Pokhara and Royal Chitwan National Park.

Set on the shores of Phewa Lake, the bustling highland town of **Pokhara** is the most romantic place in Nepal and the closest the Himalayan kingdom has to a hill station. About six hours by road from Kathmandu, the town is known for its awesome views of Annapurna and fishtailed Machapuchare, but there are plenty of ways to while away a day in the Pokhara Valley.

Shops and stalls in the bazaar area have a wide variety of Nepalese

THIS PAGE (FROM TOP): A zigzag pattern of torchlights marks the path of early morning hikers on Malaysia's towering Mt Kinabalu; yaks are often employed on the Mt Everest trekking route in Nepal; colourful prayer flags flutter above Ganden Monastery in Tibet.
OPPOSITE: Taktsang (Tiger's Nest) Monastery clings to a sheer mountainside above the Paro Valley in western Bhutan.

THIS PAGE (FROM TOP): Bhutan's Uma Paro is one of the most luxurious hotels in the Himalayas; a trekker crosses Tibet's white-water Tsangpo River.

OPPOSITE (FROM LEFT): A porter on the trail to Kanchenjunga, the world's third highest peak, in India's mountainous Sikkim region; equipment used in the first ascent of Everest (1953) on display at the Himalayan Mountaineering Institute in Darjeeling.

and Tibetan crafts, including bangles, beads, carpets and religious trinkets. The day hike to the top of Sarangkot Hill provides glimpses of local village life and spectacular views from the ancient monastery perched on the summit. Soar high above the valley in an ultralight aircraft or paraglider. Hang out for hours (reading a book, surfing the Internet, people watching) in one of the many bars and cafés along Baidam Road, or chill at the lakeside **Fish Tail Lodge** (PO Box 10 Lakeside, Pokhara, Nepal; +977.6146 5071; fishtail-lodge.com), where you can lie beside the pool, cocktail in hand, gazing at the snow-capped peaks. Reachable only by boat, the lodge has hosted many famous guests over the years (including royals from Japan, Thailand and England) and includes romantic touches – a roaring fireplace in the bar and hammocks in the garden.

Tucked at the eastern end of the Himalayas, the kingdom of **Bhutan** and its vibrant mountain culture seem virtually untouched by the modern world. The enlightened monarchy and Buddhism remain the twin pillars of the nation, whose people were recently named among the happiest on the planet in a worldwide survey. Visitors trek to ancient monasteries like Taktsang ("Tiger's Nest") poised high above the Paro Valley or attend flamboyant festivals like Thimphu Tshechu that feature traditional dance, masks, archery and religious rites.

Despite its remoteness, Bhutan also boasts some fine hotels. At **Uma Paro** (PO Box 222, Paro, Bhutan; +975.8271 597; www.uma.paro.como. bz, see pages 120–121) couples can hide away in spacious Bhutanese-style villas with wood-burning stoves, private spa treatment areas and butler service. The hotel can also arrange to have 20 monks (with drums, horns and cymbals) bless your marriage in the shrine room of the 7th-century Kyichu Lhakhang temple.

India & Sri Lanka: Tea Time

The British Raj lives on in the old hill stations of India and Sri Lanka. More than two dozen hill stations are scattered around the subcontinent, most in the Himalayan foothills, but also the Deccan Plateau of southern India and the mountains of central Sri Lanka. Given the cool climate, incredible vistas and diverse attractions, the hill resorts have long attracted local honeymooners and count among the top spots in both countries for couples.

One of the best known hill stations in **India**, **Darjeeling** lies in the rugged knot of mountains between Nepal and Bhutan, home to many exiled Tibetans and the hearty Gurkha people of British Army fame. Travellers can fly into Darjeeling or hop onto the romantic "toy train" that winds its way from steamy **New Jalpaiguri** via countless bridges, tunnels and switchbacks. Listed by UNESCO as a World Heritage Site, the line's official name is **Darjeeling Himalayan Railway** (Darjeeling Station, Hill Cart Rd, Darjeeling, West Bengal, India; +91.354.200 5734; www.dhrs.org). The full journey takes about seven hours.

Kanchenjunga, the world's third highest peak, hovers over the landscape on a bed of wispy clouds. Forest and tea plantations complete

the picture of a highland outpost that really does feel like the mythical Shangri-La. Crowded, noisy, chaotic Chokra Bazaar is the place to browse for souvenirs and photographic opportunities. The museum at the **Himalayan Mountaineering Institute** (Jawahar West Rd, Darjeeling, West Bengal, India; +91.354.225 4083; www. himalayanmountaineeringinstitute. com) chronicles the history of local climbing. And no visit to Darjeeling is complete without an early morning drive to the top of Tiger Hill to watch the sunrise over the mountains while wrapped up together in a warm blanket.

Founded in 1859 by a Scottish company, **Glenburn Tea Estate** (Glenburn Valley, West Bengal, India; +91.33.2288 5630 or +91 98.3007 0213;

www.glenburnteaestate.com) now doubles as a working tea plantation and secluded boutique hotel. Each of the estate's two Victorian bungalows features four suites with access to common gardens, verandahs and terraces, as well as a massage and steam room where spa services are rendered. Some of the suites feature four-poster beds or fireplaces, while all of them have old-fashioned clawfoot bathtubs, newfangled rainshowers and expansive views of the Himalayas.

Tea was also the original raison d'être of **Nuwara Eliya** in the central highlands of Sri Lanka. Tea aficionados around the globe prize the area's fabled "high altitude" tea, with its rich flavour and strong aroma. Recently local resorts have

taken advantage of this leafy heritage, and adapted themselves to revolve around a tea theme.

Guests are welcome to join in the harvest at a chic boutique hotel called **The Tea Factory** (Heatherset Estate, Kandapola, Sri Lanka; +94.52.222 9600; www. aitkenspencehotels.com/teafactory). Whatever they pick is processed and bagged at the on-site factory, ready to take home as a souvenir. Couples can arrange excursions to the surrounding highlands, including a climb up Adam's Peak to watch the sunrise over the Indian Ocean, or trek in wild and rugged Horton Plains National Park with its unusual alpine flora and fauna. Afterwards, the resort's Six Senses Spa soothes aching muscles.

Highland Escapes

Fresh strawberries, marvellous tea and jungle walks are among the wonders of the **Cameron Highlands** of northern **Malaysia**. With temperatures as low as 16°C at night, the contrast with the steamy lowlands cannot be more dramatic. The climate is perfect for a walk in the woods; its myriad rainforest trails meander through the region. Many of the local farms, including several that keep butterflies and bees, and plantations open their doors to visitors. Follow up a round of 18 on the old colonial golf course with tea and scones at **Bala's Chalet** (Lot 55, Tanah Rata, 39000 Cameron Highlands, Pahang, Malaysia; +60.5.491 1660; www.balaschalet. com) or homemade dessert at **Strawberry Moment Café** (23–24

THIS PAGE: *Located on the ancient Tea Horse Road between Tibet and Southeast Asia, Lijiang is one of China's best preserved historic cities.*

OPPOSITE (FROM TOP): *Samosir Island floats in the middle of Lake Toba on the Indonesian island of Sumatra; lush rice terraces cover many of Bali's highland areas.*

cooler climate than Bangkok and beachside Thailand. The renowned night market, countless craft factories and golden stupas give travellers a wide choice of urban activities. The real attraction, though, is the unspoilt countryside around Chiang Mai, where white-water rafting, elephant-back safaris and jungle ziplines are just a few of the adrenaline-packed possibilities. The city is also the main staging point for treks to visit the hilltribe villages of northern Thailand. Journeys can last from a few days to several weeks. **Siam Rivers** (17 Ratchatwitee Rd, Prasing, Amphur Muang, Chiang Mai 50200; +668.9515 1917; www.siamrivers. com) organises a wide range of adventure sports around Chiang Mai.

Just over the border from northern Thailand, the historic city of **Lijiang** in southern **China** affords a whole different take on the highland experience. Laced with canals and bridges, the Old Town is a UNESCO World Heritage Site. Founded more than eight centuries ago, Lijiang was once a key stopover on the Tea Horse Road between Southeast Asia and Tibet. Overlooking the ancient quarter is the Mu Palace compound, a miniature "forbidden city" with fabulous Ming and Qing dynasty architecture.

Also looming over the town is a cluster of 13 snow-capped peaks called the Jade Dragon Snow Mountain, home to the southernmost glaciers in the northern hemisphere. The most famous view of the mountain is from the Black Dragon Pool in

Lijiang, a much-painted vista that encompasses the lake and its white marble bridge, with the snowy Dragon hovering in the distance. Energetic couples can hike up the mountain; guided mule trains and cable cars are available for those who wish to conserve their energy for later in the day. Trout fishing is another attraction in the area.

The luxurious new **Banyan Tree Resort Lijiang** (PO Box 55, Lijiang, 674100 Yunnan, China; +86.888.533.1111; www.banyantree.com/en/lijiang) is the newest establishment in this ancient town. The design and décor of this all-suite retreat reflect Lijiang's rich cultural legacy, including sweeping roofs inspired by local Naxi dwellings and a predominance of black, red and gold fabrics and finishes. Couples can sample local specialities (like rice noodles with yak meat) during a private dining experience beneath the Moonlight Pagoda, set on a small island in the middle of the resort's lake.

Island Highlands: Indonesia & the Philippines

Lake Toba on the island of Sumatra was created 75,000 years ago by one of the largest volcanic eruptions of all time, a blast so enormous that it may have triggered the last ice age. Today, the tranquil lake area is one of Indonesia's best high-altitude escapes, homeland of the fascinating Batak people and a multi-faceted destination that combines outdoor sports, arts and crafts as well as rich local traditions.

Most visitors take the one-hour ferry over to **Samosir Island** in the

Jalan Angsana Satu, Brinchang Point, 39100 Cameron Highlands, Pahang, Malaysia; +60.5.491 2061; strawberrymoment.com), where the mouth-watering selection includes strawberry strudel, chocolate-covered berries, strawberry mousse and a strawberry cocktail named The Breeze.

The northern Thai city of **Chiang Mai** is just high enough (300 metres) to give it a noticeably middle of the lake. The island still feels like a mini Bali, the lakeshore strewn with tourist lodges, funky little cafés and open-air workshops where Batak textiles and wooden sculptures are produced by local artisans. Couples can hire motorbikes for a jaunt to the rice terraces and pine forests that dominate the island's interior, or simply laze on the beach and stare at the big puffy clouds that form over Lake Toba each afternoon.

Overnight options on Samosir run all the way from youth hostels and homestays to lakeside hotels like the **Carolina Cottages** (Tuk-tuk Siadong, Samosir Island, Lake Toba, North Sumatra, Indonesia 22395; +62.625.415 210; carolina-cottages.com) where many rooms have balconies overlooking the gardens and water. The front desk can arrange boats, motorbikes and bicycles for couples to explore up and down the lakeshore. Whether on the secluded hillside, tucked away in the jungle, or overlooking the resort's private beach, the DeLuxe Rooms are best for couples.

Rice terraces and local tribes are also an iconic feature of the Baguio Highlands on **Luzon** island in northern **Philippines**. The cool mountain climate is a refreshing surprise in a country more known for its tropical beaches and coral reefs – daytime temperatures are just right for hiking, mountain biking or horseback riding. In addition to the unique Cordillera tribes – Kalinga, Ibaloi and Kankana-ey – the region is also renowned for the endless emerald Banaue rice terraces, the Kabayan mummy caves, and spas

where couples can pamper themselves with a Baguio strawberry massage.

Perched on a pine-covered ridge, **The Manor at Camp John Hay** (Loakan Road, Baguio City, Philippines 2600; +637.4424 0931; www.cjhhotels. com) offers the region's swankiest digs, an atmosphere redolent of an American national park lodge. The resort is part of a sprawling complex that was once an R&R (rest and relaxation) base for the American GIs stationed in the Philippines. Among the camp's modern attractions are paintballing, rock climbing and an 18-hole golf course. The historic, two-storey honeymoon cottage is tucked away in its own grove of trees away from the resort, offering the privacy that newlyweds would certainly enjoy. ~ **JY**

Elope on Equatorial Slopes

Couples who enjoy extreme sports might want to consider taking a honeymoon on Puncak Jaya in eastern Indonesia. The highest permanently snowy mountain between the Andes and the Himalayas, the 4,884-metre high mountain rises from the steamy, equatorial jungle in the Irian Jaya region of eastern Indonesia. Alpine Ascents International (www.alpineascents.com) and Basecamp (www.basecamp.co.uk) can get you there and back for around US$20,000, excluding international flights. The expedition-style journey takes a minimum of two weeks, including heavy duty hiking through thick jungle to the base camp and technical climbing to reach the frozen summit.

Destination Weddings

Traditional weddings in faceless hotel ballrooms with hundreds of guests (including relatives you don't really know) are passé these days. Increasingly, couples are opting for weddings at exotic or romantic destinations away from home, celebrated with a small group of family and close friends.

Following a trend that has become popular around the world over the past decade, Asia has discovered destination weddings. As the term implies, this means getting married away from home. In days gone by, this was a major undertaking, but with more and more hotels, resorts and wedding planners throughout the region jumping onto the destination wedding bandwagon – and helping the bride and groom with every aspect of their big day – it's now easier than ever to tie the knot in distant romantic places.

Asia's most popular destination weddings are probably beach locales like Bali, Phuket and the Maldives. These types of weddings can also feature seasonal themes (Lunar New Year, Winter, Christmas), fantasy themes (vampire, medieval, Roman toga, Japanese anime), and outdoor locations (national parks, coral reefs, rainforest, mountain tops).

The wedding portal **DestinationWeddingsAsia.com** has a wealth of information on countries, types of weddings available, limousine services, patissiers, florists, wine vendors, entertainment, invitation printers and wedding planners. Even if your hotel planners are making all the arrangements, this website is a great place to browse for ideas.

In most Asian countries, some dates are considered more auspicious than others for getting married. If this is important to you, consult your wedding planner as soon as possible about securing that date. Be prepared though: it might be very difficult to get a "slot" on the most fortunate of days. You may have to compromise on what's available and you may feel rushed as planners try to fit in as many weddings as possible.

Traditional & Historical Themes

The award-winning agency **Inside Japan** (Lewins House, Lewins Mead, Bristol, BS1 2NN, UK; +44.117.314 4620; www.insidejapantours.com) can organise a destination wedding in **Kyoto** that includes traditional Japanese dress, hairstyle and make-up (for both the bride and groom), and a private ceremony at the Kamigamo Shrine. Wedding planners in **Bali** offer a number of destination choices, including a sunset beach wedding with gamelan musicians, flower girls, umbrella boys and a candlelit reception on the sand.

As its name suggests, **Regal Weddings** (109 Kamal Complex, opp Gulab Bagh, Udaipur, 313001 Rajasthan, India; +91.294.329 0228; www.regal-weddings.com) specialises in planning weddings fit for royalty in a range of palaces, mansions, forts and historical monuments in **India** at locations such as Bikaner, Udaipur, Jaipur and Jodhpur. Among the favourite wedding sites are Devigarh Palace and Samode Palace. Individualised events which include (but are not limited to) the bride and groom arriving and departing on an elephant, entertainment by fire-eaters, snake charmers and a grand wedding night fireworks display can be put together. Regal can also arrange beach weddings in Goa and Kerala.

If your dream is a ceremony that's as culturally authentic as

possible, **Lanna Weddings** (c/o Canna Cards, 61-65 Wualai Rd, T. Haiya A. Muang, Chiang Mai, 50100; +66.53.201 683; ww.northernthailand. com) in **Thailand** offers what they label "non-touristy" Lanna-style Thai nuptials. The wedding day begins at 4.45 am when the couple present offerings of food, incense and flowers to monks making their daily rounds in the city's silversmith area. Later in the morning, the couple visit a Thai Buddhist temple to get the blessing of the head monk, followed by the release of birds, fish or turtles to produce karmic "merit" for the couple.

Leading a noisy parade, the groom arrives at the wedding venue (the "home" of his bride) where he

THIS PAGE (CLOCKWISE FROM TOP): Panoramic sea views frame the wedding gazebo at AYANA Resort & Spa in Bali; a Japanese wedding is held in a shinto shrine; ring exchange during a Lanna-style wedding in Thailand.

OPPOSITE: The Renewal of Love ceremony at the Conrad Maldives Rangali Island resort can include a cruise on a romantic dhoni sailing craft.

must pass through symbolic gates and convince the gatekeepers that he is a worthy husband. The groom may be asked questions or asked to present a dowry in order to pass. The couple will then partake in the knot ceremony, performed by community elders. Afterwards, the newlyweds must show the wedding party their nuptial bedroom before the true celebrations of the day can begin during the wedding feast.

Small, Private Affairs

A wedding or blessing on a private island in the **Maldives** offers couples the chance to wed away from prying eyes and gatecrashers. With 33 suites and villas, **Cocoa Island** (Makunufushi, South Malé Atoll, Maldives; +960.664 1818; www.cocoaisland.como.bz; see pages 168–169) lends itself to being taken over by the entire wedding party. Barefoot blessing ceremonies take place on a narrow spit of white sand that snakes into the turquoise and sapphire Indian Ocean. Honeymoons unfold in aromatic over-water bungalows with nothing between you and the deep blue sea.

A beach wedding in **Malaysia** need not be a completely informal affair. **Avillion Port Dickson** (3rd Mile Jalan Pantai, Port Dickson, Negeri Sembilan, Malaysia; +60.6.647 6688; www.avillion-portdickson.com; see pages 162–165) will erect an elaborately decorated marquee on the beach with formal seating, dance floor, stage, artistic centrepieces and full-blown table settings – the works.

Hosting no more than 30 adults in 15 luxury tents, **Four Seasons**

Tented Camp Golden Triangle
(PO Box 18, Chiang Saen Post Office, Chiang Rai 57150, Thailand; +66.53.910 200; www.fourseasons. com/goldentriangle; see pages 188–189) in **Chiang Rai** is also perfect for taking over the whole resort to ensure complete privacy. Plus, you can have the dream wedding you've always wanted. Four Seasons can arrange a traditional Thai ceremony complete with traditional Lanna costumes for both you and your partner, have the ceremony led by a village elder and provide elephants as your mode of transport to and from a remote wedding site overlooking the crossroads of three countries (Thailand, Laos and Burma).

Nuptials a la Aman

Amanresorts offers a number of destination wedding options throughout Asia, including **Amansara** (Road to Angkor, Siem Reap, Kingdom of Cambodia; +855.63.760 333; www.amanresorts.com/amansara) near the Angkor temples in northwest **Cambodia**. The former guesthouse of King Sihanouk is now a sumptuous 24-suite resort (12 with private pools).

Among the ceremony options is a traditional Khmer wedding blessing conducted by a Christian priest or Khmer monk, complete with traditional costumes, musicians and dancers. After the nuptials, the wedding party can explore the amazing temples of Angkor and the gateway town of Siem Reap. Legal weddings are also possible, but necessitate more lead-time to arrange.

The **Amanwana** (Moyo Island, West Sumbawa Regency, Indonesia;

+62.371.22 233; www.amanresorts. com/amanwana) along the white sand beach comprises 20 luxurious "tents" with solid glass-and-wood walls and stone decks in a nature reserve on **Moyo Island**. The island is surrounded by pristine sea and teeming coral reefs, and is home to a variety of animals and birds, including deer, wild boar, macaque, sea eagles and ospreys. Indonesian blessings or legally binding ceremonies with Christian or Hindu priests can be arranged at Amanwana, but the latter needs to be coordinated with the local embassy or consulate.

The slightly larger **Amanpulo** (Pamalican Island, Philippines;

+63.2.976 5200; www.amanresorts. com/amanpulo; see pages 172–173) is located on a white-sand and coral-rimmed island. Accommodating up to 120 guests, this resort can arrange for a blessing ceremony on the beach. Local Filipino musicians serenade the couple with traditional guitar and harp music, and poetry is read before the couple exchange vows and rings at sunset. The reception can be held on the hotel's grounds, onboard one of Amanpulo's luxury boats or inside the island's romantic grotto.

Urban-setting Weddings

For larger weddings, the **Regent Singapore** (1 Cuscaden Rd, Singapore

THIS PAGE: The secluded Amanwana resort in Indonesia provides magical ceremony backdrops like this enchanted waterfall.

OPPOSITE (FROM TOP): Weddings arranged by Raffles Grand Hotel d'Angkor in Cambodia can have the dramatic Angkor temples as a backdrop; after an elaborate (or informal) wedding, couples at the Avillion Port Dickson resort in Malaysia can relax on their private balconies.

THIS PAGE (FROM TOP): *Fairytale weddings, complete with castles, are a dream come true at Hong Kong Disneyland; barefoot chic beach wedding at Diva resort in the Maldives.*

OPPOSITE: *The unusual Ithaa wedding chapel at the Conrad Maldives Rangali Island is located five metres below the waves, surrounded by a vibrant coral reef.*

249715; +65.6733 8888; www. regenthotels.com/singapore) offers a range of themes, from lavish affairs like the Moroccan-inspired Elements of Opulence featuring burgundy, red and black jewel tones; and Elements of Elegance which channels Hollywood glamour and sophistication with a sparkling stage backdrop and crystal centrepieces. The Regent can also lay on more subtle occasions like Jazz,

which offers gold and cream hues with soft fabrics surrounded by beautiful roses; or Seasons In The Park which transforms the hotel's Royal Ballroom into a romantic outdoor park setting.

For Disney fans, **Hong Kong Disneyland Resort** (+852.1.830 830; park.hongkongdisneyland.com) offers fairytale-themed weddings that blend East and West, including traditional Chinese-style banquets with dishes like roast suckling pig, steamed garoupa and shrimp dumplings. Other essentials – Disney-themed wedding cakes, complemented by entertainment options like costumed musicians performing Disney songs and music – complete the feel. You can even request a special appearance by Mickey Mouse and Minnie Mouse in their finest evening attire.

If you dream of an urban wedding, the **Kemang Icon by Alila** (Jalan Kemang Raya 1, Jakarta 12730, Indonesia; +62.21.719 7989; www. alilahotels.com/kemangicon) is a hip retreat in the Indonesian capital of **Jakarta**. Tucked between art galleries, bars and chic boutiques in Jakarta's trend-setting Kemang neighbourhood, this 12-suite hotel specialises in weddings where every detail is meticulously planned with the bride and groom beforehand, and then executed to perfection. The rooftop terrace beside the glass-walled infinity pool provides an ideal setting for nuptials and wedding banquets with stunning views over the city. Couples who want to celebrate with family and close friends can rent the entire hotel to accommodate their guests.

If a wedding with a colonial vibe appeals to you, **Kandy House** (Amunugama Walauwa, Gunnepana, Kandy, Sri Lanka; +94.81.492 1394; www.thekandyhouse.com) near the city of the same name offers rooms furnished with Dutch antiques and ensuite bathrooms containing romantic Victorian tubs. The grounds include a jungle-fringed infinity pool, beautiful gardens, and views of serene paddy fields. The infinity pool also

Themed Weddings Gone Wild

Some couples prefer a traditional white wedding inside a church or city hall. Others might find outdoor weddings the height of eccentricity. Still others – brides and grooms with no shortage of imagination – crave something much more off the wall. Asian wedding planners and organisers are available to comply with just about any wacky theme you can come up with. Gothic Romance, Japanese Chic, Eco Tranquillity and the fairytale-inspired Alice in Wonderland wedding are just a few of the zany possibilities at Singapore's Extraordinary Weddings (www.extraordinary. com.sg). One of its more "artsy" themed weddings is Colour Revival, a modern Pop Art ceremony that couples can stage inside the National Museum of Singapore, with the chairs covered in vintage T-shirts, Andy Warhol-like décor, etc. The company can arrange weddings in modern and historic hotels or less traditional venues such as the Singapore Botanic Gardens, Fort Canning or a converted British colonial style "black and white" bungalow.

overlooks the rice paddies. Lounge away the afternoon to the cooing of the estate's wood pigeons.

This nine-room boutique hotel started life as a Kandyan manor house. Channa Daswatte, a protégé of famed Sri Lankan architect and national treasure Geoffrey Bawa, lovingly restored the property in 2005 to the designer-savvy oasis that it is today. Honeymooners are pampered in a number of ways, including being presented with a complimentary bottle of bubbly, a pair of hand-woven designer sarongs, a candlelit dinner for two on the verandah, and an "out of body" aromatherapy bath with frangipani petals floating in the water.

Aquatic Ceremonies in the Maldives

As part of the "Underwater Unity" package at **Banyan Tree Vabbinfaru** (Vabbinfaru Island, North Malé Atoll, Maldives; +960.664 3147; www. banyantree.com/en/vabbinfaru), couples exchange vows inscribed on plastic flash cards while they scuba-dive seven metres beneath the surface of the Indian Ocean. If a wedding on land is your style, the resort can also arrange a very chic affair on a private sandbank.

Certified scuba divers can also say "I do" underwater at **Diva Maldives** (Dhidhoofinolhu South Ari Atoll, Maldives; +960.668.0901; www.

naiade.com) with the coral reef as your chapel and hundreds of tropical fish in attendance. A Maldivian celebrant (part of the resort's Euro-Divers team) leads this non-religious exchanging of vows. Afterwards, the whole wedding party emerges from the water to don traditional Maldivian wedding attire and enjoy champagne and canapés onboard a traditional wooden dhoni (boat), before heading to the celebratory banquet at a private location of the couple's choice. Upon returning to the resort, the couple are taken back to their flower-adorned villa on a specially decorated golf cart to enjoy a pre-prepared warm aromatherapy bath.

Couples can have the thrill of getting married underwater without actually getting wet at the **Conrad Maldives Rangali Island** (Rangali Island, 2034, Maldives; +960.668 0629; www.conradhotels1. hilton.com). The resort's Ithaa restaurant – located five metres underwater – is magically transformed into a wedding chapel, complete with an amazing 180-degree view of the surrounding reef.

Indonesia's Eclectic Wedding Locations

Resorts don't get more remote than **Nihiwatu** (+62.361.757 149; www.nihiwatu.com) on the island

Destination Weddings

THIS PAGE: The cliff-edge overhanging cabana is one of the favoured ceremony spots at the Alila Villas Uluwatu in Bali.

OPPOSITE (FROM TOP): Romantic features of the Banyan Tree Phuket include magical pool villas and soaking tubs; enjoy Intimate Moments – specially prepared for the newlywed at Banyan Tree Phuket.

of **Sumba** in eastern Indonesia, which is best described as rustic, eco-luxurious and a surfer's paradise. Seven bungalows and three villas assure privacy. You can have your wedding anywhere within the resort's 177 hectares, which comprise tropical forest, rice terraces and grasslands wrapped around the long, white Nihiwatu beach. There is an on-site non-denominational minister to preside over your ceremony while a *rato*, an animist priest, blesses your union in traditional Sumbanese style.

Losari Spa Retreat & Coffee Plantation (PO Box 108, Magelang 56196, Central Java, Indonesia; +62.298.596 333; www.losaricoffeeplantation.com) near Yogyakarta in **central Java** offers spectacular views of the eight volcanoes that surround the resort. Traditional Javanese décor and antiques, large Mediterranean-style bathrooms and spacious balconies with traditional daybeds are just some of the features of this secluded mountain resort. The resort's planners are on hand to arrange

anything your heart desires, from a romantic proposal dinner to an ornate and elaborate wedding celebration, whether civil or religious.

Alila Villas Uluwatu (Jalan Belimbing Sari, Banjar Tambiyak, Desa Pecatu 80364, Bali, Indonesia; +62.361.848 2166; www.alilahotels.com/uluwatu) in **Bali** combines eco-chic with a touch of minimalism. Weddings can be held throughout the property. The signature venue is a cliff-edge overhanging cabana, with the Indian Ocean providing a breathtaking backdrop.

Tying the Knot Thai Style

Modern, tropical minimalist design and barefoot luxury are the trademarks at **Costa Lanta** (booking office: 12/24-26 Sukhumvit Rd., Soi 33, Klongton Nua, Wattana, Bangkok, Thailand; +66.75.668 186; www.costalanta.com) on the island of **Koh Lanta Yai** near Krabi in southern Thailand. Simple, elemental villas embrace the outdoors with retractable walls and see-through ceilings, creating an overall ambience of peace, serenity and solitude. Both Western and Thai beachfront ceremonies are possible.

The Library (14/1 Moo 2 Chaweng Beach, Bo Phut, Koh Samui, Suratthani 84320, Thailand; +66.77.422 767; www.thelibrary.co.th), a hip boutique hotel in **Koh Samui**, also offers Western and Thai wedding ceremonies, as well as an "Ocean" wedding package where the ceremony takes place on a private yacht at sunset. What makes this hotel unique? Breakfast is served on mattresses on the beach, the pool is

blood-red rather than the usual blue, and the hotel gets its name from an air-conditioned library with great sea views through its glass walls, as well as books, music CDs and movie DVDs on the floor-to-ceiling shelves.

Adjacent to Khao Yai National Park in central Thailand, **Muthi Maya** (1/3 Moo 6 Thanarat Rd, Moo-Si, Pakchong, Nakorn Ratchasima 30130, Thailand; +66.44.929 999; www.muthimaya.com) offers misty mountains, a chance to see tigers in the wild and a serene atmosphere. Thai or Western weddings unfold on the main lawn or in a luxurious marquee that mingles easily with the resort's Asian-inspired open architecture. Guest villas, fashioned from natural materials, boast a large Jacuzzi, private pool and sundeck.

Perhaps the best part of the wedding packages at the **Banyan Tree Phuket** (33, 33/27 Moo 4, Srisoonthorn Rd, Cherngtalay, Amphur Talang, Phuket 83110, Thailand; +66.76.324 374; banyantree.com/en/phuket) is what comes after the actual ceremony. A setup known as Intimate Moments awaits in a villa bedroom, complete with scented candles, aromatic oils, fragrant flowers, wine and tranquil music, complemented by a drawn sunken bath with flower petals. ~ JC

honeymoonescapes

Romantic train journeys, all-inclusive cruises, indulgent spas, eco-chic resorts, smart city hotels, and beach and mountain escapes, these are just some of the unforgettable experiences that await honeymooners in Asia.

Azamara Club Cruises

THIS PAGE: Head to the pool on the open deck for a late night swim under the stars.

OPPOSITE (CLOCKWISE FROM TOP): The Club World Owner's Suite offers a spacious bedroom and living area, with floor-to-ceiling glass doors; an aerial shot of the eleven-deck cruise ship; feast on a delicious breakfast with a sea view.

Azamara Club Cruises is a boutique cruise line combining a sophisticated yet relaxed way of travelling and exquisite fine dining cuisine with, most notably, a first-class level of service. Azamara's two 694-guest ships – **Azamara Journey** and **Azamara Quest** – provide the perfect ambience for romantic voyages to destinations in South America, the Mediterranean and the Caribbean, as well as Asia. The relatively intimate setting of Azamara cruises means a more personalised service for the discerning traveller, with one staff member catering to every two guests. Couples staying in suites additionally receive the undivided attention of an English-style butler. Expect fresh flowers in your room daily, Elemis toiletries, soft European bedding, Egyptian cotton bathrobes and turn down treats in the evening.

For couples celebrating their honeymoon, the staff are happy to create your dream vacation, both onboard and on land at the destination of your choice, whether you want a spa getaway, a learning cultural vacation or a gustatory experience. Those getting married can customise their wedding to reflect the elegant and stylish event they envision. With its standard of personal service and variety of specially designed packages to enhance the romantic experience, Azamara was awarded 1st prize in the Best for Couples category in 2009 by Cruise Critic Editors' Picks Awards.

As destination specialists, Azamara Club Cruises provide immersive experiences that allow guests to learn about the cultures, histories and traditions of the cities they visit, with a wealth of insider knowledge given on the must-see places at each destination. In Asia, couples can marvel at the craftsmanship of the Taj Mahal in Agra, climb the Great Wall of China or travel to Xi'an to get up close to terracotta warriors. For naturally romantic locations of picture-postcard beauty, take in the mountain scenery of Kagoshima in Japan

or the dramatic karst structures at Halong Bay. Onshore, Azamara Cruisetours also offer trips to explore more remote regions, with a chance to see some rare inland sights.

After the day's exertions, head to the **AquaSpa** back onboard for a couple's spa

package to loosen tired muscles and rejuvenate the body. Indulge in a hydralift facial, herbal wrap, lime and ginger scrub or hot stone massage and, for some extra pampering, choose to have your spa treatment in the privacy of your suite. The exclusive Thalassotherapy Pool offers an alternative soothing therapy using the relaxing properties of warm salt water, while Azamara's **Acupuncture at Sea** provides licensed acupuncturists to help restore your body's natural balance and energy.

To satisfy tastebuds in a different sensory experience, the speciality restaurants on the ship, **Aqualina** and **Prime C**, serve beautifully presented mouth-watering cuisine, from tender cuts of beef to freshly grilled seafood. Couples will find plenty of intimate corners around both venues, as well as in the main dining room, to enjoy their gourmet dinner along with the stunning ocean view.

Azamara Journey/Azamara Quest

rooms
42 suites and 311 staterooms

food
Discoveries Restaurant (international) · Aqualina (Mediterranean) · Prime C (steak and seafood) · Windows Café (casual dining) · Pool Grill (Western) · Cova/Mosaic Café · Sushi Café on *Azamara Journey* (Japanese)

drink
Looking Glass · Discoveries Lounge · Martini Bar · Pool Bar · Sunset Bar

features
AquaSpa · Acupuncture at Sea · Cabaret Lounge · The Journey/Quest Shop · Indulgences Shop · Casino Luxe · pool · Thalassotherapy Pool · fitness centre · jogging track · photo shop · library

destination highlights in Asia
Singapore · Hong Kong · Taipei · Shanghai · Tianjin · Xiamen · Kagoshima · Nagasaki · Kyoto · Seoul · Jeju Island · Phuket · Ko Samui · Bangkok · Bali · Lombok · Halong Bay · Ho Chi Minh City · Hue · Mumbai · Chennai · Goa

contact
3 Anson Road, #13-02 Springleaf Tower, Singapore 079909
telephone: +65.6305 0033
facsimile: +65.6536 2282
email: APACRes@rcclapac.com
website: www.azamaraclubcruises.com

Eastern & Oriental Express

The Orient-Express conjures up images of high society and glamour of a bygone era, where train travel was as much a social event as it was a means of transportation. Think perfectly coiffed women, dressed in evening gowns, exchanging the gossip of the day while their tuxedo-clad husbands discuss affairs of the world, a glass of whisky in hand – all in the comfort of wood-panelled train cabins decorated with exquisite marquetry and fitted with luxe furnishings.

You do not need to go back in time in order to experience the elegance and romance of a luxury train journey. While the original Orient Express carried its passengers to Paris and Istanbul, the **Eastern & Oriental Express** takes its discerning travellers through the lush landscape of Southeast Asia. Take in the dense rainforests and tropical jungles, endless vistas of paddy plantations dotted with farmers, remote indigenous villages, beautiful mountains and ancient temples as the 400-metre-long train wends it way through countries such as Singapore, Malaysia, Thailand, Laos and Cambodia.

Large picture windows in your private Cabin, as well as in the **Dining Car** ensure guests never miss out on the views. For an even more intimate way to take in the scenery, head to the Observation Car right at the end of the train. Here, the décor takes on the feel of a colonial verandah, with teak

THIS PAGE (FROM TOP): All cabins are furnished in glamorous old-world style; during the day, the Pullman Cabin provides a private lounge area with a banquette sofa; head to the Bar Car for a drink and some light musical entertainment.

OPPOSITE (FROM TOP): Enjoy the views together from the privacy of your cabin; 24-hour steward service is available.

wood flooring and panelling, rattan chairs and potted plants. The outdoor portion of this car offers unobstructed views, perfect for photo taking, especially as the train passes through local villages where friendly village children wave and run alongside the train as it passes their homes.

To maintain the air of sophistication, dinner in the Dining Car is strictly a black-tie affair. Breakfast, brunch and lunch are also served in the Dining Car while tea can be served in the privacy of your cabin. The **Bar Car** is the place to go at the end of the day to socialise with fellow passengers and enjoy a cocktail while listening to live piano music.

Couples who favour their alone time, however, can spend the evening in their room, which takes on a lounge arrangement by day,

converting into a bedroom at night. All cabins are air-conditioned and come with their own ensuite bathroom. And the 24-hour steward service means there is no rush to leave the comfort of your cabin. Honeymooners are treated to a celebration cake, champagne, caviar and gifts from the onboard boutique.

Trips range from two to six nights, and every route whisks you away on a different exotic experience. Epic Thailand takes passengers on a six-night journey through northeastern Thailand, including a visit to an Isan village and Khmer ruins at Prasat Sikhoraphum and Phanom Rung. Legends of the Peninsula takes you through the cities of Singapore, Kuala Lumpur and Bangkok, to the quiet beaches of Trang and an elephant camp near River Kwai.

cabins
30 Pullman Cabins · 28 State Cabins · 2 Presidential Suites

food
Dining Car (international and Asian gourmet)

drink
Bar Car

features
Observation Car · live piano music in Bar Car · boutique · library · 24-hour personal steward service

destinations and other journeys
Singapore – Bangkok · Bangkok – Singapore · Others: Epic Thailand · Fables of the Hills · Legends of the Peninsula · Tales of Laos

contact
100 Beach Road # 32-01/03 Shaw Tower, Singapore 189702
telephone: +65.6392 3500
facsimile: +65.6392 3600
email: oereservations.singapore@orient-express.com
website: www.orient-express.com

Road to Mandalay

Stand in awe as you take in the vision of thousands of ancient temples rising solemnly and silently from an endless expanse of misty vegetation in Bagan. Admire the gleaming stupa of Yangon's famed Shwedagon Pagoda, fashioned with gold and adorned with an incredible number of diamonds, rubies, sapphires and other precious jewels. Embark on a side trip to Lake Inle to witness the lifestyles of the Intha – indigenous farmers and fishermen who live in houses built on stilts over the water and cultivate gardens that float on the lake. A trip through Burma is all this and more.

The charm and natural beauty of Burma, officially known as Myanmar, has remained unspoiled for generations. The customs and traditions of this largely Buddhist population have hardly varied over the centuries. Dissecting this intriguing land from north to south – and serving as an important artery for transport and commerce – is the Irrawaddy River, or the Ayeyarwady River, as it is known locally, and cruising the river in a luxury ship such as the *Road to Mandalay* must be one of the best ways to experience Burma. Owned and operated by Orient-Express, this river cruiser takes passengers on a voyage through the royal city of Mandalay and mystical Bagan and also to Bhamo, near the Chinese border, depending on your chosen cruise. All routes start and end at Yangon. The shortest trip, Highlights of Myanmar, lasts three nights while the longer Gorges of the Far North takes you on a 12-day journey of discovery.

THIS PAGE (FROM TOP): Enjoy the view together with a drink on the observation deck; take in the surroundings while swimming in the outdoor pool; the Governor's Suite is perfect for couples with its ample space and luxurious amenities.

OPPOSITE (FROM LEFT): The four-deck cruise ship provides passengers with a range of entertainment at night; explore the spiritual World Heritage Site, Bagan.

cabins
1 Governor's Suite · 18 State Cabins · 4 Superior Cabins · 16 Deluxe Cabins · 4 Single Cabins

food
Western and Asian gourmet

drink
Piano Bar · Observation Lounge

features
wellbeing centre · pool · observation deck · boutique · library · medical room

destinations
Mandalay · Bhamo · Bagan · Extensions: Lake Inle, Yangon, Ngapali

contact
100 Beach Road # 32-01/03 Shaw Tower, Singapore 189702
telephone: +65.6392 3500
facsimile: +65.6392 3600
email: oereservations.singapore@orient-express.com
website: www.orient-express.com

Few things can be more romantic than admiring the views together from the Observation Deck as the ship glides gently down the river. To make the occasion even more memorable, couples can order a bottle of champagne to their table to watch the sunset, as a harpist sets the mood with a soothing melody. Come night-time, when the ship is moored, the staff can arrange a candlelit gourmet dinner under the stars. At Bagan, take a horse-drawn carriage through the temple-filled plains or a hot-air balloon ride to savour the view from above.

At the end of the day, couples can retire to the privacy of their cabins. Regardless of which cabin you are in, you can expect the best of traditional comforts – woven fabrics in natural tones, fine linen and soft towels. The artwork featured in each room was specially commissioned while local antiques were sourced to give an authentic Burmese touch to your luxury cruise experience. All the cabins are spacious, fully air-conditioned and come with ensuite bathrooms and large picture windows to take in the views. The ship underwent a total refurbishment in 2009 to expand the size of its cabins, even though this meant reducing its maximum capacity from 102 to 82. The entire craft can be booked for a wedding or celebration.

Royal Caribbean International

THIS PAGE (FROM TOP): *The spacious bedrooms are decorated with flower petals for couples; the ship's open deck houses the main swimming pool and whirlpools.*

OPPOSITE (FROM TOP): *Head to the Day Spa for a range of pampering treatments; Royal Caribbean International caters to a wide range of destinations around the world.*

For a sense of adventure, nothing comes quite close to a romantic getaway onboard a luxury cruise liner bound for exotic destinations. **Royal Caribbean International** offers couples a wide range of itineraries and locations with its fleet of 22 innovative ships in six different classes sailing on various routes around the world. Discover the rugged wilderness and untamed wildlife of Alaska; take a cultural cruise through Europe, stopping by the romantic cities of Paris and Rome and the coastal resorts of Ibiza and Malta; tour Australia and the Fijian islands in the South Pacific; or enjoy the relaxing beach destinations in the Caribbean. For your romantic voyage through Asia, the eleven-deck **Legend of the Seas** cruise ship caters specifically to the region, covering exciting destinations such as Langkawi, Bali, Hong Kong, Phuket, Halong Bay, Taipei, Kagoshima, Shanghai and Seoul.

While onshore, couples can savour the distinct sights, sounds and tastes of Asia from bustling open-air markets to some of the world's most beautiful temples. The journey is a delight in itself, thanks to the complete range of entertainment and leisure activities available. Your home onboard comes in the form of spacious staterooms or suites, furnished in soft, calming colours for a relaxing atmosphere – a welcome retreat after a day of exploration. Most suites come with a lounge area and private outdoor balcony to take in the view, as well as personalised services and priority privileges. The most exclusive Royal Suite additionally

offers a separate bedroom with a king-size bed, a whirlpool bathtub and a baby grand piano. Guests also have the luxury of ordering all their meals in should they not be in the mood to leave their rooms. Alternatively, the elegant two-tier glass-walled **Romeo and Juliet** main dining room on *Legend of the Seas* provides mouth-watering international cuisine along with views of the ocean.

Explore the open decks and pool areas together or relax and take in the scenery from the **Viking Crown Lounge**. Perched high above the sea with stunning 360-degree panaromic views, this is the perfect place to unwind with a cocktail and watch the sunset. For a unique vantage point of the surroundings and a more energetic activity for two, scale the ship's 9-metre-high rock-climbing wall.

Couples can also enjoy ballroom dancing, wine tasting or theatre performances. To pamper the body, indulge in a couple's massage or treatment at the luxurious **Day Spa**. Other Royal Caribbean ships have different onboard highlights – Oasis Class ships come with lush gardens, Freedom Class with cantilevered whirlpools and Voyager Class with ice-skating rinks.

For couples celebrating a special occasion such as a honeymoon, anniversary or for those who want to get married at sea, Royal Caribbean's event coordinators and wedding planners will create an unforgettable moment for you. A wedding chapel is available on selected ships with beautiful views of the open water, providing a dreamy location in which to exchange vows.

Legend of the Seas

rooms
902 staterooms, including 231 suites and balcony staterooms

food
Romeo and Juliet Dining Room (formal) • Windjammer Café (casual buffet)

drink
Viking Crown Lounge • Schooner Bar • Anchors Aweigh Lounge • Champagne Bar • Pool Bar

features
Day Spa • Centrum boutiques • Entertainment Theatre • Casino Royale • adult-only solarium indoor pool • 4 whirlpools • rock-climbing wall • mini golf • main pool • fitness centre • jogging track • card room

destination highlights
Singapore • Penang • Malacca • Kuala Lumpur • Langkawi • Hong Kong • Shanghai • Tianjin • Xiamen • Sanya • Taipei • Tokyo • Fukuoka • Beppu • Osaka • Jeju Island • Seoul • Busan • Phuket • Halong Bay • Hue/Danang • Ho Chi Minh City

contact
3 Anson Road, #13-02 Springleaf Tower, Singapore 079909
telephone: +65.6305 0033
facsimile: +65.6536 2282
email: APACRes@rcclapac.com
website: www.royalcaribbean-asia.com

Amankora

The spiritual journey that Bhutan offers is by no means diluted by the country's growing range of luxury properties. Standing out from most is **Amankora**. The first foreign company to open hotels in Bhutan, Amanresorts is well versed in the ways of this beautiful and mystical place.

"Aman" means peace in Sanskrit while "kora" means circular pilgrimage in Dzongkha (Bhutan's official language) and so it follows that Amankora comprises a circuit of five lodges – **Paro**, **Thimpu**, **Gangtey**, **Punakha** and **Bumthang** – that leads its guests to many corners of Bhutan. With this comes a choice of settings from mountain backdrops to forested knolls and itineraries that are tailor-made to suit each couple. At this perfect

honeymoon destination everything is taken care of – Amankora staff pass on your priorities and preferences as you travel from lodge to lodge, so there is no need to go through it all again. In fact there are no check-in procedures; couples are simply handed the key when they arrive and are warmly treated as if they have been there all week. It gives guests a feeling of staying at one large hotel, with rooms intimately strewn around the country. But with each resort actually being so small, the exclusivity keeps the honeymoon as luxe as can be.

Upon arrival, a driver and guide greet guests at the airport and remain at their side for the entire trip, discreetly of course. Providing transportation between lodges,

THIS PAGE (FROM TOP): The Paro Suite at Amankora Paro is a stylish blend of light and dark furnishings; the bathroom features clean wooden panelling; enjoy the forest view with your meal in the Amankora Paro dining room.

OPPOSITE (FROM TOP): Spend an evening in the courtyard of Amankora Bumthang with drinks in front of the fire; the Gangtey lodge is set in a picturesque area of Bhutan.

rooms
Paro (24 suites) • Thimphu (16 suites) •
Gangtey (8 suites) • Punakha (8 suites) •
Bumthang (16 suites)

food
Dining Room (Bhutanese, Western, Indian, Thai)

drink
Living Room

features
spa • unique circuit • archery • nature hikes •
mountain treks • yoga • bespoke itineraries

nearby
Paro: Drukgyel Dzong fortress • Mount
Jhomolhari • Kyichu Lhakhang temple •
Taktsang Lhakhang monastery
Thimphu: museums • shopping • Tashichho
Dzong fortress
Punakha: Punakha Dzong fortress • Phuntsho
Pelri Palace
Gangtey: Gangtey Goemba monastery •
wildlife sanctuary
Bumthang: Jakar • temples and monasteries •
royal sports ground used for archery

contact
Amankora Reservations Office
Balakha, Chento Geog
Near Drukgyel Dzong, Paro
Kingdom of Bhutan
telephone: +975.8.272 333
facsimile: +975.8.272 999
email: amankora@amanresorts.com
website: www.amanresorts.com

they also make arrangements for picnics, dinners, mountain treks or any other daytrips. For couples on that special romantic break, Amankora can cater for the ultimate experience, offering everything from nature hikes in the Himalayas or visits to medieval monasteries, to private dinners in local farmhouses or spa treatments such as a traditional hot stone bath. The magical setting, the lodges and the service all create a very unique and unforgettable journey for two. For weddings, hotel staff can arrange a traditional Buddhist ceremony, including traditional Bhutanese wedding outfits, a traditional blessing at the temple and a local dance troupe for entertainment.

Dining at each Amankora lodge is done with utmost style and sophistication; the food lives up to the setting, which is no mean feat considering the terrain. The dining room in each lodge serves a choice of two set menus for every meal: Bhutanese or Western, Indian or Thai. The glass-enclosed space overlooking the valley at Amankora Gangtey is perhaps one of the most impressive.

The lodges themselves are striking in their beauty; a traditional Bhutanese exterior belies the modern comfort within. Warm wooden panels, a traditional Bhutanese wood-burning stove, local woollen tapestries and a deep-soaking tub set the tone for a suite that is ideal for relaxation. While each lodge has its own personality, the seamless experience of the Amankora circuit makes this a true journey and the perfect start to a couple's life together.

Uma Paro

It has been called the last Shangri-La of the modern world, a mystical peaceful land steeped in tradition that lies enclosed within towering ancient mountains. Bhutan, a landlocked country located east of the Himalayas, is a relatively secluded and unspoilt place, for it has long controlled the influx of visitors in order to preserve its distinctive culture and beautiful landscapes.

The approach towards Bhutan's only airport in Paro, via the national carrier Druk Air, is a sight to behold. The pilot skilfully skirts hilltops while making tight turns as the aircraft descends in ever-decreasing circles. A ten-minute drive away from the airport, **Uma Paro** sits atop a tree-lined hill overlooking the town and the fertile Paro Valley. One may see farmers tending to their crops, as well as local inhabitants engaging in a favourite national pastime: a friendly archery contest.

All the rooms and suites at this resort, part of the award-winning COMO Hotels and Resorts group, incorporate indigenous aesthetics and have been embellished by traditional artisans. The same building techniques and materials – handcrafted stone, wood and tiles – which the locals have employed throughout the years, are responsible for the resort's structure. Guests will appreciate the resort's attention to detail: the "bukhari" wood-burning stove in each villa; the flower-motif artwork that decorates many a wall, eave or bracket; and the Shesham wood furniture, hand-stitched Indian cotton bedcovers and gorgeous hand-knotted Nepali rugs.

At the resort's **Bukhari** restaurant, guests can savour hearty local fare such as dried local pork (sicum paa) with Bhutanese chillies and handmade noodles in soup (bathup). Those who favour organic produce will be pleased to note the use of local cheeses, apple vinegar, honey and wild mushrooms in the kitchen. Couples wanting to dine in private can choose to have a candlelit meal for two in the comfort of their villa, or in the courtyard or archery field – the staff are happy to assist in making your romantic stay at Uma Paro an unforgettable one. The resort also offers a marriage-blessing ceremony for couples, with monks conducting ceremonial prayers in an intimate shrine room.

In keeping with the natural theme of the resort, a range of recuperative Ayurvedic treatments and holistic rituals is available at the **COMO Shambhala Retreat**. Two private massage rooms perfect for couples are located in a small hct stone bath house out in the nearby pine forest. The popular Bhutanese Hot Stone Bath and Massage is a traditional therapy using hot river stones, which helps relieve deep-set muscle aches and pains, followed by a relaxing massage.

Off-site, there is a wide range of activities for guests, including hiking, customised tours and yoga retreats to immerse couples in nature and in Bhutanese culture. Within walking distance are some of the country's most historic attractions, including the gravity-defying Taktsang Goemba.

rooms
9 Superior Double Rooms • 9 Deluxe Rooms • 2 COMO Suites • 8 One-bedroom Villas • 1 COMO Villa

food
Bukhari (Bhutanese, Indian, Western) • COMO Shambhala healthy cuisine

drink
hotel bar

features
COMO Shambhala Retreat • gym • indoor heated pool • library with Internet access

nearby
Taktsang Goemba (monastery) • Drukgyel Dzong (fortress) • Kyichu Lhakhang (temple) • Rinchen Pung Dzong (fortress) • Ta Dzong (National Museum) • Paro town

contact
PO Box 222, Paro, Bhutan
telephone: +975.8.271 597
facsimile: +975.8.271 513
email: res.paro@uma.como.bz
website: www.uma.paro.como.bz

Song Saa Private Island

In Cambodia's Koh Rong Archipelago, off the coast of Sihanoukville, two pristine islands lie side by side, like lovers, washed by sparkling clear waters. Locals call the twin islands The Sweethearts, and as far as weddings and honeymoons are concerned, it's impossible to imagine a more idyllic place to embark on your new life together. Alabaster white beaches and turquoise waters along with reefs and rainforests teeming with life enclose a sustainable sanctuary of uncompromising luxury. While

Song Saa Private Island feels like a world away from civilisation, it is only 30 minutes by boat from Sihanoukville International Airport, offering privacy and seclusion with the convenience of easy accessibility.

For Melita and Rory Hunter, the couple behind Song Saa Private Island resort, the islands are the epitome of romance. For most of their married life, they have been driven by a vision to create an environmentally and socially responsible haven of pure indulgence. "The beauty of this place really does take your

breath away and it's why we've worked so hard to ensure that the luxury that we offer treads lightly on the fragile ecosystems that make this place so special," Melita says. "What bride wouldn't love to step aboard an elegant cruiser and set off over aquamarine waters to meet her groom at a Buddhist monastery, or exchange vows in the splendour of a natural rainforest cathedral or on one of the island's exquisite beaches at sunset?"

Song Saa Private Island offers everything a discerning couple could possibly desire from a wedding venue or honeymoon experience. The venue is the ultimate in eco-chic, promising both luxury and privacy, as well as a deep commitment to conserving the environment. Couples can choose from a collection of 27 over-water, rainforest and beach villas, all built using environmentally conscious and sustainable materials.

Dine in absolute seclusion on your own private beach? That can be arranged. Enjoy a massage in a rainforest setting or an indulgent pampering package at a luxurious spa and wellness centre? Of course. Doze away the day in a king-size bed, followed by a long shower in the open air? Check. There are ample opportunities for relaxation, including leisurely fine dining at the resort's over-water restaurant, **Vista**. Couples can also enjoy a refreshing cocktail at either the **Beach Bar** or **Champagne Bar**. There is also the option of selecting your own special venue for a romantic private dinner. The resort chef can

THIS PAGE (FROM TOP): *The design of the villas blurs the lines between the indoors and out; rough-hewn timber details in the villas complement the natural environment.*

OPPOSITE (FROM TOP): *Enjoy the sunset from the over-water observation deck; Song Saa Private Island is surrounded by more that 20 deserted islands.*

prepare a personalised menu for couples at any location, such as a quiet stretch of beach or in the privacy of the couple's villa. For those who are planning to have a destination wedding, the resort can organise a traditional Buddhist blessing or civil ceremony on nearby Koh Toch (Intimate Island), with its magical setting and picturesque views.

Guests will have the opportunity to learn about the island's marine and terrestrial environments that Melita and Rory have worked so hard to protect. The resort's resident marine biologist will happily show you around and explain the reef and rainforest conservation projects that are at the core the resort's vision. Since acquiring the site, Melita and Rory have successfully established a marine reserve around the islands – a no-take zone where fishing is prohibited – managed to international standards. The Hunters have plans to expand the reserve even further to safeguard the reef for future generations. With help from the resort, scientists are currently working with Cambodian authorities on a series of marine audits that track the health of the reef and its precious marine life. The water quality is also constantly monitored, and on land a flora and fauna study has been completed, which identifies, among other things, roosting sites for large ranging birds such as hornbills, sea eagles and owls. The resort's corporate social responsibility efforts also extend to the local community; it organises educational forums

to teach fishermen about sustainable practices, and collects donations to support the education of local children.

On Song Saa Private Island, everything possible has also been done to minimise the impact of the resort on the environment. Its eco-friendly buildings have been constructed with sustainable, low-emission materials, and the island's water recycling system ensures that nothing harmful goes anywhere near the pristine sea.

On the island, guests can be as active, or as lazy, as they like. Couples may choose not to set foot outside the comfort of their villas, but

rooms
27 villas

food
Vista: Asian with a modern French twist

drink
Champagne Bar • Beach Bar

features
spa and wellness centre • infinity pool • yoga
and meditation centre • sailing • diving •
kayaking • snorkelling • ecological programme
• weddings • two boutiques

nearby
more than 20 deserted islands

contact
Koh Ouen, Sihanoukville, Cambodia
telephone: +855.77.777 439
email: info@songsaa.com
website: www.songsaa.com

for a meal and a cocktail under the stars. Alternatively, couples may chose to tour the nearby islands by private yacht and spend the day relaxing in private day huts, with a butler on hand to service their every need. For the more energetic, a wide range of water sport activities are on offer, from kiteboarding and windsurfing to night diving and twilight snorkelling to experience the awesome night-time marine spectacle of light-emitting bioluminescence in the tropical waters. An open-air yoga pavilion and a fitness room perched over the water offer beautiful views of the natural surroundings while guests exercise or stretch their limbs. Tailor-made experiences like a private helicopter tour to take in the breathtaking aerial views of the seascape followed by an authentic Khmer cookery class can also be arranged.

The Hunters are passionate about Song Saa Private Island and its environment. "We've really made it our mission to provide every kind of experience our guests might want, with a focus on the natural assets that made us fall in love with this place," Melita says. "We hope that what we're doing here will be a template for the future. We want to show that when you safeguard your environment and your community, you also safeguard prosperity for generations to come."

Raffles Hotel Le Royal

THIS PAGE: The majestic dining room is ideal for wedding banquets or private dinners.

OPPOSITE (CLOCKWISE FROM TOP): The Personality Suites are decked out in old-world style; tables are beautifully set up in the hotel's restaurant; relax in Le Royal Suite living room appointed with Cambodian and French furnishings.

Phnom Penh is a much celebrated holiday destination not only for the rich cultural heritage that binds the place together but also for its lively atmosphere and welcoming people. For a honeymoon, or a romantic trip, that offers a relaxing yet enriching experience, Phnom Penh is a great choice. And a stay at the **Raffles Hotel Le Royal** is one of the best ways to indulge in utmost class and style. True to the Raffles name, this

hotel comes steeped in old-world charm mixed with all the modernity one would expect from the world's best. Sure enough, Le Royal did enjoy a heyday in the 1920s, just as the Raffles of Singapore did. This was a grand period when the hotel welcomed the world's glitterati including adventurers, writers, journalists, royalty and dignitaries. Now in the 21st century, the celebrities continue to arrive, with more recent guests including Bill Clinton, Queen Sophia of Spain and Hugh Jackman.

The hotel has been brought right up to date with a thorough renovation. And inside, the old has been preserved but brought to life with modern sleek lines and soothing colour palettes. Rooms are serviced by a personal valet and feature all the amenities that befit a Raffles Hotel. For the ultimate in luxury and style, Le Royal Suite is located on the fourth floor with views of the gardens outside. Alternatively, the Personality Suites, which are named after their famous residents from long ago, are sumptuously appointed and feature memorabilia connected to their namesakes.

Venturing out is easy enough. Happily situated at the heart of the city, guests can come and go from the comfort and tranquillity of their top-class accommodation to their own adventures outside, absorbing the local street life and colours.

For couples wanting to get married here, Raffles Le Royal is well prepared with a selection of venues from a grand ballroom

rooms
160 rooms • 10 suites

food
Café Monivong (Asian and Western) •
Le Royal Restaurant (Khmer and Western)

drink
Elephant Bar • The Conservatory • Pool Bar

features
Raffles Amrita Spa • pool • souvenir shop •
24-hour room service • airport limousine
service • concierge service

nearby
Royal Palace • National Museum of Cambodia •
Central Market • Russian Market •
S21 or Genocide Museum

contact
92 Rukhak Vithei Daun Penh,
Sangkat Wat Phnom, Phnom Penh, Cambodia
telephone: +855.23.981 888
facsimile: +855.23.981 168
email: phnompenh@raffles.com
website: www.phnompenh.raffles.com

or a poolside terrace, to a choice of private dining rooms and more intimate spaces, all complete with elegant furnishings. Couples can opt for a Khmer or Western style ceremony, with menus that are carefully tailored along with the flowers, style of photography and the cake. A Romance Specialist ensures that everything is monitored for the perfect dream wedding.

This kind of dedicated service applies to honeymooners and proposal parties too. The hotel can arrange private candlelit dinners, a private boat charter, daytrips and tours or any other requirement. And a butler and 24-hour room service will ensure couples' day-to-day requests are taken care of. Special touches include a Spa Signature experience. For him, a herbal mineral salt scrub, Khmer massage and a fresh cell facial. For her, a gentle body exfoliation followed by an Aromatherapy Massage and a fresh cell facial. After three hours of pampering within the confines of the luxurious **Raffles Amrita Spa**, a romantic stroll to Wat Phnom is just the ticket.

Raffles Grand Hotel d'Angkor

THIS PAGE: The large pool is located in the inner gardens of the hotel.

OPPOSITE (CLOCKWISE FROM TOP): The suite, with its romantic lighting, elegant interior design and cosy canopied bed, presents the perfect retreat for couples; unwind with a pampering spa treatment; enjoy an al fresco breakfast on your private terrace.

Now almost a century old, the stately **Raffles Grand Hotel d'Angkor**, Cambodia's answer to the Grand Dame Hotel, continues to stand with all the charm and elegance it had at its inception. This is a hotel steeped in Art Deco style and colonialism which it embraces at every turn. The original caged elevator still operates – with regal charm, it carries up to four people at a time. The conservatory, with all its old-world glamour, has been extended into the lobby and metalwork from one of the original doorways now frames the entrance to the **Elephant Bar**. But while the Art Deco touches and French colonial architecture combine for an elegant design, it is the Khmer objets d'art that give the Raffles Grand an identity that befits its location. Located in the heart of Siem Reap, with the UNESCO World Heritage site Angkor Wat just 8 km down the road, the hotel offers couples the perfect base from which to explore the cultural attractions of this historical city.

The facilities and activities available at the Raffles Grand truly lend themselves to a romantic getaway. Starting with accommodation, the newly renovated Cabana Suites were designed with couples in mind. The two bathrooms (one with a rainshower, one with a standalone, claw-footed bathtub), private balcony, direct access to the pool and private butler service see to the newlyweds' newly established requirements.

For seeing the sites, the hotel can organise romantic hot-air balloon trips and horse rides. A helicopter is available if the desired pace is a tad quicker.

In training for domestic bliss, the hotel's traditional Khmer cookery classes provide a valuable skill that, even in years to come, will take couples back to their honeymoon. And for dining, romance abounds. Start the evening on a private boat on the lake with canapés and champagne while the sun sets before you. Later, retreat to your suite for a

rooms
98 rooms • 21 suites

food
Café d'Angkor (international) • Le Grand
(Khmer and Western) • Apsara Terrace (Asian)

drink
The Elephant Bar • The Conservatory/
The Celebrity Bar • The Traveler Bar •
Pool Side Terrace

features
Raffles Amrita Spa • gym • beauty salon •
tennis court • pool • library • souvenir shop •
24-hour room service • butler service

nearby
Angkor Wat • Angkor National Museum •
Psaar Chaa market • Siem Reap International
Airport

contact
1 Vithei Charles de Gaulle, Khum Svay Dang
Kum Siem Reap, Cambodia
telephone: +855.63.963 888
facsimile: +855.63.964 223
email: rga.sales@raffles.com
website: www.raffles.com/siemreap

special and intimate room service, including a candlelit dinner for two with a sumptuous menu, complete with fresh flowers, your favourite music and the gentle waft of jasmine. Alternatively, couples can be taken off-site to the Athakon Architectural House or to the stunning temple complex itself. There, a cultural performance, a bottle of fine champagne and a gourmet meal from the executive chef ensures something truly enchanting and memorable.

For some extra pampering, visit the **Raffles Amrita Spa** where tailor-made packages can be put together based on guests' needs. After a massage in the double treatment room couples are served a(nother) bottle of champagne, this time by the poolside. The Raffles Grand Hotel d'Angkor, a regular feature in the *Condé Nast Traveler* Gold List of World's Best Places to Stay, knows how to treat you like royalty – exactly what you want on your romantic getaway.

Brilliant Resort & Spa, Chongqing

The highlight of a trip to Chongqing in China is a visit to North Hot Spring Park. Even though the park comprises a small area occupying just 10 hectares, Chongqing's most picturesque park offers many rich and diverse natural sites to explore with your loved one – hills, woods, ancient temples and palaces, volcanic hot springs, caves, gorges and the majestic Jialing River.

The best news for travellers is this: if you want to stay in the park itself, you can do so at **Brilliant Resort & Spa Chongqing**. Located at the foot of the Jinyun Mountains and facing the Jialing River, the buildings that make up the resort are hidden among the thick foliage and interconnected by zigzagging wooden corridors.

Trees and bamboo groves surround the suites so couples feel truly cocooned from the rest of the world. Much care has been taken to ensure that the buildings do not interfere with the growth of the trees – holes have been cut into the buildings to allow for branches to poke through in many areas, making the resort feel like an organic living thing and very much part of nature.

Taking full advantage of the healing waters of the natural hot springs in the area, the entire resort is dotted with 26 outdoor hot spring pools, with each mineral-rich spring

said to treat different ailments. All suites come with at least one private hot spring and some come equipped not only with two hot spring pools – one indoor and one outdoor – but also a spa treatment room or a private swimming pool. To complete the ambience, each room is filled with fragrance from an essential oil burner.

Your days at Brilliant Resort Chongqing start by the gong of the ancient temple nearby as your personal butler summons you for a morning yoga session. Here, your mental and spiritual well-being is given high priority. The session provides couples with an intimate time for bonding and allows them to fully commune with nature and take in the spirituality of the area – famed monks from the Song, Ming and Qing dynasties are buried here.

In the afternoon, culture and tradition take centre stage during the resort's tea performance ceremony. The demonstration gives guests an insight into the traditions and history behind tea making in China.

Evening time is a great time to book a session at the spa. Treatments incorporate spiritual and Taoist elements. In the Endless Love from Buddha therapy, a figurine of Buddha is hung in your treatment room, filled with incense from a burner. Before the actual massage, couples are taken through some meditation exercises to help relax the mind. This treatment is so calming that it is almost guaranteed to make you fall into a deep slumber.

This Brilliant world is a precious one filled with a reverence for history and culture, a deep-rooted spirituality and a love for nature.

rooms
31 suites

food
Jia Ling Xuan (Chinese fusion) •
Tepansu (Japanese)

drink
Long Bar • Tea House • Wine House

features
spa • outdoor forest hot spring area • gym •
yoga centre • tea house

nearby
Jinyun Mountain • Jialing River • Fishing Town •
Wen Tang Gorge • Shaolong Taoist Monastery

contact
North Hot Spring Park, Beibei District,
Chongqing 400702, China
telephone: +86.23.6822 9666
facsimile: +86.23.6822 7777
email: lisa@brillianthotels.cn
website: www.brilliantspa.com

Brilliant Resort & Spa, Kunming

THIS PAGE: *The bedrooms feature floor-to-ceiling windows for a bright and airy feel as well as a view of the gardens.*

OPPOSITE (CLOCKWISE FROM TOP): *Take in the calming view while stretching by the pool; each hot spring offers a mystical and romantic atmosphere; learn about the traditional Chinese tea ceremony at the Pu'er Tea Club.*

Like its sister resort in Chongqing, **Brilliant Resort & Spa Kunming** is all about its hot springs – 25 to be exact, not counting the private hot spring bath that comes with each villa. Each of its hot spring pools, drawing from natural volcanic springs in the area, is themed and targeted at the different needs and moods of guests. The Yangzong Hot Spring is a large pool that meanders among beautifully landscaped rocks and

trees. Here, couples can soak in the healing waters while enjoying the view of the mountains around the resort. At your request, yoga sessions can be conducted at the wooden tea pavilion at one end of the pool.

At the Fragrant Hot Springs, couples soak in a pool completely blanketed with fragrant flowers, with a view of the calm Yangzong Lake. The resort is located on the shores of the lake and all its thatched-roof villas and rooms enjoy the lake view.

The air is filled with mystical and spiritual calm at Forest Hot Springs, as vapours rise from the waters and curl around religious stone sculptures. This pool, surrounded by trees and flowers, creates a romantic nook for couples to enjoy some quiet time together.

At the Physiotherapy Hot Spring, the warm spring waters are channelled through pipes to create powerful jets of water which you can stand under. The pressure and pounding effect of these jets help ease tired and tense muscles.

Similarly, guests are spoiled for choice when it comes to where they want to have their spa treatment. The Lakeview Spa provides views of the lake while the Wetland Spa simulates a marshy environment, complete with reeds and the live sounds of frogs and cicadas. If you love water, the resort's over-water Spa Cabins, accessible via a narrow wooden walkway extending into Yangzong Lake, are highly recommended. Of course, you can also choose to have your

spa service in your own room. Treatments range from volcanic rock oil therapies to international favourites such as French-style aromatherapy massages, body wraps using mineral-rich mud from the Dead Sea, and Thai and Swedish massages.

Many of the Brilliant spa treatments are integrated with yoga exercises, based on the belief that physical and mental well-being are intricately related – yoga helps calm the mind while spa therapies relax the body. Lessons in tai chi, a form of Chinese martial arts said to improve blood circulation and agility, are held in the open as it is believed that the essence of the earth and the sky need to be absorbed in order to realign the chakras.

To replenish your energy, the **Wetlands Restaurant** serves both Western and Chinese cuisine. Couples can also arrange for an in-villa meal with a personal chef who can prepare a sumptuous barbecue feast or healthy spa menu.

A vacation at Brilliant Resort & Spa Kunming is not just a romantic spa holiday. It is one that will refresh your senses and awaken your spirituality.

rooms
23 villas

food
Wetland Restaurant (international)

drink
Pu'er Tea Club

features
spa • pool • tennis court • freshwater fishing • jogging track • butler service • wireless Internet

nearby
Spring City Golf Course • The Stone Forest • Yunnan Nationalities Village • Jiu Xiang caves • Green Lake • Da Guan Park

contact
Yangzonghai area, Yiliang, Kunming City, Yunnan Province 652103, China
telephone: +86.871.767 1666
facsimile: +86.871.767 3666
email: tsong@brillianthotels.cn
website: www.brilliantspa.com

Grand Hyatt Shanghai

Everything about the **Grand Hyatt Shanghai** is redolent of wealth and prosperity. Located within the Jin Mao Tower in the heart of Lujiazui, Shanghai's financial district, the hotel literally sits in the centre of Shanghai's apex of wealth. Its address, 88 Century Avenue – and the fact that the building rises 88 stories over Shanghai – further cements the sense of good fortune (8 being considered a lucky number by the Chinese).

The hotel, which occupies the 53rd to 87th storeys of the Jin Mao Tower, evokes the essence of traditional China by incorporating age-old Chinese art into its décor. Combining this with contemporary Art Deco design and a dash of modernity, the final visual result is a blend of East and West, old and new. Each bedroom is furnished in the Art-Deco-meets-old-Shanghai style, complete with all locally made furnishings, from the ceramic ice buckets fired in Chinese kilns to the headboards engraved with Tang Dynasty poetry and the paintings that adorn the walls. After a long day viewing the sights at ground level, retreat to your sky-high room to be greeted with stunning aerial views of Shanghai, with floor-to-ceiling glass windows providing unobstructed vistas of the cityscape. The building has a total of 60 elevators – including six high-speed elevators that transport hotel guests from the basement to the very top in only 45 seconds.

THIS PAGE (FROM TOP): *Wrap up in the soft down duvet and admire the Pudong skyline from your bed; there is a range of stylish suites, complete with a separate lounge area; enjoy the cosy atmosphere and live jazz music at the Piano Bar.*

OPPOSITE (FROM TOP): *The curvilinear ceiling adds to the dynamics of the skypool area; the hotel provides an elegant venue for wedding receptions.*

The award-winning hotel houses some of Shanghai's best dining and entertainment venues. On the 56th floor guests will find a unique three-in-one restaurant which incorporates **The Grill**, **Kobachi** (Japanese restaurant) and **Cucina** (Italian restaurant). In 2010, *Shanghai Tatler* listed Kobachi and Cucina as two of the top restaurants in the city. Couples can also enjoy haute Cantonese cuisine in a private dining room at **Canton**, the hotel's speciality restaurant, before taking in the 360-degree view from the popular **Cloud 9** bar on the 87th floor. This futuristic sky lounge is one of the highest points in Shanghai, and it has won numerous awards, including being named one of the World's Best Hotel Bars by Forbes.com. Those who want a little more privacy can treat themselves to the in-room dining service,

complete with romantic candlelight, roses and champagne. The Grand Hyatt Shanghai, with its ten function rooms, two ballrooms and a well-trained events management team, can also just as easily put together grand gala wedding dinners as intimate affairs for two.

For some extra pampering, take a trip to the **Club Oasis Spa**. A temperature-controlled skypool stretches from window to window, giving guests the illusion of swimming in the sky, while the spacious spa areas – lined with white and silver Italian marble and mosaics – make for an elegant, palatial atmosphere. Enjoy a massage together in this wellness centre, with sliding picture windows for you to watch the rest of the world go by. The spa also has an on-site Traditional Chinese Medicine masseur to help restore the balance of energy flow in your body.

rooms
555 rooms · 45 suites

food
Canton (Cantonese) · Cucina (Italian) · Grand Café (Western and Chinese) · The Grill (Western) · Kobachi (Japanese) · Club Jin Mao (Shanghainese)

drink
Cloud 9 · Patio · Piano Bar

features
Club Oasis Spa · pool · sauna · fitness centre · executive lounge

nearby
Oriental Pearl TV Tower · Shanghai World Financial Centre · Shanghai Centre · Super Brand Mall

contact
88 Century Avenue, Pudong New Area, Shanghai 200121, China
telephone: +86.21.5049 1234
facsimile: +86.21.5049 1111
email: shanghai.grand@hyatt.com
website: shanghai.grand.hyatt.com

JW Marriott Shanghai

Rising majestically 60 storeys above downtown Puxi, the **JW Marriott Shanghai**, housed within the architectural marvel that is Tomorrow Square, provides a perfect landmark in which to celebrate your own landmark occasion with your loved one.

Designed by Richard Nixon of John Portman & Associates and completed in 2003, Tomorrow Square is a visual masterpiece. At the 38th floor, the building deviates from its solid base by rotating 45 degrees along the Nanjing Road and People's Park axis. Because of this rotation, Tomorrow Square can appear radically different from various perspectives, even appearing to swell and shrink as you walk around it from a distance.

Being right in the heart of Shanghai's commercial shopping district means that couples staying at this hotel are within easy reach of what the city has to offer, including attractions such as the Shanghai Grand Theatre, the Shanghai Art Museum and The Bund. Xintiandi – Shanghai's newest shopping, dining and entertainment hot spot – is also within walking distance.

After a day of activity, guests can unwind in the cosy surroundings of **JW's Lounge** or return to their sky-high refuge – rooms are located on the 41st to 59th floors. On a clear day, enjoy breathtaking 360-degree views of the city centre, with uninterrupted panoramas over People's Square, across the river to Pudong and down towards the old French Concession.

Various on-site restaurants, a spa, indoor and outdoor pools, a 24-hour health club and 24-hour concierge and room service ensure that guests get their every need catered to. In addition, there is a 1,650-sq-metre function space, complete with captivating views and natural sunlight – perfect for special occasions such as weddings and ceremonies.

The hotel's **Mandara Spa**, with interiors reminiscent of an old Shanghai village, offers a full range of pampering treatments, including its signature "four hand massage". The Mandara Spa Suite for Two, designed for couples, features an oversized private spa tub, steam showers, private changing rooms and relaxation lounges.

While there are plenty of dining options nearby, the hotel's in-house restaurants are not to be missed. The **Wan Hao Chinese Restaurant**, serving traditional Cantonese dim sum and Shanghainese cuisine, and **JW's California Grill**, with its "Californian-Asian" creations, are listed among the 2010 Top 150 Best Restaurants in Shanghai in *Shanghai Tatler*. All restaurants offer tables with stunning city views.

For a romantic getaway, couples can stay in a Studio Suite with executive floor benefits – access to the executive lounge serving breakfast, all-day refreshments and evening cocktails, a complimentary bottle of champagne and a 60-minute Aromatic Flower Bath at the Mandara Spa. Packages for couples also include a romantic candlelit dinner at the "World's Highest Library" on the 60th floor.

rooms
156 Deluxe Rooms • 52 Deluxe Corner Rooms • 35 Executive Suites • 42 Executive Rooms • 14 Executive Corner Rooms • 41 Studio Suites

food
Wan Hao Restaurant (Cantonese, Shanghainese and dim sum) • Marriott Café (International) • JW's California Grill (meat, seafood) • 360 Gourmet Shop (traditional deli items)

drink
Lobby Lounge • JW's Lounge

features
Mandara Spa • business centre • florist • gym • pools • whirlpool and Jacuzzi • sauna and steam rooms • meeting facilities and services

nearby
People's Park • People's Square • Shanghai Grand Theatre • Shanghai Art Museum • Xintiandi • Huaihai Road • The Bund • Huang Pu River • Yu Yuan Garden • Lujiazui Financial District • The Oriental Pearl TV Tower

contact
399 West Nanjing Road, Huangpu District, Shanghai, 200003, China
telephone: +86.21.5359 4969
facsimile: +86.21.6375 4357
email:
mhrs.shajw.reservations@marriotthotels.com
website: jwmarriottshanghai.com

Amanusa

A teakwood carving, engraved with scenes from the *Ramayana*, highlights the welcome at the resort's open-air entrance and sets the inspiration for the décor. Couples can have their pick from 35 suites – eight with private pools – that each feature wooden four-poster beds, outdoor showers built into moss-covered *paras* stone walls and garden courtyards that offer cosy intimacy for al fresco dining, day or night.

Located nearby the desirable beaches and the many varied shopping and dining options of Legian, Seminyak and Sanur, Amanusa is a self-contained destination that offers a bounty of dining and relaxation experiences. From a sunrise breakfast on the beach or a poolside candlelit affair to a traditional 10-course Indonesian tasting dinner, couples can follow whatever the heart and appetite desires. Fine Thai and Italian fare are also available on-site, but if you prefer the

Twilight, the magic hour as the sun wends its weary way toward the horizon, and the sound of gamelan music soothes the senses. In the distance, the Indian Ocean sings refrain upon refrain of its ancient song while indigenous birds chime in with their chorus. Relaxing and immersing yourself in nature is not difficult at **Amanusa**. The resort is perched on a seaward rise on the southern Balinese peninsula of Nusa Dua, the lush green of the adjacent tree-lined golf course offering a gentle buffer to the coastline. Bougainvillea blossoms and frangipani trees, along with fine examples of the artistry of the native people are recurrent features of the resort. All this combined with the peaceful atmosphere and signature Amanresort service promises couples an unforgettable romantic getaway.

THIS PAGE (FROM TOP): The bright and airy bedroom is fitted with marble flooring, a four-poster canopied bed and wooden furnishings; savour a romantic meal for two in the garden courtyard.

OPPOSITE (FROM TOP): The resort has a distinct rustic charm to its design; enjoy an aromatic soak in the oversized flower-filled bath.

rooms
35 suites

food
The Terrace (Thai, Indonesian, Continental) ·
The Italian Restaurant (Italian) ·
Pool Terrace (snacks)

drink
The Bar

features
The Beach Club · spa suite · library · boutique ·
pool · gym · tennis courts · cookery classes

nearby
Bali Golf and Country Club · Nusa Dua Beach ·
cycling · island tours

contact
Nusa Dua, Bali, Indonesia
telephone: +62.361.772 333
facsimile: +62.361.772 335
email: amanusa@amanresorts.com
website: www.amanresorts.com

simplicity of a romantic picnic in the sun, feel free to request a wine hamper. The kitchen staff can assemble a selection of nibbles to accompany the wine of your choice, including breads and spreads, and a variety of cheeses, vegetable sticks and cured salmon with crème fraiche, fit for nearby Nusa Dua beach or anywhere in the resort.

You can also request for lunch or tea packed to go for sightseeing trips. Visit a local village, pore over bargains at bustling markets or learn more about the spirituality of the Balinese people at a number of picturesque temples. A helicopter charter to the temple of Pura Luhur Uluwatu is recommended for those with a penchant for flights of fancy, with other awe-inspiring routes taking sightseers into the fertile heartlands of Ubud and over tiered rice paddies and the yawning crater of a volcano. Further thrills can be had white-water rafting or on trips out to sea to cruise, snorkel or dive.

When body and mind are in need of comfort, seek out one of Amanusa's skilled masseuses, who employ a mix of traditional Balinese and Swedish massage techniques. The resident Reiki master can redress any energy imbalances, while a reputed local blind reflexologist offers his healing services once a week.

AYANA Resort & Spa

THIS PAGE (FROM LEFT): *Enjoy a floating brunch served to you in the sunshine; while away the afternoon in the river pool; the resort's wedding chapel, Tresna, features glass panels so you can take in the view with your vows.*

OPPOSITE (FROM LEFT): *Rock Bar is the perfect place for cocktails at sunset; black and white décor set the tone in the bedroom.*

Sitting atop limestone cliffs above Jimbaran Bay, **AYANA Resort & Spa** overlooks mysterious coves and crashing surf while commanding grand expansive views of the Indian Ocean. In this sprawling 77-hectare resort, you can choose from 290 hotel rooms or 78 free-standing private cliff-top villas. These Ocean or Cliff Villas, situated far apart for maximum seclusion, are set in traditional Balinese compounds and come with a private pool – making each villa a true *ayana*, meaning place of refuge in Sanskrit.

For the ultimate in exclusivity, the resort offers the AYANA Villa. Situated on 3000 sq metres of landscaped tropical gardens on the edge of the cliff, the grounds of the luxurious three-bedroom villa can also be transformed into a romantic wedding venue. This allows you to start your honeymoon right after your wedding. After the ceremony, retreat to your villa to enjoy panoramic views while sitting in your own infinity-edge pool. Choose to have an in-villa pampering spa treatment in the separate spa room or indulge in some private yoga and meditation classes.

At AYANA, romance is always in the air with a trained army of staff who are experts at putting together a romantic event. The resort provides six different wedding venues dotted along its private 1.3-km-long coastline. So whether you are looking for a garden wedding in an outdoor gazebo with sea views, hoping to say "I do" in a cliff-top all-glass chapel, or planning to have an intimate affair at the end of a secluded jetty, the resort will make it possible.

Apart from helping you to manage every aspect of your event – from catering, decorations, hair, make-up, entertainment and transport – other thoughtful touches

AYANA provides to make a romantic occasion even more memorable include a shower of scented rose or frangipani petals, fireworks over the Indian Ocean and a horse-drawn carriage for riding off into the sunset.

At this resort, the cliff and sea are not just beautiful backdrops. Incredible effort has been put into the construction of the resort to enhance the experience of nature. AYANA's **Rock Bar** is built right into the base of the towering cliffs, hovering 14 metres above the ocean. Here, you can sip refreshing cocktails to the sound of the waves. Designed by renowned Japanese architect Yasuhiro Koichi, Rock Bar is accessible only via a special cliff-side elevator. Don't miss this unless you suffer from severe vertigo.

Over at its **Thermes Marins Bali Spa**, the focus is on the therapeutic effects of natural seawater. It is home to one of the world's largest aquatonic seawater jet pools and features a Spa on the Rocks – spa villas built on rocks surrounded by the sea.

With such attention to detail, it is no wonder that AYANA Resort & Spa continues to win a string of awards. In 2010 alone, it won, among others: Asia's Leading Luxury Resort for the second year running, as well as Asia's Leading Luxury Villa (AYANA Villa) at the World Travel Awards.

rooms
290 rooms • 78 private villas

food
Dava (modern, international) • Kisik (seafood and grill) • Padi (Thai, Indian and Indonesian) • Sami-Sami (Italian) • Honzen (Korean barbecue and Japanese) • Langit Theatre (Indonesian buffet) • Spa Café (healthy cuisine) • Damar Terrace (international and Asian) • Pesta Lobster (romantic dinner on pier)

drink
C- Bar • H2O • The Martini Club • Rock Bar

features
Kubu Beach • Thermes Marins Bali Spa • ocean beach pool • 18-hole golf putting course • tennis pavilion • handicraft shops • gallery • villa library • aerobics and yoga pavilion

nearby
Tanjung Benoa Water Sports Centre • Uluwatu Sacred Temple with Kecak dance performance • Jimbaran Beach • traditional fish market • Bali Golf and Country Club and New Kuta Golf Course • Jenggala Ceramic and Pottery Centre • Shopping Gallery at Nusa Dua • cookery classes

contact
Jalan Karang Mas Sejahtera, Jimbaran, Bali 80364, Indonesia
telephone: +62.361.702 222
facsimile: +62.361.701 555
email: reservation@ayanaresort.com
website: www.ayanaresort.com

Komaneka at Bisma

THIS PAGE: *Lounge on the sun deck before the sleek lap pool whilst taking in the vast forest surroundings.*

OPPOSITE (FROM TOP): *When night falls, the airy lounge area of the villa turns into your own curtained pavilion; enjoy a dreamy morning in the large canopied bed.*

Built on the hillside by the Campuhan River valley in Ubud, the newest Komaneka resort, **Komaneka at Bisma**, offers a tranquil, romantic spot to enjoy the natural beauty of its surroundings. The hotel's contemporary design incorporates modern sophistication with traditional Balinese architecture, using locally sourced materials and elegant furnishings in warm, earthy tones. Each of the stylish Pool Villas feature a 12-metre-long plunge pool and a terrace, and guests can admire the panoramic view of the rice fields and coconut groves either from the privacy of their rooms or from the resort's half Olympic-size infinity-edge pool. The 500-metre jogging track located within the compound takes runners on a scenic route under a canopy of trees and along the river and paddy fields. For that perfect wedding, the on-site glass wedding chapel tucked into the lush greenery provides a beautiful backdrop in which to exchange vows.

The resort's pride in Balinese cultural heritage is reflected in the range of activities lined up for guests. In addition to a candlelit dinner, a traditional Balinese massage and a honeymoon cake, the honeymoon package features a visit to the Neka Art Museum, known for its collection of artwork by Balinese, Indonesian and foreign artists, each piece inspired by the life, charm and culture of Bali. Couples are then taken on a tour to the village of Petulu, where thousands of white herons descend every evening. It is said that the birds represent the souls of innocent men killed during anti-Communist activities in the 1960s. The herons are considered to be symbols of good luck and are protected by the community. For a touch of cultural creativity, couples can learn to make religious offerings using coconut leaves, take a woodcarving lesson or learn the art of Balinese dance.

rooms
32 Bisma Suite Rooms • 6 one-bedroom Pool Villas • 2 family Pool Villas • 1 two-bedroom Pool Villa • 1 three-bedroom Pool Villa

food
Indonesian and Western fusion

drink
Lobby Bar • Pool Bar

features
Komaneka Spa at Bisma • pool • gym • jogging track • library

nearby
Ubud palace • Ubud market • Sacred Monkey Forest of Padangtegal • art studios • galleries and museums • markets

contact
Jalan Bisma, Ubud, Gianyar 80571, Bali, Indonesia
telephone: +62.361.971 933
facsimile: +62.361.971 955
email: sales@komaneka.com
website: www.komaneka.com

The hotel's fine-dining restaurant serves up Indonesian and Western fusion cuisine. Its chefs have won several awards over the years, including a silver medal at the Bali Food Festival at Nusa Dua (2004) and a bronze medal at the Ubud Food Festival (2008). If you would like some cooking tips from Komaneka's illustrious chefs, sign up for a cookery lesson, which includes a tour to a morning market, recreating dishes from local recipes and a personalised apron as a gift.

The **Komaneka Spa at Bisma** is a serene wellness oasis, nestled in the riverside. Enjoy traditional Indonesian massages, herbal body scrubs and wraps, and other pampering treatments to the sound of flowing water. The spa has three double treatment villas, perfect for couples. Indulge in a Fruit Body Mask treatment or a body scrub with Javanese lulur. Traditionally for royals, this luxurious body scrub of rice and spices is a skin-softening elixir that naturally exfoliates rough and dry skin. For massages, a range of aromatherapy oils have been created exclusively for the Komaneka Spa, including Komaneka Spice which is a blend of warming clove combined with cassia, ginger and ylang-ylang to soothe all the senses.

Matahari Beach Resort & Spa

Hidden away in a remote and unspoiled corner of Bali, sandwiched between the Java Sea to the north and a beautiful backdrop of mountains to the south, the **Matahari Beach Resort & Spa** epitomises the ideal seaside retreat – secluded, quiet and tranquil.

Here, it is easy to leave everything behind to immerse yourself in nature. The resort, located in the Pemuteran area on the northwestern coast of Bali, sits on an interesting natural feature – a black volcanic sand beach. This beach is also known for its excellent diving and snorkelling conditions, with large areas of colourful coral reefs.

The resort itself is thoughtfully and harmoniously integrated into the pristine countryside and beachfront. It features 16 traditional Balinese-style bungalows – Garden View, Premium Garden View, Deluxe and Super Deluxe – that were constructed using only locally sourced materials, such as sandstone, marble and wood. Hundreds of local artists and craftsmen were involved in creating the intricate Balinese woodwork, statues, mural decorations and ornate stone carvings that adorn the buildings. Highlights in each bungalow include marble terraces, handcarved Balinese two-winged wooden doors, a king-size four-poster bed and rich traditional furnishings. For those who like being close to nature, each bungalow has an outdoor shower in a private garden. Couples staying in the Super Deluxe Bungalow will also love taking in the quiet surroundings from their own private pavilion in the middle of a lotus pond.

In line with Matahari's sensitivity towards the environment, its two restaurants – **Dewi Ramona Restaurant** and **Leon Beach Bistro** – use mostly locally produced ingredients. In fact, the organic vegetables used are grown high in the mountains near Bedugul by the resort's partner farms. The restaurants serve traditional Balinese fare, as well as international, fusion and vegetarian cuisine.

For a touch of romance, couples can arrange to have a candlelit champagne dinner served by the pool, accompanied by live music. Or if you love the sound of lapping waves as you dine, opt for an evening meal on the beach, with food prepared right at your table.

To pamper the body, visit the resort's **Parwathi Spa**, built to resemble an ancient royal palace. This atmospheric spa, complete with fountains, mood lighting and the scent of lotus and frangipani flowers, offers its own signature treatments designed to both relax and rejuvenate. The four-hand Royal Bali Massage is particularly popular.

For newlyweds, Matahari offers some romantic activities in harmony with nature. Couples can be blessed by a priest in the resort's temple followed by a tree planting ceremony in the garden to celebrate their marriage. To discover the beauty of unspoiled Bali, take a guided tour through a Sacred Garden, passing secluded farms and rivers, and several cascading waterfalls. Enjoy a refreshing dip in the natural waterfall pool together, and afterwards, unwind with a one-hour traditional Balinese massage in an open-air pavilion by the river and a romantic al fresco lunch.

rooms
16 bungalows, each comprising 2 units: 20 Garden View rooms • 6 Premium Garden View rooms • 4 Deluxe rooms • 2 Super Deluxe rooms

food
Dewi Ramona Restaurant (Euro-Asian) • Leon Beach Bistro (Balinese and Western)

drink
Wayang Bar • wine cellar

features
Parwathi Spa • pool • gym • gallery • library • cookery classes • Werner Lau Diving Centre

nearby
Menjangan Island • Bali Barat National Park • Pulaki Temple • Melanting Temple • trekking • horse riding

contact
Jalan Raya Seririt, Gilimanuk,
Desa Pemuteran, Kecamatan Gerokgak,
Kabupaten Buleleng 81155, Bali, Indonesia
telephone: +62.362.92312
facsimile: +62.362.92313
email: info@matahari-beach-resort.com
website: www.matahari-beach-resort.com

Maya Ubud Resort & Spa

THIS PAGE: *Enjoy complete privacy at the most exclusive Presidential Villa, nestled in the hillside.*

OPPOSITE (FROM LEFT): *A fragrant flower bath will leave you feeling calm and balanced; tuck into a delicious sunrise breakfast at Maya Sari; the spa pool provides beautiful views of the river below.*

Ubud has long been the spiritual centre of Bali, its mystical and spiritual energies a draw for many. **Maya Ubud Resort & Spa** capitalises on this by creating an ambience that helps you fall easily into a relaxed and serene state.

The resort sits on a strip of land that slopes dramatically down to the Petanu River. To the east are the villages of Bedulu and Pejeng, and to the west, the rice fields of Peliatan. The resort – a tranquil haven of tropical gardens and thatched buildings, private pool villas and luxury guestrooms – embeds itself in the verdant hillside foliage.

The architecture maximises its proximity to the swirling and sacred waters of Petanu River. The resort's **River Café** and **Maya Sari** restaurant overlook the river, while its spa is built on the Petanu's banks. The award-winning **Spa at Maya** is made up of a cluster of enchanting double and single thatched treatment pavilions suspended 30 metres down the cliffside. Walkways wind through lush greenery to the pavilions, which are complete with daybeds overlooking the valley. Canopied bathtubs overhang the waters of the river below. Its spa treatments using

essential oils and natural herbal ingredients are aimed at balancing the senses and refreshing the skin.

To help guests de-stress from everyday life and find spiritual balance, private meditation classes are conducted in secluded Balinese pavilions or *bale* overlooking the river. Special classes are also available for Pilates and couples yoga – which teaches couples how to centre each other's spiritual energy through touch.

For dining, the resort serves a wide variety of cuisine. Maya Sari offers a sumptuous sunrise buffet with river valley views, while the innovative **Asiatique** features regional dishes from Thailand, China, India, Japan, including teppanyaki grill and Indonesian delights from across the archipelago. The resort is happy to set up more intimate

arrangements for couples. These include a six-course dinner under the stars on its starlight deck and a picnic lunch by the river in one of the resort's riverside gazebos.

The bustling artist village of Ubud, with its central market, art galleries and trendy eateries is only a 20-minute walk away from the resort. Complimentary bus shuttle services are available every hour. Nature lovers can take a guided tour through the rainforest, past ancient temples, traditional Balinese villages and through rice terraces.

Romantic activities for two offered at Maya Ubud Resort & Spa range from photo sessions and breakfast in bed, to countryside drives in a private car and tree planting in the riverside garden. For those looking to get married in this magical and serene setting, the resort can arrange for you to say "I do" in a number of venues, at the edge of the river valley or in the tropical temple garden.

rooms
48 rooms • 60 villas

food
Maya Sari (international and Indonesian) • River Café (healthy spa cuisine) • Asiatique (Asian)

drink
River Café • Bar Bedulu

features
Spa at Maya • main pool • spa pool • library and business centre • fitness and yoga centre

nearby
artist village of Ubud

contact
Jalan Gunung Sari, Peliatan, Ubud
80571 Bali, Indonesia
telephone: +62.361.977 888
facsimile: +62.361.977 555
email: marketing@mayaubud.com
website: www.mayaubud.com

Tugu Bali

"Tugu", in the language of Indonesia, means monument, and true to its name, the **Tugu Bali** is a living monument of all that is beautiful in the classic representation of Bali through art and culture. Monumental too is the devotion of the hotel owners to create amongst this grandeur an all-encompassing romantic destination whose authenticity remains unmatched.

The location of the resort, at Canggu Beach on the southwest coast of Bali, was specifically selected for its privacy and romantic ambience. Thatched-roof buildings nestle against the dune line and the sound of waves is ever present. Watching the sunset while walking hand in hand across the sand alongside the swell of the Indian Ocean is one of the simplest yet most romantic things to do here.

Like the other members of the Tugu Hotel family, authentic antiques and artwork from Java, Bali and the surrounding islands are featured throughout the hotel. Each collection tells its own story; be it myth or legend, they bring the romance of the past to life. One of the most romantic suites, the Puri Le Mayeur villa, was built around the true love story between Belgian painter Adrien-Jean Le

THIS PAGE (FROM TOP): The beautifully decorated rooms are designed with couples in mind; the stunning Bale Sutra dining room reflects both Peranakan and Balinese culture; the Puri Le Mayeur suite sits in the middle of a lotus pond.

OPPOSITE (FROM TOP): Enjoy a private al fresco picnic in bed; a romantic dinner can be had in the garden.

rooms
1 Honeymoon Villa: Puri Le Mayeur Villa •
9 Dedari Suites • 9 Rejang Suites •
1 Kampong Suite • 1 Walter Spies Pavilion

food
Bale Agung (Western, Babah Peranakan, Indonesian) • Bale Sutra (Babah Peranakan and Chinese) • Bale Puputan (Royal Balinese) • Waroeng Tugu (Javanese and Balinese) • Black Chamber (Western, Chinese, Indonesian)

features
spa • pool • private plunge pool • Jacuzzi • art shop • surfing • snorkelling • diving • fitness centre • wireless Internet • cookery classes

nearby
Nirwana golf course • Tanah Lot Temple • surfing • Seminyak shopping and restaurant district

contact
Jalan Pantai Batu Bolong, Canggu Beach, Bali, Indonesia, 83352
telephone: +62.361.731 701
facsimile: +62.361.731 708
email: bali@tuguhotels.com
website: www.tuguhotels.com

Mayeur and Ni Polok, the legendary Balinese dancer. As the story goes, Le Mayeur visited Bali in 1932, intrigued by its fascinating culture. He started painting and took Ni Polok and two other dancers as models and inspiration for his paintings. Although he only intended to stay for eight months, he soon fell under the spell of Bali and that of Ni Polok, whom he wed after a three-year courtship. They lived the rest of their lives in Bali and their romance resonates today in the Puri Le Mayeur villa which houses some of the original Le Mayeur paintings and wood carvings of their first home, crafted by a blind man who worked for the couple. Everything about this villa, also the hotel's dedicated honeymoon suite, speaks of love, from the red and gold colour theme in the bedroom to the ornate wood panelling and timber columns.

One of the most attractive features of this villa is its position in the centre of a large lotus pond. A small bridge over the pond leads guests to a dining pavilion. In the evening, lit only by candles and flare torches, this alcove sets the perfect mood for a romantic dinner.

Choosing from a range of gourmet, traditional and modern cuisine, couples can indulge in their favourite foods or venture into the undiscovered and new. In the Peranakan-inspired room, Balinese dancers can entertain couples while they dine or guests can take part in a theatrical re-enactment of a Majapahit King's parade, complete with entourage and grand dinner. The hotel also has a "point where you wish" policy – point to where you want to have your dinner, and a table will appear, almost magically, upon your command.

Uma Ubud

THIS PAGE: *Relax with a cocktail by the Pool Bar in the evening.*

OPPOSITE (CLOCKWISE FROM TOP): *Indulge in a massage in the double treatment room at the COMO Shambhala Retreat; light colours in the bedroom complement the lush greenery outside; the highlight of the Uma Pool Suite is the private plunge pool with views of the Balinese jungle.*

For a place that has become associated with revitalisation, rejuvenation, restoration and healing, the etymology of its name is both telling and apt. The idyllic pastoral region of Ubud, located in the heart of Bali and persisting, it seems, at an unhurried pace of its own rhythms, gets its name from the word "ubad", which in local vernacular means medicine. Medicinal herbs that grow wild among the flora, fresh organic produce from bountiful fields, and the daily catch from the encompassing seas are some of the special elements that help make a stay at **Uma Ubud** such a curative pleasure.

An intimate encounter that will not be forgotten, coming to this resort, in a region that is also known for the handicraft of its talented artists and artisans, is like stepping into a vibrant painting of the rich and dynamic indigenous island landscape. The artfully crafted hotel – part of the award-winning COMO Hotels and Resorts group – lies on the threshold of dramatic geographical features, a five-minute drive or 20-minute walk from town. A picture of luxury, Uma Ubud overlooks the paddy-lined Tjampuhan Valley and is backdropped by mountain scenery, with the River Oos winding its frenzied way down below.

Sweet solitude, for lovers who treasure their alone time, is easily attainable here. Be it for your honeymoon or a dream getaway, guests can take their pick of 29 bright and airy rooms – including five suites, four with private pools – and also request the most secluded table at dinner as well as personal tours of Ubud.

Couples can avail themselves of exclusive body care treatments at the resort's **COMO Shambhala Retreat**, which was named Spa Retreat of the Year by Asia Spa Awards in 2009. Fresh air and inspiring sights, coupled with customised yoga classes in an open-air studio, and guided morning walks every day,

rooms
14 Terrace Rooms • 10 Garden Rooms •
1 Uma Suite • 3 Uma Pool Suites • 1 COMO Suite

food
Kemiri Restaurant (Balinese and Asian) •
COMO Shambhala healthy cuisine

drink
Pool Bar

features
COMO Shambhala Retreat • pool • gym • yoga
pavilion • business centre with Internet access

nearby
ARMA centre of visual and performing arts •
Njana Tilem Gallery • Seniwati Gallery • Neka
Art Gallery • Agung Rai Gallery • Komaneka
Fine Art Gallery • Kintamani at Mount Batur •
white-water rafting

contact
Jalan Raya Sanggingan, Banjar Lungsiakan,
Kedewatan, Ubud, Gianyar 80571,
Bali, Indonesia
telephone: +62.361.972 448
facsimile: +62.361.972 449
email: res.ubud@uma.como.bz
website: www.uma.ubud.como.bz

make for a sure-fire formula for leaving the troubles of daily life behind. Beauty rituals and treatments, in the best local tradition, offer a means to wellness derived from home-grown ingredients; consider the retreat's signature massage, the COMO Shambhala Bath or the COMO Shambhala Ritual.

Ally your treatments with a suitable diet, if you so desire. Guests may order healthy dishes made from organic foods from the COMO Shambhala menu, or they can enjoy the nourishing culinary creations of the resort's **Kemiri Restaurant**, named after the candlenut that is a constant in Indonesian cuisine. Here, modern interpretations of Southeast Asian cuisines, married with Western technique and infused with native and Indian spices, abound.

Beyond the warm embrace of the resort, couples have a multitude of activities to choose from. Take a walk through the paddy fields and visit temples; go exploring on a biking or rafting adventure; trek through forests or up a volcano; go shopping or stop to admire the customs, cultural performances and colourful festivals of the friendly and gentle Balinese people.

Villa Babar

THIS PAGE: The luxurious villa provides the perfect wedding setting, with beautiful surroundings and spacious grounds.

OPPOSITE (FROM TOP): Soft lighting in the living room complements the picture windows offering expansive views of the ocean; featuring clean lines and minimalist décor, each bedroom portrays a theme inspired by Indonesian culture.

Built on a secluded headland beside a pristine beach along Bali's west coast, **Villa Babar**, with its open concept and subtle elegance, celebrates a special oneness with its surroundings while offering an unrivalled experience in luxury.

Right on the beachfront, with panoramic views of the Indian Ocean that extend all the way down to Uluwatu on Bali's southwestern tip, Villa Babar could not be located in a more spectacular spot. Guests staying in rooms facing inland are treated to views of lush rice fields, with the mountains rising majestically in the distance evoking a feeling of calm spirituality. It is said that the place emanates a palpable mystical energy, making it an ideal site for those seeking peace through meditation or yoga.

The two-storey villa marries Indonesian and European styles seamlessly with the walls made of white stone imported from Yogyakarta, cream terrazzo tiled floors, limewashed timbers and a colonnaded walkway, on both ground and upper floor levels. Located in the Tabanan Regency – the most agriculturally productive area in Bali and home to Mount Batukaru – the villa is a convenient base from which to explore Bali's natural treasures. At 2,276 metres above sea level, Mount Batukaru is the island's second highest peak. Local guides will accompany you on gentle hikes through the forests and

rooms
6 bedrooms

food
International and Balinese

features
open-air living room • air-conditioned lounge •
media room • pool • Internet access •
helicopter pad

nearby
beach • mountain biking • mountain trekking •
golf • horse riding • surfing • rice fields •
traditional village visits

contact
Banjar Pondok, Desa Beraban, Kecamatan
Selemadeg Timur 82162, Tabanan,
Bali, Indonesia
telephone: +62.361.730 596
facsimile: +62.361.730 596
email: info@balivillababar.com
wbsite: www.balivillababar.com

jungle or challenging treks up the mountain, depending on your predilection. The area also features great biological diversity, affording animal lovers sightings of rare species. And a trip to the breathtaking Jatiluwih rice terraces, a UNESCO World Heritage Site, is definitely worth making. Standing at the top of Bali's terraced green paddy fields and taking in the endless contours stretching over the hills and valleys will make you feel like you are the only two people in the world.

Couples spending the day in the villa can indulge in special open-air massages or enjoy the property's tranquil gardens, including the Ganesha garden and the Sumba garden, the latter distinguished by a cluster of sculptures from Sumba in eastern Indonesia. While away the afternoon sipping champagne by the swimming pool in the front garden, which is,

in turn, mere steps away from the beach. The villa's spacious lounge – decorated with Indonesian stone carvings, wooden statues and tribal shields – is equipped with a sophisticated music system, billiard table and a selection of books and games. Villa Babar also has its own helipad and can arrange private helicopter tours for guests, providing a unique opportunity for couples to discover parts of Bali that few tourists get to see.

Fresh meals are prepared daily at the villa by a personal chef using local organic produce and imported meats. Anything from a light snack or a romantic candlelit dinner, to a grand banquet or wedding reception can be arranged. So whether you are looking for a secluded romantic getaway or a beautiful wedding venue, Villa Babar is an excellent choice.

Villa de daun

THIS PAGE (FROM TOP): The lavish Ixora Room at the DaLa Spa; luxuriate in a hot bubble bath for two; warm earthy hues and wooden furnishings provide subtle elegance and charm.

OPPOSITE (FROM TOP): Enjoy a spot of tea overlooking the private pool; thousands of fresh flowers complete the romantic setting as you dine.

Villa de daun is a cosy and stylish Balinese hideaway right in the heart of Bali's most vibrant tourist area, Kuta. Surrounded by tropical landscaping within the resort's 1-hectare property are 12 contemporary villas designed to embrace the outdoors and capture the spirit of a traditional Balinese village. Each villa is set within its own compound, with living spaces that open directly to the outdoors and a private swimming pool.

Just a few minutes' walk from this calm sanctuary lies the frenetic Kuta beach, as well as a myriad of shopping, dining and entertainment venues. Guests looking for a quiet retreat, while at the same time hoping to indulge in some retail therapy and sightseeing, will find Villa de daun a convenient base from which to venture out.

For those who do not wish to leave the resort, the **de daun Restaurant** offers fine Indonesian cuisine prepared with fresh produce in a relaxed garden setting. There is also an in-villa barbecue service, where a private chef grills a selection of meats and fresh seafood to perfection for guests.

Couples looking to create romantic moments will not be disappointed. The resort's staff are willing to go the distance. If you want your villa garden completely decked with candles, or thousands of fresh flower petals to cover your whole pool, or even a private dinner for two in your villa – it can be arranged.

rooms
4 one-bedroom Pool Villas • 6 one-bedroom Deluxe Pool Villas • 1 two-bedroom Deluxe Pool Villa • 1 three-bedroom Deluxe Pool Villa

food and drink
de daun Restaurant (Indonesian cuisine) • in-villa dining

features
DaLa Spa • library • butler service • personal chef, car and driver on request

nearby
downtown Kuta • Kuta Beach • international airport • restaurants • bars • shops

contact
Jalan Raya Legian, Kuta, Bali, Indonesia 80361
telephone: +62.361.756 276
facsimile: +62.361.750 643
email: info@villadedaun.com
website: www.villadedaun.com

In fact, couples on their honeymoon are treated with the utmost attention. In addition to a foot bath on arrival, they will receive a delicious de daun honeymoon cake. The canopied bed will be adorned with flowers and a special flower bath will be prepared for them. For extra pampering, every villa comes with a butler to cater to every need, while a car and driver are available on demand.

The **DaLa Spa** is undoubtedly the highlight of this resort. For the new brides, the spa recreates a traditional Javanese beauty wedding rite. Aptly named the Royal Wedding Ritual treatment, the highlight of this nurturing ritual is a Javanese lulur exfoliation, where a paste of turmeric, sandalwood and rice powder is applied to the body to soften and heal the skin. This is followed by a hydrating yogurt body polish and a milk bath infused with seven different flowers, which recreates the ceremonial rite where a Javanese bride is lovingly bathed by her parents before the wedding.

Other signature treatments offered in the opulently decorated spa include the DaLa Aromatherapy Massage, which focuses on the art of healing through touch and smell; the Tutti Fruity Spa, which nourishes with fresh fruit; and the Empress Facial Ritual.

In 2008, Villa de daun was voted Best Boutique Hotel Spa by SpaAsia Crystal Awards, while the resort's DaLa Spa won Best New Spa in the Asia Spa & Wellness Ritual 2007 Gold Awards.

Villa Sungai Bali

THIS PAGE (FROM TOP): Relax together on the poolside sunbeds; enjoy a delicious breakfast served in the thatched-roof dining pavilion; the bedroom is a cosy hideaway for couples, overlooking the private pool.

OPPOSITE (FROM TOP): Lounge by the sleek horizon lap pool and take in the lush surroundings; Villa Sungai Bali provides Acqua di Parma toiletries in the bathroom.

Certain elements make for a great romantic vacation – a quiet location within an interesting and beautiful area, lavishly appointed rooms complete with luxurious amenities, delicious wholesome food whipped up by gourmet chefs using fresh ingredients and in-house spa services. **Villa Sungai Bali**, named top Best Overseas Boutique Property by *Luxury Travel* in their Gold List Awards 2010, is one high-end standalone villa that provides all these. However, it is the personalised service provided by the dedicated staff and the attention to customer care that elevate Villa Sungai to a different class altogether.

Overlooking a tributary of the Ayang River, set deep in a tropical rainforest in the village of Cepaka, Villa Sungai comes with twice-daily housekeeping services, a butler, a house manager and a personal chauffeur and car.

Chefs are on call to cook up anything you desire, 24 hours a day, whether you want some pre-dinner canapés by the pool, a four-course dinner paired with wine, a wedding reception for 10 guests, or a simple bowl of noodles for supper.

The pampering continues in the private treatment room where a team of masseurs and therapists deliver massages, including the popular couple's massage, body scrubs, facials and other relaxing spa treatments incorporating traditional Balinese herbs.

Guest privacy is never compromised, even with such a large pool of staff at your command. Wait staff seem to materialise magically to fulfil your needs, and melt away when their services are not required. The concierge can arrange romantic in-house touches such as a freshly drawn bath for two

rooms
Villa Sungai: 3 guest suites
Sungai Gold: 1 guest suite

food
private dining pavilion

drink
private bar

features
in-villa spa services • pool • WiFi • personal
concierge • butler • chauffeur and car

nearby
Tanah Lot • Nirwana Golf Course •
Ubud (35 minutes) • Seminyak (20 minutes) •
markets • temples

contact
Villa Sungai Bali, Cepaka, Tabanan,
Bali, Indonesia
telephone: +61.410.324 535
email: info@bali-villasungai.com
website: www.bali-villasungai.com

or a gamelan orchestra to serenade couples with their pre-dinner cocktails. It also organises some inspiring activities around the area for guests to connect with nature, including jungle hiking, white-water rafting, elephant safaris and scuba diving. Volcanoes, bright green paddy fields and forests surround the untouched village of Cepaka, affording an idyllic setting for romance.

The villa itself exudes a raw beauty reflecting the serenity and rustic charms of the region, with a sophisticated chic design in neutral tones and the use of natural materials. Soak up the atmosphere while sitting in the thatched-roof dining pavilion and watching the private 18-metre pool seemingly cascade into the forest and river

below. For indoor comfort, each of the three suites in Villa Sungai features a king-size four-poster bed, draped with billowing fabric and made up with imported Egyptian cotton bedsheets and plush duvets.

A separate smaller villa, **Sungai Gold**, is perfect for honeymooners. Like the main villa, the interiors are a blend of white terrazzo floors, white walls and cool khaki furnishings, with sliding glass doors filling the room with natural light. It has one bedroom and its own pool and is accessed via a pathway through a lush tropical garden. Couples can host an intimate wedding ceremony with family and friends at Villa Sungai, and then shut themselves away for a honeymoon in blissful seclusion at Sungai Gold.

Tugu Lombok

THIS PAGE: *The atmospheric Bale Kokok Pletok dining hall serves a wide variety of cuisine.*

OPPOSITE (FROM LEFT): *The Bhagavat Gita Suite is furnished in romantic tones, complete with a canopied bed; spend an afternoon lounging on a daybed by the sea; the natural surroundings of the Hening Swarga Spa make it the perfect place to find tranquillity for the body and soul.*

It is hard, even for a well-seasoned traveller, not to feel impressed on entering **Tugu Lombok**. A deep reverence for local history and a passion for art are clearly shown in the intricate details that characterise every corner of the hotel. The building that leads to the lobby used to serve as a reception house during the Dutch colonial era. It was removed from where it stood in Lombok's old capital, Ampenan, and painstakingly reconstructed to form the hotel's entrance.

Everything from the construction of the buildings and the use of original artwork, to the incorporation of local myth and legend into the design, manifests the hotel's deep devotion to Lombokian culture and mythology and a mission to share it with others. In fact, the owners set the hotel up here to dispel the misconception that Lombok has no romantic history or past.

Each accommodation option reflects an aspect of Lombok history. The Bhagavat Gita Suites are rooms in a colonial-era building with thatched roofs, antique doors and private plunge pools. The most interesting feature in these suites is the large stone

bathtub, carved out of a boulder. The Aloon Aloon Garden Villa offers a private garden, outdoor dining area for a candlelit dinner for two, a unique tree trunk bed and an oversized copper bathtub. The Kampoeng Lombok Bungalows are designed to feel like native village houses with the use of wood and bamboo, but still fitted with modern luxuries.

Most honeymooners reserve the Puri Dadap Merah suite, named after the sacred Red Dadap trees that surround it. Built to resemble an ancient temple, this villa exudes an exotic temple-like feel using deep red and green tones. Ancient antiques from Madura, Java and Bali are featured here while local wood carvings and brocade adorn the walls. Couples could spend an entire day in this room. From their private plunge pool they can enjoy the view of the ocean and spacious gardens, before indulging in a couple's massage later on in their own spa area. When night falls, a romantic dinner on the rooftop terrace can be prepared especially for them.

Guests can also sign up for classes to learn more about Lombokian culture first-hand. See how villagers make the alcoholic palm wine called *tuak*, or learn about the process of cultivating pearls. Other activities include the Terracotta Class and the Gendang Beleg Drum/Dance Class.

For more active cultural exploration, couples can spend the afternoon snorkelling or diving in the Gili Islands – there is a wide range of sea and water activities nearby to choose from – or learning about local life on an excursion to a traditional village. For a touch of romance, treat yourself to breakfast onboard a traditional wooden dragonhead boat as the sun rises over Mount Rinjani, Indonesia's second highest volcano.

rooms
1 Honeymoon Suite: The Puri Dadap Merah •
7 Bhagavat Gita Suites • 6 Aloon Aloon Villas •
5 Kampoeng Lombok Bungalows

food
Bale Kokok Pletok (Western, Chinese and Indonesian)

drink
Lara Djonggrang Bar

features
Hening Swarga Spa • pool • Jacuzzi •
private plunge pool • art shop • canoeing •
snorkelling • diving • private boat trip to Gili
Islands • fitness centre • wireless Internet

nearby
Kosaido Golf Course • The Gili Islands •
Pura Medana temple • Tiu Pupus Waterfalls •
Tanjung village • Rinjani National Park

contact
Jalan Pantai Sire, Desa Sigar Penajalin
Kecamatan Tanjung Lombok Utara,
Indonesia 83352
telephone: +62.370.612 0111
facsimile: +62.370.612 0444
email: lombok@tuguhotels.com
website: www.tuguhotels.com/lombok

Amantaka

When the Laotian town of Luang Prabang was named a UNESCO World Heritage Site in 1995, the UNESCO report called it the best-preserved traditional town in Southeast Asia. Filled with beautiful French colonial buildings and ancient Buddhist temples, coupled with many spectacular natural sites and a slow pace of life that has remained unchanged for decades, it is no wonder many consider Luang Prabang to be the "jewel in Laos' crown".

Right in the heart of town is the stately and serene **Amantaka**. As one of the few Amanresorts located near a UNESCO World Heritage site, Amantaka takes upon itself the responsibility of promoting local culture and endeavours to recreate an authentic Lao-French ambience within the resort. The high ceilings and open verandahs create a spacious and breezy feel throughout the building. The lobby opens up to a large courtyard where the main pool is located. The smallest suite features a roomy 70 sq metres of indoor and outdoor space while the largest suites, the Amantaka Pool Suites, give you 120 sq metres of blissful living in the form of a spacious bedroom and lounge area, private verandah, sala and a pool in your own garden.

However, as with all Amanresorts around the world, it is the superlative personal service and the staff's little thoughtful touches that are winning the hearts of travellers everywhere. There even exists an exclusive

THIS PAGE (FROM TOP): The Aman Spa offers a private treatment room for couples; the living room provides an elegant space for lounging; the four-poster bed is the focal point of the bedroom.

OPPOSITE (FROM TOP): The white exterior of the main resort building complements the blue of the mirror-like pool; relax with a sensual soak in the large bathtub.

rooms
8 Suites · 4 Pool Suites · 8 Khan Pool Suites ·
2 Mekong Pool Suites · 2 Amantaka Pool Suites

food
Dining Room (Lao-French) ·
Pool Terrace (light meals)

drink
Lounge Bar

features
Aman Spa · library · boutique · art gallery ·
gym · yoga studio · pool · cookery classes

nearby
Pak Ou Caves · Kuang Si Waterfall · Tad Sae
Waterfall · Hmong Village · Ock Pop Tok's
Living Crafts Centre · Xieng Thong Temple ·
Mount Phousi · Royal Palace Museum

contact
55/53 Kingkitsarath Road, Ban Thongchaleun
Luang Prabang, Lao PDR
telephone: +856.71.860 333
facsimile: +856.71.860 335
email: amantaka@amanresorts.com
website: www.amanresorts.com

breed of traveller, dubbed the "Amanjunkie", so moved by the Aman experience that they prefer to only stay at Amanresorts when travelling. At Amantaka, every time you enter or leave the hotel, you are presented with an icy cool towel and a warm smile. The staff greets you by name and no request is ever too extraordinary for them to handle – perfect for organising that romantic surprise for your loved one.

You might be hard-pressed to think of something the resort has not already anticipated. Want to witness the procession of monks who gather along the streets at 5.30 am every morning? Amantaka can not only arrange for you to attend this spiritual experience – which sees locals paying respect to monks by placing food into their alms bowls – but also provides a portion of sticky rice for you to present as your own offering. Want to travel upriver to see the sacred Pak Ou caves? Amantaka takes you there in a private boat, and plans your journey such that on your return trip, you get to enjoy the view of the sun setting as a butler serves you a refreshing aperitif. Similarly, elephant rides, blessing ceremonies, excursions to hilltribe villages and temples as well as trips to waterfalls for a scenic swim have all been thoughtfully planned for you. There is simply no better way than the Amantaka way to take in this magical gem of a town.

Avillion Port Dickson

THIS PAGE: The chalets built over the water at Tumasek Beach offer a serene setting, perfect for romance.

OPPOSITE (FROM LEFT): Take in the calming sea view together; the Village Court Restaurant by the pool serves both Western and local dishes, with fresh grilled seafood as its speciality.

Simple pleasures enrich the soul and ignite the senses, and at **Avillion Port Dickson** in Malaysia, every tiny detail has been orchestrated to enhance your sense of well-being and pleasure. Set along the 3rd mile of Port Dickson beach, about an hour away by car from Kuala Lumpur, the resort, named best Luxury Boutique Hotel by World Luxury Hotel Awards 2010, is designed to resemble a Malay fishing village. Wooden chalets reminiscent of traditional *kelongs* – offshore huts built above the water – branch out from the beach and into the warm waters of the Straits of Malacca.

All the Premium Chalets come with large private sea view balconies, allowing couples to sneak in plenty of private moments – watching the sunset, enjoying the breeze with a glass of wine or a spot of stargazing – accompanied by the sounds of the sea. The accommodation interiors, decorated in a contemporary style but keeping traditional

Malaysian elements, feature plenty of spaces for lounging, from the four-poster king-size bed to the queen-size pangkin daybed.

The blue mosaic bathroom comes with a large bathtub, and an open-air rainshower means guests can enjoy a refreshing shower outdoors with a sky view. The luxury toiletries are formulated with 100% natural, plant-based ingredients and the same reverence for high-quality natural products can be found at the resort's **Avi Spa**. This two-storey pavilion built directly over the water offers a complete range of soothing and rejuvenating treatments. The spa, which has won numerous awards for its treatments as well as for its design, has a "low-tech high-touch" philosophy, rooted in the belief of the healing nature of human touch. The spa suites, including two designed for couples, have big open windows facing the sea. The caress of the soft breeze will put you at ease even before your treatment begins.

Guests can later venture out for a romantic stroll and explore the many restaurants, shops and activities along the bustling Port Dickson stretch of coast, or for a particularly relaxing evening, choose to stay within the resort grounds, with its own pools, including an adult-only pool, and private beach. Find your own quiet niche along the beach, or hide away in the many scenic nooks around the award-winning resort – it won the Excellence Award in Architecture from the Malaysian Institute of Architects in 2000.

Serving a mixture of local and Western cuisine, the resort's **Village Court Restaurant** offers a casual poolside atmosphere. For a great overview of the terrain, ask for a balcony table at **Crow's Nest Restaurant**, which reflects a contemporary Malaysian design with its teakwood ceilings and rattan furnishings.

Couples and honeymooners receive special treatment when they opt for one of the resort's packages, including an airport transfer, a bottle of sparkling wine, a box of chocolates, a candlelit dinner and a therapeutic treatment at Avi Spa.

THIS PAGE (FROM LEFT): *Indulge in a session of pre-wedding pampering at the spa with its floor-to-ceiling sea views; enjoy the comfort of the soft white four-poster canopied bed.*

OPPOSITE (FROM TOP): *The cocktail lounge suspended in the water is a great place to unwind at sunset; a wedding set-up reflecting a summer ocean theme with shells and blue glass table decorations.*

Avillion Weddings

Avillion Port Dickson loves to host weddings. Its natural beach setting provides a beautiful outdoor setting for your special event. Picture walking barefoot down a flower-strewn beach, towards a specially built archway adorned with local orchids, with hanging crystal hearts and butterflies twinkling brightly in the sunlight.

Avillion's Tumasek Beach venue can hold up to 500 people while its Riau Beach can take 200 guests. At your command, either beach can be transformed into whatever dream

setting you desire. A popular choice is the blue-themed wedding to reflect and complement the sea, with blue chiffon draped over wooden posts fluttering romantically in the sea breeze, blue table linen, blue floral decorations and wedding cupcakes with blue icing. A traditional all-white wedding, in a white purpose-built marquee – with white linen, white chairs and great lengths of billowing white fabric – is also a favourite among couples getting married at Avillion.

If a beach wedding is not to your taste, the resort also has manicured grounds for a garden wedding as well as a ballroom for an indoor event that can seat 180 people. Alternatively, the ballroom can be used to hold the cocktail reception or wedding dinner after your beach solemnisation ceremony.

Couples can use the Avi Spa lounge to host their hen or stag parties. Other themed pre-wedding parties such as an open-air picnic under the stars can easily be arranged

rooms
44 Premium Water Chalets · 162 Water Chalets ·
32 Garden Chalets · 7 Two-bedroom Water
Villas · 2 One-bedroom Water Villas ·
15 Beach Rooms · 9 Beach Studios

food
Crow's Nest Restaurant (international) ·
Village Court Restaurant (local and
international)

drink
The Galley Bar & Lounge · Jungle Fringe
Karaoke & Bar · Avi Spa Floating Lounge

features
Avi Spa · spa garden · private beach · gym ·
pools (24 hours) · water sports centre · pet
farm · spice farm · tennis court · activity hut ·
orchid hut

nearby
Kampung Sungai Timun (crocodile sighting &
fireflies) · Kampung Sekawang (Malay fishing
village) · Cape Rachado Lighthouse · army
museum · ostrich farm · homestay village

contact
3rd Mile, Jalan Pantai, 71000 Port Dickson,
Negeri Sembilan, Malaysia
telephone: +60.6.647 6688
facsimile: +60.6.647 7688
email: res@avillionportdickson.com
website: www.avillion.com

too. The roomy Avi Space that sits on the upper deck of the spa building is a good spot for pre-wedding makeover and manicure sessions or spa parties, with a calming ocean view. Treatments include leg massages and wraps, hydrating hand massages and head and shoulder massages. This space can accommodate 45 guests.

And while the bride-to-be enjoys her party at the Avi lounge, the groom-to-be and friends could head to the **Jungle Fringe Karaoke & Bar** for the stag party. There are four private rooms in this African-themed bar, furnished with safari-style décor.

When it comes to food, whether you require a simple cocktail menu, a traditional Chinese dinner, an international buffet or a four-course gourmet Western lunch, all can be arranged with ease, thanks to Avillion's team of experienced catering staff. Other preparations, such as flowers and decorations, table seating and guest lists are adeptly handled by the resort's wedding experts so you have nothing to worry about on your big day. The resort also has a panel of professional wedding photographers on hand to capture each memory on camera.

After the wedding, retreat to your room to be greeted with little surprises left by Avillion. Apart from a chilled bottle of champagne, your chalet will be decked with wedding decorations and your bed blanketed with flower petals – a loving touch designed to set you in the right mood.

Coco Palm Dhuni Kolhu & Coco Palm Bodu Hithi

THIS PAGE (FROM LEFT): Sunset Lagoon Villas, the largest and most exclusive at Coco Palm Dhuni Kolhu; enjoy an all-natural soak at the Coco Spa.

OPPOSITE: The spacious bathrooms in the Escape Water Villas at Coco Palm Bodu Hithi feature a designer bathtub made for two.

Mention the Maldives and heavenly images of snow-white sand, rippling turquoise water and decadently luxurious hotels enter the mind. Those who have experienced this Indian Ocean paradise will know that the reality is as picture-perfect as the postcard. The Coco Palm resorts by Coco Collection offer a truly tranquil getaway experience for couples, with a range of "Uniquely Coco Experiences" – activities just for two, from a delicious picnic on a sand bank to a romantic night's stay on a deserted Maldivian island.

Coco Palm Dhuni Kolhu (Baa Atoll)

Located a 30-minute seaplane transfer away from the capital Malé, **Coco Palm Dhuni Kolhu** is a sanctuary, ideal for couples seeking a quiet retreat on a secluded island. Guests are treated to stunning views of the sunset as they take the wooden boardwalk down to the Lagoon Villas. Inside, the crisp white bedspreads and wooden furnishings complete the feeling of luxurious comfort.

Step out of bed and straight into the lagoon for a refreshing, early morning swim, or wander into the heart of the island to the **Coco Spa** for some indulgent pampering. More energetic types can head to the water sports centre to enjoy activities such as snorkelling, surfing and waterskiing, or to the PADI-certified dive school, where a trip to the mesmerising underwater world of tropical species and absolute serenity awaits.

Guests can choose to spend the morning watching dolphins, followed by a trip to a local village to experience the essence of

Maldivian culture. Those seeking a little more privacy, however, can treat themselves to a sunset dinner for two under the pergola on the tip of the island, before strolling down to the beachside private cinema to enjoy a classic movie under the stars, complete with canapés and champagne.

Coco Palm Bodu Hithi (North Malé Atoll)

This hideaway resort, 40 minutes by speedboat from the capital, incorporates modern style while sharing the same Maldivian charm as Coco Palm Dhuni Kolhu. Having previously won first place for the most beautiful spa-resort worldwide (VIP International Traveller Reader's Travel Award 2008), **Coco Palm Bodu Hithi** offers couples a romantic trip to remember. All the villas come with their own personal bar, flatscreen television with DVD player, music system and wireless Internet connection – perfect for couples wanting home comforts while cosseted in glorious seclusion.

The most exclusive residences, the 184-sq-metre Club Coco Palm Villas, provide true privacy, set apart from the island with a car transfer service. Sink into an indulgent, specially prepared bath, wrap yourself in a Coco silk robe and savour personalised meals served in the privacy of your villa, with a butler on hand for any other requests. Alternatively, guests can dine at **The Stars** floating restaurant after enjoying a complimentary sunset cruise around the surrounding islands.

Coco Palm Dhuni Kolhu (Baa Atoll)

rooms
57 Beach Villas • 27 Deluxe Villas •
12 Lagoon Villas • 2 Sunset Lagoon Villas

food
Cowrie Restaurant (international) • Cornus Restaurant (Thai) • Cornus Grill • in-villa dining

drink
Conch Bar • Lagoon Bar

features
Coco Spa • recreation centre • Internet café • fitness centre

Coco Palm Bodu Hithi (North Malé Atoll)

rooms
44 Island Villas • 16 Water Villas • 16 Escape Water Villas • 24 Club Coco Palm Villas

food
Air (fusion cuisine) • Tsuki (Japanese) • Aqua (Asian) • Breeze (al fresco casual dining) • The Stars (Asian) • in-villa dining

drink
Latitude • Altitude

features
Coco Spa • activities space • spa boutique • library • yoga and tai chi pavilions

nearby
local village visits • scuba diving • snorkelling • sailing • canoeing • waterskiing

contact
04-01, STO Trade Centre, Orchid, Magu, 20-188 Malé, Republic of Maldives
telephone: +960.334 5555
facsimile: +960.334 6666
email: reservation@cococollection.com.mv
website: www.cocopalm.com

Cocoa Island

Imagine being stranded with your loved one on a desert island filled with swaying palm trees encircled by cobalt waters, with warm powdery white sand beneath your feet and endless stretches of horizon as far as the eye can see. There are no roads, no shops, no hint of industry save for the occasional fishing boat on the open sea. This is **Cocoa Island**.

Located in South Malé Atoll, Cocoa Island is a convenient 40-minute speedboat transfer from Malé. Apart from its seclusion and exclusivity, couples coming to this resort, part of the renowned COMO Hotels and Resorts group, will be taken by its clean and sophisticated design. On the southern side of the 350-metre-long island, strung out along a wooden platform like jewels on a necklace, are the resort's 33 suites and villas. Access to your room requires a pleasant stroll atop this over-water platform, where the crystal clear waters below teem with abundant marine life. The suites and villas are designed to resemble boats docked along a pier. Inspired by Maldivian fishing boats called dhonis, with curved hulls made of wood, the unique Dhoni Suites and Dhoni Loft Suites feature large airy living and sleeping areas and outdoor decks with direct access to the sea – guests have been known to simply jump off their decks to snorkel. Interior spaces are elegantly furnished in a contemporary style, using natural textiles and materials, with floor-to ceiling white muslin curtains for a cool, breezy feeling.

THIS PAGE (FROM TOP): *The Dhoni Suites resemble Maldivian fishing boats; enjoy the natural light and cool breeze in this tranquil haven; the villas are surrounded by clear turquoise waters.*

OPPOSITE (FROM TOP): *An aerial view of Cocoa Island; couples can practise yoga on the beach against a calming backdrop.*

rooms
17 Suites • 10 Loft Villas •
4 One-bedroom Villas • 2 COMO Villas

food
Ufaa (Indian and Mediterranean) •
COMO Shambhala healthy cuisine

drink
Faru

features
COMO Shambhala Retreat • PADI dive centre •
pool • hydrotherapy pool • yoga pavilion •
gym • guest lounge with Internet access

nearby
Cocoa Thila Dive Site • Kuda Giri Underwater
Wreck • Guraidhoo Corner • Kandooma Caves •
sand dunes

contact
Makunufushi, South Malé Atoll,
Republic of Maldives
telephone: +960.664 1818
facsimile: +960.664 1919
email: res@cocoaisland.como.bz
website: www.cocoaisland.como.bz

Couples who are looking for a restful holiday will be pleased to note that here, doing nothing is encouraged. Spend the day lounging by the pool, or in the privacy of your own sundeck, dipping into the sea when the mood takes you, then ordering a meal to your room when you get hungry.

To rejuvenate, couples can head to the **COMO Shambhala Retreat** which houses four treatment rooms overlooking the ocean, including one for couples, a steam room and a hydrotherapy pool. Guests can choose from a wide range of treatments and massages based on Asian and Ayurvedic techniques. There is also an open-air yoga pavilion which faces the sunrise – perfect for that relaxing routine at the break of dawn. For its attention to detail and holistic therapies, the retreat was named Best Hotel Spa (Africa, Middle East and Indian Ocean) by Condé Nast Traveller Reader's Spa Awards in 2010.

When you feel rested enough for some activity, Cocoa Island has its own water sports centre where you can find kayaks, catamarans and windsurf boards. A PADI-certified dive centre also awaits divers keen to explore the much-lauded diving sites of the Maldives, some of which are said to be the world's best. Depending on the season, guests can discover a hidden world of bright corals and tropical fish, manta rays, turtles and even whitetip sharks, all beneath the surface of the ocean.

Honeymooners are treated to a bottle of champagne upon arrival, a private yoga class and a souvenir, as well as a complimentary sunset cruise to watch dolphins at play.

Shangri-La's Villingili Resort & Spa

Located on one of the southernmost islands that make up the Maldives, **Shangri-La's Villingili Resort and Spa** is literally a private tropical island paradise in the middle of the ocean. Set amidst stunning white sandy beaches, lush vegetation, 17,000 coconut trees and towering banyan trees, the luxury resort features 142 contemporary Asian villas imbued with Middle Eastern and Indian touches.

In addition to pool and beach villas, the resort also offers some more unusual accommodation options: tree house villas and water villas. Its tree house villas – the first of their kind in the Maldives – were constructed on stilts 3 metres above the ground, among the treetops of the jungle.

Guests in tree house villas can soak in the treetop experience and the views of the ocean from their elevated infinity pools and outdoor bath areas, as well as the spacious wooden decks. The resort's open and airy water villas offer a different sensory experience. Enjoy the sound of waves lapping gently whilst lounging on the sundeck, with a backdrop of endless, glistening sea. Perfect for privacy, this haven is accessible via a walkway over the turquoise blue waters, home to a host of marine life.

The 3-km-long Villingili island is part of a larger group of islands called the Addu Atoll, which extends across the equator and into the southern hemisphere. Getting to the resort involves an hour-long flight from Malé

THIS PAGE (FROM TOP): Enjoy a private meal for two on the beach; the spacious and airy Shangri-La bathrooms are the epitome of chic; neutral colours and elegant furnishings create a relaxing atmosphere in the bedroom.

OPPOSITE (FROM TOP): The secluded Villa Muthee provides the perfect getaway experience; watch the sunset together from the Fashala Lounge.

rooms
142 villas including 2 presidential villas

food
Javvu Restaurant (Western, Mediterranean) •
Dr. Ali's Restaurant (Middle Eastern, Chinese
and Maldivian) • Fashala Lounge (seafood)

drink
Manzaru Bar • Endheri Bar

features
CHI, The Spa • entertainment centre •
Shangri-La Eco Centre • pool • dive centre •
health club • beauty salon • yoga and
meditation pavilion • shops • badminton court

nearby
snorkelling • scuba diving • waterskiing •
parasailing • surfing • kayaking • biking •
night fishing

contact
Villingili Island, Addu Atoll, Republic of Maldives
telephone: +960.689 7888
facsimile: +960.689 7999
email: slmd@shangri-la.com
website: www.shangri-la.com/en/property/
male/villingiliresort

International Airport, followed by an eight-minute boat ride from Gan International Airport on Addu Atoll. Its proximity to the equator is a draw for many couples, who mark their special occasion by dining right on the equator, onboard the resort's luxury yacht.

Shangri-La's innovative Dine by Design service has created every romantic setting you can imagine for a meal. These include a candlelit dinner in the middle of the jungle, under the banyan trees; a specially prepared picnic on a nearby uninhabited island; and a daytime snack on the beach under a private cabana. The resort prides itself on having a whole range of secret dining locations around the island for couples to choose from.

For relaxation and healing, **CHI The Spa** offers a spa concept based on traditional Chinese medicine and Himalayan healing philosophies. Set on the highest geographical point in the resort spanning over 16,700 sq metres, the secluded sanctuary is its own spa village. There are eleven spacious treatment villas, five of which are for couples, including a CHI villa which is dedicated to offer the Himalayan Tsangpo Ritual, a signature bathing and cleansing ritual that uses ingredients based on the Sowa Rigpa, the 1,500-year-old Hima ayan healing tradition.

The honeymoor package includes a stay in one of the resort's presidential suites, Villa Muthee, a dolphin cruise onboard the resort's luxury sailing yacht, a blessing ceremony by the beach, a private photo session and a 90-minute Kandu Boli Ritual – an indigenous spa treatment using cowrie shells.

Amanpulo

THIS PAGE (FROM TOP): Amanpulo can organise a romantic beach barbecue for couples; relax on the comfortable sun loungers by the Beach Club.

OPPOSITE (FROM TOP): Each casita is a private haven, furnished with rich cream fabrics and mood lighting; an aerial view of Pamalican Island.

Your luxury experience with **Amanpulo** begins the moment you touch down at Manila International Airport in the Philippines. You will be whisked away to a private charter plane that will transport you to a little island called Pamalican, located among the Cuyo Islands southwest of Manila.

This idyllic island is a quintessential paradise blessed with tantalisingly clear blue waters, powdery sand so white it gleams in the bright sunshine and coral reefs teeming with marine life. Amanpulo occupies the entire island so guests are free to roam wherever they like, either on foot or in their own private golf buggy provided by the resort.

Here, couples will find plenty to do and many opportunities to create romantic memories. The long swathes of white sand under clear blue skies provide a dream backdrop for a beach wedding. Great weather and perfect setting aside, Amanpulo's in-house team will ensure that everything you need and want for your special day will be delivered to you.

Honeymooners who just want a calm and peaceful time together can spend their days in a swaying hammock, lounging by the pool or taking walks on the beach. At night, restaurant staff can set up a special torch-lit dining area in front of a private fire so that you and your loved one can dine in romantic

seclusion under the starry sky to the accompaniment of the gentle surf. If you opt for one of Amanpulo's romance packages, you will also find yourself sailing away to watch the sunset on one of the resort's luxury boats – live musicians and cocktails included.

Surrounding the island are 7 sq metres of coral reef in shallow waters. A little beyond are sandbanks and a channel where guests can catch a glimpse of whales, dolphins and sea cows. A snorkelling trip to take in the marine wonders is a must and diving expeditions or PADI certification courses can be arranged.

Reflecting the style of traditional *bahay kubo*, or huts, dwellings at this resort are called casitas. The distinctive four-sided

pitched roofs built atop wooden frames can be seen from the air as you fly towards the island. There are 40 casitas offering different settings: Beach Casitas with private paths leading to the beach, Hillside Casitas built on elevated land offering views of the Sulu Sea and neighbouring islands and Treetop Casitas, rising just above the foliage. Every casita features a king-size bed, an outdoor terrace, a sundeck with comfortable loungers and a huge bathroom with a Cebu marble bathtub.

For longer stays, couples can rent the resort's one-bedroom villa, complete with a pool, spacious living and dining areas, outdoor lounge and kitchen, with housekeeping and a private chef provided.

rooms
40 casitas • 11 villas

food
The Restaurant (international and Filipino) • Lobby Terrace (casual dining) • Beach Club (seafood and Spanish) • Lagoon Club (Vietnamese) • Windsurf Hut (Italian)

drink
The Bar

features
Aman Spa • gym • Beach Club • Lagoon Club library • pool • tennis court • sea sports hut • boutique

nearby
diving • snorkelling • fishing • windsurfing • cruises to nearby islands • cycling

contact
Pamalican Island, Philippines
telephone: +63.2.976 5200
facsimile: +63.2.976 5204
email: amanpulo@amanresorts.com
website:
www.amanresorts.com/amanpulo/home.aspx

Capella Singapore

Top-tier travellers are assured of nothing but the best at one of Singapore's latest super luxury hotels, **Capella Singapore**. Designed by Pritzker-award-winning architect Lord Norman Foster, and outfitted by the renowned Jaya Ibrahim, this colonial masterpiece sits among 12 tropical hectares on the island of Sentosa. Just 20 minutes away from Singapore's main island, Capella is a luxurious retreat, where the best of the old meets the best of the new. There are 112 rooms in all, with a range of options from a one- or two-bedroom villa to a premier guestroom or free-standing Colonial Manor.

The setting and the design are as chic as can be, but does the hotel deliver? With a focus on Personalised Service (with a capital P), yes it certainly does. Taking pride in what they do, the Personal Assistants who cater to each guest are trained and skilled in the fine art of personalised service. Making contact before the arrival, the PA prepares for and remains the main point of contact for guests, arranging any romantic extras such as a private candlelit dinner, a yacht charter, special requirements for a magical proposal and so on.

Combine this level of Personalised support with the dream honeymoon, wedding or proposal, and couples are sure to be more than delighted. For the perfect wedding, a special Celebration Team offers

THIS PAGE (FROM TOP): Enjoy the view from your oversized bathtub or the lounge area on the terrace; the dining area is furnished in chic tones; the modern design and neutral décor complement the surrounding greenery.

OPPOSITE (FROM TOP): An aerial shot of the main pool in the evening; take in the scenic view from the bathroom.

rooms
61 Premier Guestrooms • 11 Suites • 38 Villas •
2 Colonial Manors

food
The Knolls (local and Mediterranean) •
Cassia (fine dining Chinese)

drink
Bob's Bar

features
Auriga Spa • 3 pools • 24-hour gym •
24-hour library • Capella Signature Tours

nearby
Resorts World Sentosa • Universal Studios •
Sentosa Golf Club • restaurants • shops •
cruising • sailing

contact
1 The Knolls, Sentosa Island, Singapore 098297
telephone: +65.6377 8888
facsimile: +65.6337 3455
email:
reservations.singapore@capellahotels.com
website: www.capellasingapore.com

both guidance and creativity and ensures that all complexities are choreographed with finesse, minimising the stress and making the dream a reality.

For the wedding itself, the circular ballroom, complete with a glass-domed skylight, can seat up to 400 guests or there is the more intimate Gallery, which can seat 100. In close vicinity is the Bridal suite, Bliss, where the bride can get ready while watching her guests arrive on the live TV feed. Designed in shades of cream, ivory and honey yellow, this space offers a little calm before the main event. There is, of course, a spacious dressing table with professional lighting for the make-up stage, and the large-scale three-way mirrors complete with a raised platform, the head massage and hair spa and the private walk-in wardrobe add the finishing touches to the behind-the-scenes luxury wedding experience.

With Capella's attention to detail, couples can rely on great food for their event too. The Celebration Specialist crafts personalised dinner menus alongside the chefs, while sommeliers select the wines to pair them with. Not forgotten, a sensational wedding cake is created by the hotel's patissier.

Lastly, there is the **Auriga Spa** to melt away any tension or anxiety (if any). Adopting a genuinely holistic approach to well-being, couples can enjoy spa services in the serene Couples Suite and can even choose a Relationship Enhancement Programme, which includes a variety of relaxation and learning activities for two.

Amanwella

A sea turtle laying eggs on the beach, crocodiles basking in the salt pans, elephants plodding along the open plain and migratory birds making themselves at home. The sight of nature's splendour at its best is priceless. And these sights are eminently accessible from **Amanwella**, located near the village of Tangalle in southern Sri Lanka. Built in a coconut grove, fronting a crescent beach, the resort lies within easy reach of several national parks, wildlife reserves and temples.

Its name reflects its immediate surroundings: "aman" is Sanskrit for peace while "wella" is the Sinhalese word for beach. Overlooking the beach, the resort has been designed with an architectural philosophy that recalls Sri Lanka's own Geoffrey Bawa, with the use of stone, timber and clay tiles and coupled with an overall aim to meld the building into the natural environment.

The creature comforts available to each couple are numerous – pleasingly well-appointed contemporary interiors, private terraces on which to savour the sumptuous vistas while lounging in the sun and plunge pools for invigorating dips.

Comfort and well-being are also on the minds of the staff at the resort spa. Facials, massages and body treatments, including therapeutic soaks with a serving of fresh coconut juice or a champagne flute in hand, are all available. Pick a palm under which to

THIS PAGE (FROM LEFT): Enjoy an al fresco meal with a sea view at The Restaurant; the bedroom is a stylish model of contemporary minimalism.

OPPOSITE (FROM TOP): Lounge on the oversized daybed on the terrace and take in the view; cool off in the suite plunge pool.

rooms
30 suites

food
The Restaurant (Asian and Mediterranean) ·
Pool Terrace (light meals) · Beach Club
(Asian and Mediterranean)

drink
Lounge and Bar

features
library · boutique · spa · pool

nearby
Wella Wathuara Village · Yala National Park ·
Mulgirigala Rock Temple · Uda Walawe
National Park · Bundala National Park ·
Rekawa Turtle Conservation Project

contact
Bodhi Mawatha, Wella Mawatha, Godellawela,
Tangalle, Sri Lanka
telephone: +94.47.224 1333
facsimile: +94.47.224 1334
email: amanwella@amanresorts.com
website: www.amanresorts.com

receive a healing massage or request treatment in a spa suite or your own room.

On an island where fresh fish is gathered from the sea each day, it's no wonder that **The Restaurant** serves up delectable seafood as part of the local and Mediterranean cuisine. Meanwhile, the **Beach Club** is a good alternative for lunch and dinner, with cold granitas and freshly churned ice cream surely in demand, especially on warm days.

While couples may, understandably, be perfectly content to remain at Amanwella, there are experiences aplenty worth exploring beyond the resort. Start with the famous rock temple at Mulgirigala, a scenic 35-minute drive away and situated impressively atop a 210-metre-tall rock, rising up amidst the forest.

In the winter, when the seas are amenable, guests can swim in the waters – "sea bathing" as Sri Lankans call it – or indulge in a spot of snorkelling. A visit to one of the national parks and wildlife reserves is a must on any agenda. Witness all manner of creatures in their own habitat at parks such as Uda Walawe, home to large elephant herds and animals such as the spotted deer, langur monkey and jackal, and Bundala, a haven for birdwatchers, famed for its large flocks of flamingos.

Closer to the resort is the Rekawa Turtle Conservation Project, one of the most important sea turtle nesting sites in the country. Five species lay their eggs every night on many a peaceful beach, and visits are recommended during full moon.

Aleenta Resorts & Spa

THIS PAGE (CLOCKWISE FROM TOP):
*Aleenta provides a beautiful
setting for your dream
beach wedding;
enjoy the calming ocean and
pool view from the bedroom;
the Frangileela Suites at
Aleenta Hua Hin come with a
large private pool and
sunbeds for two.*
OPPOSITE: *The idyllic beach
backdrop and chic villa design
at Aleenta Phuket set the
romantic tone in the evening.*

The laid-back and relaxing atmosphere at the award-winning **Aleenta Resorts and Spa** allows guests to appreciate what the Sanskrit word "aleenta" signifies: a blessed life, a sense of contentment and time well spent with loved ones. Both resorts offer specially designed romantic getaways, honeymoon retreats and wedding packages, with a selection of secluded villas and suites for couples to choose from.

Aleenta Hua Hin – Pranburi

A three-hour drive south from Bangkok takes you to **Aleenta Hua Hin – Pranburi**, where you will find 23 rooms and villas built in an array of Mediterranean-meets-Asia styles. The luxury two-storey beach bungalow features a private verandah and plunge pool on the ground floor and an upper level with front and rear balconies, as well as a private rooftop deck, perfect for an evening of cocktails and stargazing. The most romantic option for couples is the Penthouse – a spacious circular room set high above the resort. Guests staying in this room can enjoy an uninterrupted view of the Gulf of Siam and Khao Sam Roi Yot national park. This room also includes a sunken stone tub built for two and couples can indulge in special aromatic baths, arranged by the resort's spa.

Guests are only 30 minutes away from Hua Hin town, but many choose to dine at the on-site restaurant which serves healthy Thai and international food. The menu changes daily, depending on the freshest ingredients and seafood on hand. For those who want to dine in private, in-villa candlelit dinners or barbecues with a private chef on

the beach can be arranged. Spend an evening at the **Pool Lounge** with dazzling views of the Gulf of Siam; lucky couples might even be able to spot pink and grey dolphins in the distance. Thailand's largest national park, Kaeng Krachan, and Khao Sam Roi Yot, Thailand's first coastal park, are both nearby, perfect for a romantic stroll amidst nature.

Aleenta Phuket – Phang Nga

Following the success of the Hua Hin resort, Aleenta expanded into Phuket in 2006. Located along the stretch of white-sand Natai beach, 20 minutes north of Phuket International Airport, **Aleenta Phuket – Phang Nga** continues in the tradition of plush oceanfront villas, each with a distinct style. Aleenta's "Outside Living-in" concept means that all rooms can be opened up so couples can get the most of the surrounding scenery and sea views while enjoying a champagne breakfast in bed.

The **Chef's Table Seafood & Grill** is a private bistro where guests can savour inspiring cuisine featuring fresh seafood and choice cuts of meat. The chef has won rave reviews for his innovative creations, including winning the Selected Hot List Tables Asia award by *Condé Nast Traveler* in 2008. Couples can sign up for customised cookery classes, or for more relaxing activities, visit **Spa IV** for a range of recuperative body treatments.

Aleenta Hua Hin – Pranburi

rooms
23 suites

food
Asian-European fusion

drink
Pool Lounge • bar

features
Spa IV • pool • plunge pools • library • bike hire

nearby
kayaking • jet-skiing • boat trips • waterfalls • national parks • elephant riding • Klai Kangwon palace • Hua Hin night market

Aleenta Phuket – Phang Nga

rooms
44 villas

food
Aleenta Restaurant (Thai and European) • Chef's Table Seafood & Grill (European and Asian)

drink
Sunset Lounge

features
Spa IV • pool • gym • library • boutique

nearby
national parks • turtle sanctuary • jungle and nature safari

contact
3 Soi Ladpraw 95, Ladpraw Road, Wangthonglang, Bangkok 10310, Thailand
telephone: +66.2.514 8112
facsimile: +66.2.539 4373
email: reservation@aleenta.com
website: www.aleenta.com

Siri Sathorn

Bangkok, with its exotic blend of old and new, historical and commercial, spiritual and bawdy, makes for an exciting and unforgettable destination for a honeymoon or romantic getaway. Whether you want to learn about culture and religion, enjoy some entertainment and shopping or simply desire a place to rest and relax, Bangkok offers its own wonderful and bewildering mix.

One of the best locations to base yourself in Bangkok is the upmarket Silom-Sathorn area – the commercial and business heart of the city. And **Siri Sathorn**, a Beaufort serviced residence, is truly a luxury home away from home. Long-term residents and short-term visitors can all agree the warmth and friendliness of the staff and management are unmistakable. At Siri Sathorn, all the staff, from the duty manager to the doormen, as well as reception staff, greet you by name and welcome you with big smiles when you walk in the door.

Stepping into your apartment here is like entering a cosy and sheltered cocoon, thanks to the double-glazed windows that shut out the street noise and ozone purifiers that keep the air fresh. All suites come with separate living areas and fully equipped modern

kitchens, which means that couples can look forward to planning and cooking their own romantic meals. If you choose a room with an outdoor terrace, you can also dine outside while enjoying great views of the city.

If you don't feel like cooking, the on-site **Liquid Bar and Café**, which also provides room service until midnight daily, serves up Thai and Western cuisine both inside and in the garden by the outdoor pool. The streets nearby are also filled with varied eating choices, from chic restaurants serving Japanese, Indian and Vietnamese food, to local fare from night markets. Trendy pubs and upscale nightclubs abound here too.

Both Saladaeng Skytrain station and Silom MRT station are conveniently within walking distance for easy sightseeing. But you do not have to venture too far to experience a taste of what Bangkok has to offer. Silom shopping complex is close by for a little retail therapy, though it is the street vendors along Silom, with their colourful stalls, that attract many tourists. Couples can take a five-minute stroll to Lumpini Park, Bangkok's first public park built on royal land, which was given to the people by King Rama VI. Relax here with a spot of birdwatching or rent a row boat for a leisurely paddle around the lake.

At the end of the day, when you are well and truly tired from exploring the streets of Bangkok, retreat to Siri Sathorn's **Seven Eden Spa** for some much-needed downtime. Couples can enjoy treatments in the privacy of their own spa rooms, with therapists on hand to suggest the packages best suited to your needs, whether you are looking for rejuvenation, detoxification or relaxation.

rooms
111 one- and two-bedroom suites

food
Liquid Bar & Café (Thai and Western)

drink
Liquid Bar

features
Seven Eden Spa • outdoor pool • karaoke lounge • fitness club • complimentary shuttle bus service

nearby
Lumpini Park • Suan Lum Night Market • Saladaeng Skytrain station • Silom Complex • Silom MRT station

contact
27 Soi Saladaeng 1 Silom Road, Silom, Bangrak, Bangkok 10500 Thailand
telephone: +66.2.266 2345
facsimile: +66.2.267 5555
email: reservation@sirisathorn.com
website: www.sirisathorn.com

Four Seasons Resort Chiang Mai

The cultural capital of northern Thailand, Chiang Mai, was part of the Lanna Kingdom in the 13th century. At one time sharing a common history and territory with Burma and Laos, the region gets its distinctive charm and traditions from the resulting blend of cultures. Located on fertile plains, the area is covered with vivid green rice fields. In fact, Lanna means "the land of a million rice fields".

Four Seasons Resort Chiang Mai, located in the lush Mae Rim Valley just 20 minutes north of Chiang Mai, recreates the beauty and majesty of a traditional Lanna village. The Resort is set within 8 hectares of landscaped gardens and terraces, which feature two small lakes, lily ponds, waterfalls and a working rice farm, complete with its own family of water buffalo. Rice from the farm is harvested three times a year, and is stored in traditional barns before being donated to a local temple. These barns are considered holy places where Mae Phosop, the Thai rice spirit, is believed to reside.

This tiny "kingdom" of Lanna-style dwellings comprises a range of pavilions and pool villas, as well as resort villas and luxurious residences. All feature rooms with soft, white bedding and teakwood flooring and furniture, complemented by delicate Siamese artwork.

THIS PAGE (FROM LEFT): Al fresco meals can be leisurely enjoyed in the dining sala; the Pool Villa is just one of the lavish yet cosy residences available.

OPPOSITE (FROM LEFT): Rice paddies and majestic mountains form the backdrop of this Resort; unwind with a pampering session at the spa.

rooms
64 pavilions · 12 pool villas · 22 resort villas and residences

food
Sala Mae Rim (Thai) · Terraces (Mediterranean) · Rice Barn (private dining) · Chef's Table (private dining) · in-pavilion dining

drink
Elephant Bar · Ratree Bar

features
spa · pools · fitness centre · tennis courts · library · yoga · cookery school · kick-boxing · Lan Sai Village boutiques · mountain biking

nearby
Sai Nam Peung Orchid Farm · Tiger Kingdom · Wat Pa Darabhirom temple · Darabhirom Palace Museum · Mae Sa Elephant Camp · Mae Sa waterfall · Queen Sirikit Botanical Garden · golf courses

contact
Mae Rim-Samoeng Old Road, Mae Rim, Chiang Mai, 50180 Thailand
telephone: +66.53.298 181
facsimile: +66.53.298 190
email: reservations.thailand@fourseasons.com
website: www.fourseasons.com/chiangmai

Lounging on the daybed on the Thai-style verandah, couples can take in the picturesque gardens, rice paddies and mountain landscape stretching out into the distance. Night time at this establishment is a magical experience: gardeners light up over 300 torches in the rice fields and around the Resort, creating a mesmerising, mystical atmosphere of twinkling lights.

This traditional yet fairytale-like setting is the perfect backdrop for creating a romantic memory. The Breakfast in the Land of a Million Rice Fields package offers an exclusive treat for only one couple a day. This delicious private breakfast, paired with a bottle of pink Prosecco, allows you to start the day in the **Rice Barn**, in the middle of the Resort's own rice fields. The barn is decorated in traditional Lanna style, with a low table and cushions for comfortable lounging. Alternatively, in the evening, couples can opt for a five-course dinner in the Rice Barn, complete with candles, flower arrangements and soft background music. After the meal, take a scenic walk around the lush gardens and float coloured wishing lanterns on the lake together. Depending on the season, couples can watch the sun rise in a hot-air balloon, taking in the stunning Chiang Mai landscape from above, or they can make a trip to an exclusive elephant camp for a ride on these gentle giants.

For those who want to celebrate matrimony the traditional Lanna way, a local wedding complete with Thai music and blessings by village elders can be arranged.

Kaomai Lanna Resort

Starting life as a tobacco drying plant, **Kaomai Lanna Resort** has outlived its numerous competitors who once dominated the northern part of Thailand. Its survival is due to the determination of its owner, Mr Thawat Cherdsatirakul. It was his mission to keep this little piece of history alive in the form of a beautiful boutique resort.

This calm hideaway is located in a town called Sanpatong, just 20 km south of Chiang Mai. Although this is no tourist Mecca, Sanpatong does have its own cultural and historical identity as an old commercial hub of the north. It lies on the route to Doi Inthanon, Thailand's highest mountain, and Kaomai Lanna has embraced this idyllic mountain location, creating a perfect piece of romantic real estate.

A keen gardener, Mr Thawat started work on turning the barns into 36 guest rooms during the 1990s. Throughout, the renovation was completely focused on keeping the growing guesthouse harmonious with its surroundings. True to his passion, the tall shady palms stayed and the surrounding gardens became a veritable oasis and indeed, the love with which Kaomai Lanna was built has remained a permanent feature.

The answer to the eco-warrior couple's honeymoon dilemma, this delightful haven is nature-loving and community-conscious. The resort's policy is to employ local people – not only are the staff from Sanpatong, but only local craftsmen worked on the renovation and the construction material was locally sourced. Environmental measures include the laundry

THIS PAGE (FROM TOP): Enjoy a delicious Thai meal overlooking the garden; the pool is particularly inviting at night; start the day with a relaxing yoga session in the studio.

OPPOSITE (FROM TOP): The exteriors of the buildings are covered in lush greenery; the romantic canopied bed is perfect for honeymooners.

rooms
36

food
Kaomai Lanna Restaurant (Thai, Chinese and international)

drink
The Tamarind Bar

features
Thagarn Spa • yoga studio • cycling • Jacuzzi • outdoor pool

nearby
Doll Making Museum • Saa Paper Village • Maewang Soft Trekking (bamboo rafting and elephant riding) • Doi Inthanon Mountain • Baan Tawai Wooden Artefact and Furniture Shop • Ganesha Museum • Vieng Tha Garn historic site

contact
1 Moo 6, Chiang Mai-Hod Road Banglang, Sanpatong, Chiangmai 50120, Thailand
telephone: +66.53.834 4705
facsimile: +66.53.834 480
email: service@kaomailanna.com
website: www.kaomailanna.com

drying greenhouse that cuts the need for tumble drying (sheets dry in half an hour in that little baking hut), and the creeping fig trees that surround the barns reduce the need for air conditioning.

Everything is kept quintessentially Thai; the owner's personal collection of Lanna antiques decorates the rooms, the food served at the restaurant is 100% locally sourced, and treatments administered in the homely **Thagarn Spa** are done with ingredients grown in the lush garden. Rose, lemongrass, kaffir limes and tamarind are as natural as they come. Couples can indulge in the resort's signature massage, the Royal Classic Massage, which uses the traditional Luk Pra Kob (Herbal Ball) to calm the meridian points,

or partake in a relaxing yoga session in the designated studio. Morning classes are given by local yogis, and yoga workshops and retreats are also available.

The haven that is Kaomai Lanna is all about the personalised experience. Guests are catered for not by some pre-arranged package. Instead, the owners remain flexible in serving and providing guests with what they want. This makes for the perfect wedding, honeymoon or romantic break with an added special touch from the resort. Honeymooners can expect the norm – a bottle of champagne, flowers, a candlelit dinner and so on – but it is the thoughtful and kind-hearted nature of the owners and the staff that makes a stay here unforgettable.

Mandarin Oriental Dhara Dhevi

To stay at the **Mandarin Oriental Dhara Dhevi** in Chiang Mai is to immerse yourself in the culture and history of traditional Thailand. Couples stepping into the resort's carefully landscaped 24-hectare grounds will find themselves magically transported back in time to the historic Lanna Kingdom, a period which lasted from the 13th to 16th century in northern Thailand.

The team of designers, led by Rachen Intawong, came up with the idea of recreating an ancient city. Among the paddy fields, lakes and landscaping lie Lanna-style villas – characterised by steeply sloping, multi-tiered roofs – wooden rice barns and colonial mansions in small clusters. Adorning these buildings are locally crafted decorations and artwork, hilltribe textiles and Thai silks, evincing the fact that designers meant for the resort to be a "working museum".

Couples will find it easy to soak in the atmosphere, lying on a daybed in the Thai sala of their teakwood villa, overlooking lush tropical gardens and rice fields. Or while the day away in the private Jacuzzi or plunge pool – after getting a relaxing massage in the outdoor massage area. Colonial suites offer a different experience, with Victorian-style furnishings, tiled floors, glass chandeliers and marbled bathrooms. But for a true palatial experience, couples can stay in one of the resort's exclusive residences.

The cultural immersion continues at the **Dheva Spa**. Built in the style of an ancient Burmese palace with seven-tiered roofs, ornate mouldings and Buddhists sculptures, the spa exudes a sense of earthy spirituality, helping to ease guests into a calm and relaxed state of mind. The spa specialises in Ayurvedic treatments and guests can consult its specialist Ayurvedic doctor for healing treatments. For instance, Kati basti is designed to ease body tensions: a specially formulated and warmed Ayurvedic oil is poured onto the spine to alleviate blockages. This is followed by a gentle back massage and an application of a warm herbal compress.

For wedding and receptions, a variety of options is available. The Royal Residence, a complex with six bedrooms in six private Lanna-style pavilions, three swimming pools and private gardens, is ideal for that intimate wedding with select family and friends. Drawing inspiration from a mythical Buddhist legend of the Himmaphan Forest, the garden houses impressive rain trees, frangipani trees and a wall of life-size elephant sculptures.

For larger celebrations, the resort has extensive lawns, as well as an ethereal Lanna prayer hall for that Lanna-inspired wedding affair. All other arrangements – catering, flowers, decorations and transport for guests – are handled by the resort's staff, so that you can have an anxiety-free dream wedding, ending with (if it suits your fancy) you and your beloved drifting away in a hot-air balloon, or riding off into the sunset in a horse-drawn carriage.

rooms
69 Villas & Residences • 54 Colonial Suites

food
Le Grand Lanna (Thai) • Farang Ses (French) • Fujian (Chinese) • Akaligo (international buffet breakfast) • Oriental Shop (cakes)

drink
Horn Bar • Loy Kham Pool Bar • Colonial Pool Bar

features
Dheva Spa • fitness centre • library • pools • tennis court • craft village

nearby
Sankampaeng Craft Village • golf course • adventure activities • elephant camp

contact
51/4 Chiang Mai – Sankampaeng Road, Moo 1 Tambon Tasala, Amphur Muang, Chiang Mai 50000, Thailand
telephone: +66.53.888 888
facsimile: +66.53.888 999
email: mocnx-inquiry@mohg.com
website: www.mandarinoriental.com

Four Seasons Tented Camp Golden Triangle, Thailand

Four Seasons Tented Camp Golden Triangle in northern Thailand recreates the romance and splendour of classic adventure, complete with luxurious tented accommodations, elephants and guides, but without the hardship or the hunting. In fact, this experience is all about immersing yourself in nature and learning to appreciate wildlife.

Located on elevated land in the heart of the Golden Triangle, near the confluence of the Ruak and Mekong rivers, this jungle camp overlooks Thailand, Burma and Laos and is accessible only by riverboat. Accommodation comes in the form of 15 luxury air-conditioned tents complete with handcrafted furniture, mosquito nettings and hurricane lamps. Guests enter the tent through a wooden door but all other areas within the tent are constructed with soft materials and opened with zippers. Unique, beautifully coordinated furnishings characterise the living and sleeping area. An old-fashioned, two-person, hand-hammered copper bathtub stands in the middle of the tent, and a sun deck and an outdoor rainshower add to its old-world charm. All the tents are anchored into the hillside, offering guests unobstructed views of the jagged mountain ridges and sweeping floodplains of the Mekong River, verdant rice fields that cover the valley floors and tribal villages that dot the hillsides.

The Camp can host a maximum of 30 guests at any one time. Its all-inclusive packages come with accommodation, all meals and beverages, a spa treatment, an excursion to the Golden Triangle and private round-trip transfers from Chiang Rai airport. The highlight for many would be the elephant training lessons conducted by an elephant specialist and local mahouts, expert trainers versed in the 2000-year-old Thai tradition of elephant care. All guests will get

rooms
15 luxury tents

food
Nong Yao Restaurant (Thai, Laotian, Burmese and Western) • Wine Cellar (private dining) • Elephant Camp (private dining)

drink
Burma Bar

features
spa • pool • whirlpool • boutique • library • outdoor shower • sun deck • elephant activities

nearby
Hall of Opium • Sop Ruak (Golden Triangle) • Mae Sai and Tachilek border towns • Chiang Saen National Museum • gateway to explore northern Thailand, Burma, Laos • temples

contact
PO Box 18, Chiang Saen Post Office, Chiang Rai 57150, Thailand
telephone: +66.53.910 200
facsimile: +66.53.652 189
email: reservations.thailand@fourseasons.com
website: www.fourseasons.com/goldentriangle

a chance to feed, bathe and ride on these gentle creatures. The Camp's Asian elephants were rescued from city streets in Thailand as part of an ongoing programme to provide domesticated elephants with a humane and natural environment.

A variety of authentic cuisine is offered at the main **Nong Yao Restaurant**, a thatched-roof open-air pavilion with rustic hardwood floors by the riverside. The **Burma Bar**, within sight of the **Elephant Camp**, is the perfect place to enjoy views of the sun setting over the Ruak River. Decorated with trekking and navigation equipment, maps, books, tribal antiques and a tripod-mounted telescope, the atmospheric bar serves delicious local delicacies and cocktails.

The Camp's free-form pool and whirlpool provide guests with a relaxing break between activities, while an on-site spa offers a selection of traditional Thai massages and restorative treatments which incorporate the use of natural mountain plants and herbs.

For couples wanting private moments together, the Camp has many arrangements in place, including in-tent spa treatments and meals, or private excursions to the hilltop for breakfast. The torch-lit Elephant Camp dinner, followed by the release of traditional Thai floating lanterns on the river for good luck, is a favourite activity among many couples. The more adventurous can go on a rafting adventure ending with a private picnic meal on the riverbank.

Let's Sea Hua Hin Al Fresco Resort

THIS PAGE: This tranquil resort provides the perfect escape, with an intimate design but maximum privacy.

OPPOSITE (FROM LEFT): Soft plush fabrics and natural light create a warm atmosphere in the Studio Piers; enjoy a romantic evening on the moon deck under the stars; at night the Gaia Spa and lobby are beautifully lit up.

With just 40 rooms and a no-children policy, **Let's Sea Hua Hin Al Fresco Resort** seems to have been designed with couples in mind. The resort – which won Outstanding Award for Architecture by Thailand Boutique Awards in 2010 – comprises two blocks built facing each other along a 120-metre-long "canal pool". About two and a half times the length of an Olympic-size swimming pool, the pool allows all ground floor Studio Pier rooms direct access via a personal pier.

The Moon Deck Suites on the upper floors of the resort all offer a private open-air deck, yet easy access to the pool via a stairway and garden. Couples can lounge on the double-size daybed, a glass of wine in hand, and enjoy the unobstructed view of the sea, the moon and the stars at night. To get a chance to experience the uncommon sight of the full moon rising over the horizon, guests are encouraged to schedule their visits a day before a full moon is expected.

Couples will appreciate the thoughtful touches incorporated into every room – the oversized bathtubs, rainshowers built for two, a very comfortable "laZzzzz" bed, perfect

As part of Let's Sea's romance package, couples enjoy a bottle of champagne, complimentary drinks from 5–7 pm at the **Breeze Bar**, dinner for two and a spa session at the resort's **Gaia Spa**. The spa on the lobby rooftop is elegantly decorated, with statues in the veiled alcoves that transform into magical lanterns when illuminated at night. Couples can bond over a cookery class or learn how to create cocktails by the pool. The massage class teaches guests how to help their loved ones de-stress and relax by using basic traditional Thai massage techniques.

True to its al fresco theme, the resort takes its green efforts seriously. Apart from ingenious energy-saving designs, using recyclable, natural materials and landscaping to keep areas cool, the staff are encouraged to use pooled transportation to reduce vehicle emissions. For these efforts, Let's Sea has been given the Gold Class Award for Green Accommodation by the Department of Environmental Quality Promotion.

for all-day lie-ins, and mood lighting. The indulgent Bath Menu lets couples order different types of baths, according to the mood they want to create. In-room private dining, breakfast in bed or afternoon tea served on your private pier or moon deck can also be arranged.

The resort is located on Hua Hin's main beach, midway between Hua Hin town and Takieb Mountain. Couples will love the quiet charm and naturally romantic setting – the peaceful 5-km strip of beach is ideal for long strolls or jogging. The **Let's Sea Hua Hin's Beach Restaurant** is right on the beachfront, allowing diners to enjoy authentic Thai meals overlooking the sea. The **Sand Lounge** by the pool brings the beach to you, and going barefoot here is encouraged.

rooms
20 Studio Piers • 20 Moon Deck Suites

food
Let's Sea Hua Hin's Beach Restaurant (Thai, international) • Sand Lounge (light snacks)

drink
Breeze Bar

features
Gaia Spa • canal pool • al fresco fitness garden

nearby
His Majesty the King's Klai Kangwon • Marukhathaiyawan Palace • Khao Takieb • Sam Roi Yod National Park • Pa-La-U Waterfall • Kaeng Krachan National Park • Royal Hua Hin Golf Course • Hua Hin Night Market • horse riding • elephant trekking • windsurfing • fishing

contact
83/188 Soi Mooban Nonggae, Khaotakieb-Hua Hin Road, Hua Hin, Prachuap Khirikhan 77110 Thailand
telephone: +66.32.536 888
facsimile: +66.32.536 887
email: info.huahin@letussea.com
website: www.letussea.com

Four Seasons Resort Koh Samui

THIS PAGE: *Enjoy a romantic private picnic on the beach.*

OPPOSITE (FROM LEFT): *Drawing the curtains turns the outdoor villa lounge into your own thatched pavilion for maximum privacy; the four-hand Chakra Crystal massage balances spiritual energy with the use of warm stones.*

Nestled in the hillside on the northwestern tip of Thailand's third largest island is the charming **Four Seasons Resort Koh Samui**. Landscaped tropical gardens and coconut groves surround its spacious Thai villas, and as the Resort faces the Gulf of Siam, guests are also treated to glorious views of the surrounding islands, clear turquoise waters and white, sandy beach below.

The indigenous population of Koh Samui used to earn their living maintaining coconut plantations. This important heritage has been preserved by Four Seasons Resort Koh Samui – which occupies land that was once an orchard – through the careful protection of the coconut, jackfruit and mango trees around the Resort's grounds. The secluded villas are built on stilts among the greenery, and each features its own al fresco dining area and private plunge pool overlooking the ocean. Sliding glass doors in the bathroom open onto a wooden deck for a scenic bathing experience amidst nature.

Every meal can be an intimate, romantic affair at this Resort. Guests can enjoy an in-villa champagne breakfast or a picnic spread on a private beach. The private cove is a definite highlight for couples – perfect for a candlelit dinner for two, complete with fireworks, or a beautiful natural setting for lavish weddings and receptions.

Wedding packages include a three-night stay in a villa, a pampering spa treatment for the bride and groom, exquisite flower arrangements and live guitar music, with the Resort taking care of all the personalised catering and planning for the day. For those who want to celebrate matrimony with a traditional Thai wedding, a special ceremony complete with live Thai music and blessings by Buddhist monks can be arranged. As the sun sets after the wedding, retreat to your villa via a path lined with tropical flowers.

rooms
60 one-bedroom villas · 14 residence villas

food
Lan Tania (Thai and Italian) · Pla Pla (seafood and local dishes)

drink
Beach Bar · Lan Tania lounge

features
spa · pool · health club · boutique · yoga · library · tennis · pétanque · kayaking · volleyball · *Siamseas* cruise boat

nearby
Nathon Pier · Big Buddha · Angthong National Marine Park · Koh Phangan · Koh Tao · Santiburi Samui Country Club · Fisherman's Village

contact
219 Moo 5, Angthong, Koh Samui, Surat Thani 84140, Thailand
telephone: +66.77.243 000
facsimile: +66.77.243 002
email: reservations.thailand@fourseasons.com
website: www.fourseasons.com/kohsamui

For relaxation, couples can luxuriate in a massage at the Resort's spa or opt for a health and beauty treatment right on the beach. The spa is a calm sanctuary, wrapped in a lush jungle. Its five salas, with indoor and outdoor massage beds, offer a selection of treatments, including facials, body scrubs and wraps, and a wide range of alternative wellness therapies. Yoga-lovers can practise in private in the nearby yoga pavilion, with a tranquil, inspiring backdrop from sunrise to dusk. The Resort also organises some unique recreational activities, both on-site and off-site, such as a fruit and vegetable carving class at the **Lan Tania** Restaurant and beach games including takraw, a type of kick volleyball native to Southeast Asia, and coconut pétanque.

Explore the surroundings together by taking the Resort's cruise boat, *Siamseas*, to neighbouring islands or a gentle hike to a waterfall for a refreshing swim. Couples can visit the 40 paradise islands of Angthong National Marine Park, go snorkelling in the clear waters at Koh Tao and Nuangyuan, or dive in the Gulf of Siam.

SALA Samui Resort & Spa

Located at the very tip of a headland on the northeastern corner of Koh Samui, **SALA Samui Resort & Spa** is a collection of pool villas built on a quiet sandy bay along Choeng Mon beach. Bordered by rock formations on one side and surrounded by tiny islands, the bay exudes a serene ambience, perfect for romance. This cool sophistication is reflected in the architecture of the elegant villas, built in a modern contemporary style, but given a local touch with traditional Thai sloping roofs.

Interiors are characterised by wooden flooring and furnishings, contrasted against fresh white curtains and upholstery.

Each villa sits within its own enclosed garden and all, apart from the deluxe balcony rooms, come with a private plunge pool. Catch up on some reading or enjoy some private moments with your loved one in the shade of the covered poolside salas, or relax with a warm bath in the large bathtub made for two, with a scenic view of the pool and lush surrounding gardens.

Honeymooners and those celebrating their weddings with one of the resort's packages will be treated to extras such as a couple's spa treatment, sparkling wine, chocolates and red roses decorating their room. They will also get to enjoy a fresh seafood dinner paired with wine and candlelight under the stars. The resort's **Pangaea Restaurant & Bar**, as its name suggests, combines ingredients and cooking techniques from every continent, resulting in unique culinary creations, with both local and international influences. Alternatively, couples can indulge in the in-villa dining experience, with a lazy day of comfort complete with breakfast in bed and cable television.

Within the resort, there are two large beachfront pools, one of which is a 25-metre lap pool, surrounded by four massage salas, appearing to float in a lotus pond. You can get a massage or foot rub here at the poolside, but for more comprehensive spa therapies,

rooms
69 rooms, villas and suites including 53 private pool villas

food
SALA Samui Restaurant (international and Thai) • Pangaea Restaurant & Bar (international)

drink
SALA Beach Bar • Pangaea Restaurant & Bar• SALA Wine Cellar

features
SALA Spa • 2 beachfront pools • fitness centre • SALA Gift Shop • guest lounge • tour desk • wireless Internet

nearby
Big Buddha • Fisherman's Village • Samui International Airport

contact
10/9 Moo 5, Baan Plai Laem, Bo Phut, Koh Samui, Suratthani 84320, Thailand
telephone: +66.77.245 888
facsimile: +66.77.245 889
email: info@salasamui.com
website: www.salaresorts.com/samui

head to the **SALA Spa**. You will find yourself enveloped in the earthy scents of natural herbs and lulled into a relaxed state, surrounded by tropical greenery, garden pavilions and landscaped courtyards. A sanctuary in every sense of the word, the spa lets you choose from a wide variety of couple's treatments that you can enjoy together in a private spa suite.

Many places of interest are within easy reach of SALA Samui Resort & Spa. The island's most notable landmark, Big Buddha, is only 15 minutes away, as is Bophut's Fisherman's Village and the action-packed Chaweng Beach. Famed for its shallow blue waters, Chaweng Beach is one of the hottest areas for dining and nightlife in Koh Samui. The resort is also happy to organise private sightseeing excursions for guests. You can choose anything from boat tours to neighbouring islands to diving trips, elephant trekking and visits to nearby temples and historical sites.

ShaSa Resort & Residences

A well-marked spot on the backpacker trail, Koh Samui has become a more sophisticated offering for holidaymakers in recent years. Flanked by small remote islands, wrapped in sandy beaches and home to rolling hills and coconut plantations, Koh Samui fulfils the exotic holiday dream.

Full moon partying on neighbouring island, Koh Phangan, or diving off one of Asia's top spots at Koh Tao could be the draw to this idyll. But for those who really care about doing all this in style, come and stay at a place like **ShaSa Resort & Residences**. This boutique beauty sits snugly on the hillside; all rooms look out to the sea with floor-to-ceiling windows while huge private verandahs offer an alternative and stylish living space.

The accommodation options range from enormous to huge to large, with the communal living spaces – lounge, kitchen and balconies – created with company in mind. The clean and contemporary design features local materials executed with modern elements: the result is an understated style.

Out among the resort grounds there are three swimming pools: a hydrotherapy spa pool, a children's pool and lastly, one kept just for adults, the obvious choice for those on a romantic break. By day, the **Beyond the Sea** restaurant – one of the finest on the island – is a café/deli, claiming the best tea and coffee in Koh Samui and the best bakery, providing soft warm breads and pastries. After dark, however, Beyond the Sea becomes

THIS PAGE (FROM TOP): The bright and spacious suite offers a luxurious home away from home; indulge in a spa treatment by the hydrotherapy pool; Beyond the Sea provides a cosy al fresco setting for dinner.

OPPOSITE (FROM TOP): Enjoy the sea views from the comfort of your bed; an evening shot of the resort and main pool.

rooms
32 Seaview Suites • 1 Beachfront Pool Villa

food
Beyond the Sea (Thai)

drink
Beyond the Sea

features
spa • 3 pools • gym • boutique • wireless Internet

nearby
Samui Tiger Zoo • Aquarium • Lamai Beach • Chaweng Beach • Butterfly Garden • Samui International Airport • kayaking • water sports

contact
116/1 Moo 2 Tambon Mared, Laem Set,
Koh Samui, Surat Thani 84310, Thailand
telephone: +66.77.913 888
facsimile: +66.77.913 899
email: info@shasahotels.com
website: www.shasahotels.com

a superb cocktail bar with a sea breeze and calming view.

ShaSa Resort also provides an excellent wedding venue. The top-class service by the experienced and caring staff ensures all needs are seen to, whether it's a special request from the bride and groom themselves or a query from a guest. The wedding itself can be a traditional Thai or Western solemnisation ceremony, complete with a musician and a traditional drum parade. All floral arrangements are taken care of, as are the photography and catering, including a wedding cake and a candlelit dinner for after the ceremony. Honeymooners and wedding couples also enjoy a tailor-made package at the resort's spa.

The spa is elegant in its simplicity, the tradition of Thai hospitality completing the atmosphere. Treatments are based on both Thai and Asian therapies and all are administered with locally produced products.

In all, the glorious ShaSa suites with their 180-degree views of the sea are a perfectly private space. Further afield, Chaweng Beach and Lamai Beach are far enough to keep the crowds away but near enough for couples to venture to. Indoors, a private butler is available on call and intimate dinners can be set up pretty much anywhere around the resort grounds. ShaSa's owners recognise the importance of surprise rather than relying solely on the sublime setting, and that makes the resort honeymoon heaven.

W Retreat Koh Samui

On the northern edge of Koh Samui, cut off from the main island by a hill, lies a brand new entrant to the beach scene – **W Retreat Koh Samui**. To the casual observer, the scene presents a finger of land, protruding out into the blue-green waters of the Gulf of Siam, filled with dense green foliage. Only closer observation would reveal the stylish villas that make up the resort, hidden among the tropical trees and swaying coconut palms. And just as the resort melds unobtrusively into its idyllic surroundings, so too will couples lose themselves in the relaxing embrace of this luxurious sanctuary.

Stepping into the resort, you are greeted with an expansive view of the sea from the lobby while an interactive digital display dances around your feet. The lobby itself is an inspired example of chic style and contemporary design – terrazzo floors, wood panelling and high ceilings. An intriguing feature is the curved platform leading to the ocean-view circular seating areas, floating in an infinity pool.

The accommodation, in the form of 75 retreats dotting the resort's grounds, also emanates this same palpable style and glamour, where clean lines meet vibrant

THIS PAGE (FROM TOP): The spacious Extreme WOW Suite lounge is furnished in deep purple tones; the modern dining area follows the same lines; each retreat is surrounded by lush greenery, offering maximum privacy.

OPPOSITE (FROM TOP): An aerial view of Koh Samui; enjoy a soak together in the oversized bathtub.

colours. For a truly indulgent experience, W Retreat Koh Samui, the first W Retreat in Southeast Asia, presents its "WOW" and "Extreme WOW" villas. The Extreme WOW Ocean Haven provides couples with an extravagant 890 sq metres of space, decorated with custom-made furniture. The purple-themed bathroom features a circular tub and a hanging rattan lounge chair. Couples can avail themselves of the daybed, two sunbeds, outdoor dining area, patio with barbecue pit and bedrooms with balconies facing the ocean. The size of this retreat also makes it ideal for intimate wedding parties.

Every retreat comes with a private pool, outdoor shower and daybeds. And if spending the day in bed is all you really want to do, the W Retreat signature mattress and goose down comforter will ensure perfect bliss. A full-day lie-in is made even more tempting when you can enjoy your favourite shows on the 46-inch plasma-screen television.

During the day, couples will find many varied ways to re ax: work out at **SWEAT Fitness Centre**, participate in a range of non-motorised sea activ ties at **WAVE** or indulge in a pampering treatment at the **AWAY Spa**. Come night-time, the resort takes on a different kind of energy. Party the night away at **WOOBAR**, one of the hottest nightspots-with-a-view on the island, where live DJs spin dance tunes. Those looking for a quieter evening can balance their way across the stepping stones to **SIP** for tapas and cocktails.

The next day, if you are too tired to get up, simply order breakfast in bed. The staff's Whatever/Whenever policy means that your wish is their command – anytime.

rooms
75 private pool villas

food
The Kitchen Table (international) · Namu (Japanese) · in-retreat dining

drink
WOOBAR · TONIC Bar · SIP · W Lounge

features
AWAY Spa · WET (pool) · SWEAT Fitness Centre · SWING (tennis court) · WAVE (non-motorised water sports activities) · WIRED Business Centre · W The Store (gift shop) · W Library

nearby
Fisherman's Village · Big Buddha · Santiburi Golf Course · waterfall hikes · mountain biking · Thai kick-boxing

contact
4/1 Moo 1 Tambol Maenam, Surat Thani, Koh Samui 84330, Thailand
telephone: +66.77.915 999
facsimile: +66.77.915 998
email: reservations.wkohsamui@whotels.com
website: www.whotels.com/kohsamui

Pimalai Resort & Spa

THIS PAGE: *The resort's infinity-edge Horizon Pool offers a tranquil spot to admire the lush surroundings.*

OPPOSITE (FROM LEFT): *Dark wooden furnishings and soft, white fabrics set the tone in the villas; the Pimalai excursion boat will take you on trips to nearby islands and caves.*

Nestled within a lush tropical rainforest and fringed by a 900-metre-long strip of pristine white sand beach on the southwest coast of Koh Lanta, **Pimalai Resort & Spa** provides a picturesque setting for romance. This beach resort, named Best Tourist Accommodation (Southern Region) by the Thailand Tourism Authority, has the perfect mix of ingredients – five-star comforts, natural surroundings and stylish architecture and design that is sensitive to the environment. Located well away from crowded beaches and other resorts on the island and close to Lanta Marine National Park, Pimalai is, as the Sanskrit name suggests, a little place in

heaven. This unspoiled paradise, an hour's boat ride away from mainland Krabi, offers 121 accommodation units, all built in a contemporary modern Thai style. So beautiful is this resort that *The Independent* (UK) named it one of the top 50 best wedding destinations.

At Pimalai, a wedding ceremony is typically an intimate affair held on a flower-strewn beach with spectacular sweeping views of Ba Kan Tiang bay. An elegant wedding hut and archway decorated with tropical flowers is set up for the ceremony, and the wedding package includes a bouquet for the bride and corsage for the groom, a wedding cake, a souvenir photograph and two hours of pampering treatment at the **Pimalai Spa**. Optional arrangements include traditional Thai musicians and dancers, fireworks and even an elephant to take the couple to their wedding.

The resort strives to make any romantic occasion special for honeymooners. In addition to offering personalised bathrobes and a bottle of sparkling wine in the rooms, the resort can arrange a serenaded sunset cruise; boat trips to nearby islands for a picnic lunch; private candlelit dinners on the beach; in-villa barbecues; private car excursions; and helicopter tours. Three of its restaurants – **Seven Seas**, **Baan Pimalai** and **Rak Talay** – offer natural romantic outdoor settings with picturesque sea views.

Spend the day exploring the deep waters of the Andaman Sea, home to colourful soft corals and a host of tropical sea life, at some of the most remote dive sites in Thailand. The resort's own PADI dive centre offers daily dive tours, special trips and night dives from November to May in its luxurious new dive boat with air-conditioned saloons and sun decks. Diving sites include Koh Haa Island, Phi Phi Islands, Hir Daeng and Hin Muang. For a more relaxing afternoon, indulge in a pampering session at the Pimalai Spa, voted the Best Spa in the Asia Pacific Region by TTG World Travel Awards. Built around a small creek with waterfalls that flow through a lush garden, the spa has an open-air relaxation area, covered open-air treatment rooms, an outdoor Jacuzzi and a herbal steam room.

rooms
68 Rooms • 7 Beach Villas • 39 Pool Villas • 7 Pavilion Suites

food
Seven Seas (fine dining: French with an Asian touch) • Baan Pimalai (Asian and Western) • Spice N' Rice (Thai) • Rak Talay (grilled fish and seafood) • Banyan Café (light lunch dishes)

drink
Pool Bar • Lobby Bar • Seven Seas Wine Bar

features
pools • fitness room • library with books, films and Internet access • basketball • croquet • boules • water sports • dive centre • tennis courts

nearby
Lanta Marine National Park • Phi Phi Islands • Squid Safari sunset cruise • Thai cookery lessons • mangrove forests • kayaking • elephant trekking • snorkelling

contact
99 Moo 5, Ba Kan Tiang Beach, Koh Lanta, Krabi 81150, Thailand
telephone: +66.75.607 999
facsimile: +66.75.607 998
email: reservation@pimalai.com
website: www.pimalai.com

Paradise Koh Yao

Located on the small, unspoiled island of Koh Yao Noi, in between Phuket and Krabi, the **Paradise Koh Yao** is a quiet refuge overlooking 400 metres of soft, white-sand beach and the clear waters of Phang Nga Bay. The lush jungle and striking limestone cliffs that backdrop the resort form one of the most beautiful sea sceneries in Southeast Asia. The distinctive rock formations rising out of the sea house many hidden caves and lagoons, which can be explored by canoe or kayak.

Paradise Koh Yao comprises 70 tropical-style studios and villas, each designed to harmonise with the environment – the surrounding rice paddies and rubber tree plantations are thoughtfully conserved and incorporated into the landscape features. All residences have open sala living areas and semi-outdoor bathrooms for glorious views of Phang Nga Bay and the clusters of nearby islands. Just slide back the partition doors for a refreshing al fresco shower amongst nature. So picturesque is this area that it has served as the setting for movies such as the James Bond film *The Man with the Golden Gun*, as well as *The Beach*, starring Leonardo DiCaprio.

Couples on romantic packages will get to enjoy being "abandoned" on one of these secluded islands with a luxury picnic hamper and a bottle of Prosecco. Lounge on the beach mats under a bright parasol or take a dip in the glistening sea in absolute privacy. A boat will return later to bring you back to the resort for more pampering. A couple's spa session at the **Paradise Spa** is a treat for all the senses. The tropical outdoor spa features

room
1 Hilltop Pool Villa • 6 Pool Villas • 16 Jacuzzi Deluxe Studios • 20 Jacuzzi Studios • 28 Superior Studios

food
Seafood Grill (Thai, international, seafood) • Al Fresco (Mediterranean)

drink
Pool Bar • Beach Bar

features
Paradise Spa • yoga • pool • gift shop

nearby
Hong Island • James Bond Island • Muslim Village on Yao Noi Island • snorkelling • diving • canoeing • rock climbing • mountain biking

contact
24 Moo 4, Tambol Koh Yao Noi, Amphur Koh Yao, Phang Nga 82160, Thailand
telephone: +66.076.584 450
facsimile: +66.076.584 499
email: res@theparadise.biz
website: www.theparadise.biz

a waterfall Jacuzzi and a herbal steam cave sauna built right into the rock formation of the resort. Massages and spa treatments use only natural products and take place in salas overlooking the bay. Honeymooners can indulge in special spa treatments, which include a selection of body scrubs followed by an aromatherapy massage designed to balance the spiritual centre. Health-conscious couples hoping to recharge their minds and bodies can choose from an a-la-carte menu of wellness activities such as yoga sessions, Vipassana and Mantra-style meditation instruction, qigong classes and nutritional guidance.

For private dining, enjoy a delicious five-course gourmet dinner with French champagne under the palm trees on the beach. The resort's two restaurants serve international cuisine, with mouth-watering Thai dishes and grilled seafood, as well as light Mediterranean fare, including authentic wood-fired oven pizzas.

As part of the resort's honeymoon package, couples are taken on a private trip on a long-tail boat to nearby Koh Hong to explore the caves and mangrove forests, snorkel and have a picnic lunch. "Hong" in Thai means room, and the limestone landforms creating room-like, enclosed lagoons are a definite highlight. Other excursions that can be arranged include village tours, nature walks and elephant trekking. Adventurous types will love the views while biking through the jungle or rock climbing at one of 50 spots on Koh Yao Noi and the neighbouring islands.

Amanpuri

Built on the slopes of a secluded enclave on the western side of Phuket is the ultra-exclusive **Amanpuri**, Amanresorts' flagship property. Meaning "place of peace" in Sanskrit, Amanpuri lives up to its name in many ways. Accommodations here – frequented by the international jet-set, including VIPs and film stars – take the form of traditional Thai pavilions interspersed among the coconut trees that blanket the slope leading down to the beach.

The 40 pavilions and 30 villas are joined to the rest of the resort by elevated walkways. Thick surrounding vegetation ensures couples' privacy, each haven being closed off from the world and open to nature. For the best sea views, ask for Pavilion 103 or 105.

Teak wood, Thai textiles and traditional art dominate every room. On stepping into your pavilion, you feel a sense of calmness and spirituality. Apart from the spacious bedroom and oversized bathroom, each pavilion has an outdoor area with a sun deck, so you can sunbathe in private before taking a break to enjoy a meal on the dining terrace. Villas come with plunge pools as well as housekeeping services and cooks on demand.

Even though couples might not want to leave the comfort of their pavilion, a trip

THIS PAGE (FROM TOP): The Thai-style pavilions are surrounded by lush greenery; dine by candlelight with a view of the pool.

OPPOSITE (FROM TOP): The bedroom is a stylish blend of neutral tones; take the steps down from your pavilion to the private beach.

rooms
40 pavilions · 30 villas

food
Terrace Restaurant (Thai, Italian and European) ·
Beach Terrace (casual dining) ·
Naoki (French *kaiseki*)

drink
The Bar · The Beach Club

features
Aman Spa · Amancruises · gym · library ·
gallery · beach club · pool · tennis courts

nearby
island tours · diving · snorkelling · golf ·
markets · temples

contact
Pansea Beach, Phuket 83000, Thailand
telephone: +66.76.324 333
facsimile: +66.76.324 100
email: amanpuri@amanresorts.com
website:
www.amanresorts.com/amanpuri/home.aspx

to the beach below is highly recommended. A wide, open stairway cascades directly onto the thin crescent of Pansea Beach, a spot that many claim to be the prettiest in Phuket. This white-sand beach is hemmed in by natural rock formations and greenery, and is accessible only through Amanpuri and one other nearby resort, making it truly private and exclusive.

As you take your seat on one of the sun loungers that line the beach, attendants immediately appear to offer you cold refreshments. If you need to cool off, they will help you position your beach umbrella and provide cold towels and ice. Instructors are also on hand to guide you should you wish to try out some windsurfing, snorkelling, kayaking, bodyboarding or other sea activities. And if you want the whole beach to yourselves for an unforgettable proposal, wedding celebration or romantic dinner, it can be arranged.

Aman's private fleet of more than 20 sailing vessels is perfect for whisking your loved one away on a surprise cruise to see the limestone cliffs of Phang Nga Bay or to Koh Kai Nok to snorkel among the coral gardens. You can also choose to have a spa session or candlelit dinner onboard. Some luxury yachts come with bedrooms for a romantic overnight interlude.

Back on land, couples can continue the pampering at the **Aman Spa**, or energise with a workout at the gym. Balanced on the hillside with floor-to-ceiling windows for great views of the Andaman Sea, the gym also houses a Pilates studio for private or group classes.

JW Marriott Phuket Resort & Spa

THIS PAGE (FROM TOP): Relax outdoors in the comfortable shade of the sala terrace; the designated children's pool means adults are not disturbed; cosy up together under the stars at Out of the Blue Drink.

OPPOSITE (FROM TOP): The Royal Suite comes with its own pool; JW Marriott Phuket provides a beautiful venue for weddings.

JW Marriott Hotels, the higher end of the Marriott hotel portfolio, were designed for experienced travellers – those who want something distinct, authentic and luxurious, something that little bit extra. And if there was ever a time to be demanding about such things, the honeymoon would be it. For **JW Marriott Phuket Resort & Spa**, there are two factors to consider. Firstly, it is 20 km away from the famous Patong Beach. Secondly, it is enormous. But rather than these two factors dampening the dream trip, they go very much in favour of the perfect honeymoon or romantic getaway.

Party central is the other end of the island and honeymooners can opt in or opt out according to their mood. There are daily shuttle buses taking guests into Phuket Town and Patong, so a night of dancing and cocktails is never too far out of reach.

Then there is the size to consider. With 265 rooms and three huge swimming pools, the resort could appear daunting for those who want something intimate. But, there are so many quiet corners that it is easy for couples to find their own private little hideaway in a different place each day. Add to this the five-star service and lush tropical setting, JW Marriott Phuket is clearly a perfect choice.

As for the rooms, honeymooners are directed to the Oceanfront Pool Suites. This one-bedroom beauty has a large bathroom with an oversized terrazzo tub as the focal point. In true Thai style and as pleasing to the eye as the hotel surroundings, the suite is

rooms
252 Deluxe Rooms • 8 One-bedroom Suites •
4 One-bedroom Oceanfront Pool Suites •
1 Two-bedroom Oceanfront Pool Suite

food
Cucina (Italian) • Andaman Grill (American
steakhouse) • Marriott Café (buffet) •
Ginja Taste (Thai) • Kabuki (Japanese) •
Siam Deli (casual dining) • in-room dining

drink
Sala Sawasdee Lobby Bar • Rim Nam Pool Bar •
Out of the Blue Splash • Out of the Blue Drink •
Beside the Sea Pool Bar

features
Mandara Spa • health club • fitness centre •
yoga sala • shopping gallery • Ginja Cook
Cooking School • 2 tennis courts • 3 pools

nearby
Nai Yang National Marine Park • Sirinath
National Park • Patpong Beach • Phi Phi
Islands • Similan Islands • Kathu Waterfall •
orchid farm • water sports • horse riding •
mangrove forest • Blue Canyon Country Club

contact
231 Moo 3, Mai Khao, Talang,
Phuket 83110, Thailand
telephone: +66.76.338 000
facsimile: +66.76.348 348
email: jwmarriott.phuket@marriotthotels.com
website: www.jwmarriottphuketresort.com

furnished in gorgeous Jim Thompson silk. Leading outside is a large terrace with sun loungers, a sala and views of the Andaman Sea. The covered sala, complete with sunset and lapping waves, is ideal for dining with a touch of romance. To complete the scene, the suite is finished with its own infinity pool. Completely private and happily chlorine-free, it "overflows" into the sea view below. The hotel claims the only problem is leaving the room, and for a honeymoon, that sounds like just the kind of room you want.

Couples who book the honeymoon package are given a round-trip limousine airport transfer, dinner at the Andaman Grill and a spa treatment. One of the highlights of the resort is indeed the **Mandara Spa**. There are no fewer than five double luxury spa suites and 11 doub e deluxe rooms, each with a terrazzo plunge pool, private showers and spacious vanity areas. They all open to a private garden, a Thai sala and a herbal steam room. The romantic couple's package is the Mandara Spa passage of choice for honeymooners. Tne treatment includes a floral foot ritual, aromatic steam, salt scrub, floral bath, massage and facial.

For dining, the chefs promise Romance by Design as couples can select their private dinner location on the 17-km-long stretch of Mai Khao Beach for their own luxury tent. Once settled, a choice of six gourmet menus is presented, as is another of those beautiful Andaman sunsets.

Renaissance Phuket Resort & Spa

Light sandy beaches, the clear blue waters of the Andaman Sea, and vividly colourful coral reefs – there is much about the natural landscape of northwest Phuket that stirs the soul and sets the mood. It is here on the fringe of the Sirinath Marine National Park, featuring 17 km of serene beaches, that the **Renaissance Phuket Resort & Spa** is located. Little wonder, in the midst of Mother Nature's splendour that the hotel's chic design draws inspiration from the surrounding elements.

Guests will find that the vibrant colours of the stylish villas and suites mirror those found out and about, in the waters and on the shore. The stretch of Mai Khao beach that is easily accessible from the resort is just the tip of the iceberg. The impressive entirety of the beach, which may take one hour to traverse on foot, is actually Phuket's longest; yet this beach is also one of the island's less developed, offering a level of privacy and solitude that may pleasantly surprise you.

The still, mirror-like pool and smooth stone that characterise the lobby area set the elegant ambience for the rest of the resort. Individual accommodation units feature clean lines and modern furnishings, with a twist on local architecture – the unique carapace roofs of the four Ocean Front Pool Villas, for example, pay tribute to the gentle sea turtle's archetypal form.

A relaxing session at the **Quan Spa**, named for the Chinese word for pure spring waters, is a must for any couple.

Healing, rejuvenation and well-being are key objectives here; hence treatments include those of the aromatic, deep-tissue and reflexology varieties. Traditional Thai massage is of course available, as well as conditioning marine-and-mineral salt and seaweed-infused treatments.

After a visit to the spa, couples can satisfy tastebuds and stomachs with delicate Thai cuisine or contemporary fare at the eateries at the resort, with dishes predicated on the rich fresh bounty of local farmers and fishermen. Enjoy lovely sea breezes and views on the outdoor deck of **Takieng**, which specialises in simple local food. Or for that romantic al fresco beach dining experience, couples can request a private dinner for two, set out on the sand, under the stars and serenaded by the waves.

Go for a wander in the sunshine and visit ornate and spiritual Thai temples, take the Sarasin Bridge leading to the Thai mainland or spend an afternoon at the Splash Jungle water park. In fact, there are many water-based activities and sports available nearby from scuba diving trips to hidden underwater worlds to river rafting and sailing. But arguably, the most delightful finds are within the national park: mangrove forests great for hiking, jogging and biking, and snow-white beaches bearing few traces of civilisation. Walking, breathing fresh air and combing the beach for shells may be all you really need to fan the flames of romance.

rooms
21 Pool Villas • 5 Ocean Front Pool Villas •
4 One-bedroom Suites • 150 Deluxe Rooms

food
Loca Vore (casual fine dining) • Takieng (Thai) •
Sand Box (international, barbecue)

drink
Sand Box • Doppio • The Lounge

features
Quan Spa • pool • fitness centre

nearby
Wat Maikhao • Wat Chalong • Splash Jungle
Water Park • Sirinath National Marine Park •
Phi Phi Islands • Yacht Heaven Marina •
mangrove forests

contact
555 Moo 3 Talang, Maikhao Phuket 83110
Thailand
telephone: +66.76.363 999
facsimile: +66.76.363 988
email: bookmarriott@marriotthotels.com
website: www.renaissancephuket.com

SALA Phuket Resort & Spa

Even though Mai Khao beach is Phuket's longest beach, its protected status as part of Sirinath National Park means that development in the area is strictly controlled, and the stretch of golden sand remains free of the touts and hawkers who roam Phuket's more populated beaches. On a quiet stretch of Mai Khao near the northern tip of Phuket, you will find **SALA Phuket Resort & Spa**, one of the select few resorts there. This understated resort combines Sino-Portuguese architectural influences with clean lines and a contemporary open-plan design to produce a retreat worthy of its pristine setting.

The open layout of the villas – with interconnecting lounge, terrace, pool area, dining pavilion and gardens – lends an air of spaciousness, while the woodcarvings, handpainted concrete tiles and ornamental stucco reflect local heritage. Bathing areas open directly to the pool, so that you can hop straight into your free-standing circular stone bathtub after a swim. The rooms are designed for lounging: comfortable, cosy areas are to be found every few steps, from the poolside sofas and daybeds, to cushy living room settees, not to mention the plush king-size beds for that perfect night's sleep. Couples will find few reasons to leave their villas.

If you do decide to venture outside the villa, go wherever the mood takes you – a romantic stroll along the beach, a cocktail or two by the main pool or a pampering session at the tranquil **SALA Spa**, built to emulate the essence of a tropical Chinese garden. The resort also provides a range of private tours to explore the surrounding area, including a boat trip to the picturesque limestone cliffs at nearby Phang Nga Bay, where couples can enjoy a champagne lunch on a deserted beach. Depending on the season, guests may even catch a rare glimpse of sea turtles laying eggs on the sand.

Mealtimes at the resort are equally special. Its open-air restaurant, located on the beachfront, serves a delectable variety of international and traditional Thai food. The fresh seafood here is not to be missed. Request the dish you want the day before, and the staff will scour the markets early the next morning to select the freshest produce to cook in whatever manner desired. Wine connoisseurs will be pleased to note that this

dining establishment is one of very few in Phuket that boasts a Wine Spectator Award of Excellence for their brilliant selection of wines. Romantic and private dining options such as a sunset dinner on the rooftop; a beach setting under the stars; or an in-villa candlelit meal can easily be arranged.

With its excellent culinary services and idyllic setting, SALA Phuket provides a superb venue for weddings, with a number of locations available for the event. Couples could celebrate their nuptials from a rooftop vantage point or have the ceremony in the lush gardens as an alternative to the popular beach wedding. While packages are provided for a fuss-free occasion, you can also create your own dream wedding with the help of the resort's wedding planners.

rooms
79 rooms, villas and suites featuring 63 private pool villas

food
SALA Phuket Restaurant (international and Thai) • in-villa dining

drink
SALA Beachfront Bar • Lobby Bar

features
SALA Spa with salon • SALA Gym • 3 beachfront pools • SALA Gift Shop • guest lounge • tour desk • wireless Internet

nearby
Phang Nga Bay • Blue Canyon Golf Course • diving • snorkelling • mountain biking • elephant trekking

contact
333 Moo 3, Mai Khao Beach, Thalang District, Phuket, Thailand 83110
telephone: +66.76.338 888
facsimile: +66.76.338 889
email: info@salaphuket.com
website: www.salaresorts.com/phuket

picturecredits&acknowledgements

The publisher would like to thank the following for permission to reproduce their photographs:

Aaron Black/Corbis 54 (top)

Adrian Pope/Getty Images 51

Alexander Laws 89 (bottom)

Aleenta Resorts & Spa 178–9

Alilla Villas Uluwatu 86, 106, 108–9

Altira Macau 81

Amankora 118–9

Amanpulo 172–3

Amanpuri 204–5

Amantaka 160–1

Amanwana 103

Amanwella 176–7

Amanusa 138–9

Angelo Cavalli/Corbis 98

Anthony Brown/iStock 50 (bottom)

Avillion Port Dickson 102 (bottom), 162–5

AYANA Resort & Spa front cover (river pool), front flap (bottom), 10–1, 15, 101 (top), 140–1

Azamara Club Cruises front cover (cruise ship), 110–1

Banyan Tree Bintan 17 (top)

Banyan Tree Phuket 43, 75 (top), 107

Banyan Tree Ringha 18 (middle and bottom)

Ben Blankenburg/iStock 88

Brilliant Resort & Spa, Chongqing 130–1

Brilliant Resort & Spa, Kunming 132–3

Bruno Levy/Corbis 94

Buzz Pictures Ltd/Photolibrary 56 (top)

Capella Singapore 174–5

Charlie Munsey/Corbis 96 (bottom)

Christian Kober/Corbis 95 (top)

Christopher Groenhout/Getty Images 56 (bottom)

Christopher O Driscoll/iStock 89 (middle)

Christian Kober/Getty Images 54 (bottom)

Chris M Rogers/Getty Images 55 (bottom)

Coco Collection front cover (lagoon villas and sunset lagoon), 1, 4–5, 13, 17 (bottom), 24, 29 (left), 74, 78 (bottom), 166–7, back flap

Cocoa Island 29 (right), 168–9

Colin Monteath/Getty Images 92

Conrad Maldives Rangali Island 16, 100, 105, back cover (top right)

Damai Lovina Villas 85

Dave Long/iStock 90 (middle)

Dejan Sarman/iStock 57 (top)

Diva Maldives 2, 104 (bottom)

El Nido Resorts 83

Elan Fleisher/Photolibrary 37

Elena Elisseeva/iStock 90 (top)

Erkki Tasalu/iStock 71 (top)

Fadil/Corbis 39 (top)

fototrav/iStock 39 (bottom)

fotoVoyager/iStock 55 (top)

Four Seasons Resort Chiang Mai 76, 182–3

Four Seasons Resort Koh Samui front cover (bride), front flap (top), 5, 28, 192–3, back cover (lounge)

Four Seasons Tented Camp Golden Triangle 17 (middle), 82, 188–9

Four Seasons Maldives Kudaa Hura 79

Graham Klotz/iStock 40

Grand Hyatt Shanghai 41 (bottom), 134–5

Greg Elms/Getty Images 36 (bottom)

Hermann Erber/Getty Images 89 (top)

Hong Kong Disneyland Resort 104 (top)

Hou Yuxuan/iStock 50 (top)

Inmagine 21, 23, 27, 30, 33, 35 (bottom), 42 (bottom), 46, 48 (bottom), 52, 58, 59 (top), 62 (bottom right), 63, 64 (bottom), 65, 66, 67 (top), 71 (middle), 72 (top and bottom), 84, 90 (middle and bottom), 91, 101 (bottom right)

Irina Efremova/iStock 95 (middle)

Jamie Marshall-Tribaleye Images/Getty Images 72 (middle)

John Noble/Corbis 97 (left)

John Van Hasselt/Corbis 97 (right)

JoSon/Getty Images 49 (top)

Justin Guariglia/Getty Images 48 (top)

JW Marriott Shanghai 136–7

JW Marriott Phuket 206–7

Juergen Sack/iStock 93 (bottom)

Kaomai Lanna Resort 101 (bottom left), 184–5

Komaneka at Bisma 142–3

Keren Su/Getty Images 19 (bottom), 64 (top)

Kevin Miller/iStock 36 (top)

Kumarakom Lake Resort 18 (top)

Ku De Ta Singapore 44

Let's Sea Hua Hin Al Fresco Resort front cover (moon bed), 190–1, back cover (bottom left)

Luciano Mortula/iStock 47

Mandarin Oriental Dhara Dhevi front cover (couple in a field), 12, 186–7

Maria Luisa Berti/iStock 34

Mark S Cosslett/Getty Images 53 (bottom)

Martin Puddy/Corbis 99 (bottom)

Matahari Beach Resort & Spa 25 (bottom), 144–5

Maya Ubud Resort & Spa 146–7

ML Sinibaldi/Corbis 19 (top)

Macduff Everton/Corbis 67 (bottom)

Nihiwatu Sumba 87

Norbert Eisele-Hein/Photolibrary 59 (bottom)

Norbert Probst/Photolibrary 57 (bottom)

Orient-Express Trains & Cruises front cover (bottom right), 68–70, 112–5

Paradise Koh Yao 202–3

Paul Nevin/Photolibrary 99 (top)

Peter Adams/Getty Images 93 (top)

Pimalai Resort & Spa 200–201

Pudong Shangri-La, Shanghai 41 (top)

Raffles Grand Hotel d'Angkor 102 (top), 128–9, back cover (lotus)

Raffles Hotel Le Royal 126–7

Renaissance Phuket Resort & Spa 208–9

Ricardo De Mattos/iStock 31 (top)

Richard I'Anson/Getty Images 38

Royal Caribbean International 61, 62 (top and bottom left), 116–7

SALA Resorts & Spa 194–5, 210–11

Shangri-La, Bangkok 75 (bottom, left and right)

Shangri-La Tanjung Aru 80 (bottom)

Shangri-La's Villingili Resort & Spa front flap (middle), 6, 14, 60, 78 (top, left and right), 170–1, back cover (top left and bottom right)

ShaSa Resort & Residences 196–7

Shaun Egan/Getty Images 26

Wildflower Hall, Shimala in the Himalayas – An Oberoi Resort 77

WIN-Initiative/Getty Images 53 (top), 71 (bottom)

Siri Sathorn 180–1

Six Senses Ninh Van Bay 20

Sofitel Legend Metropole Hanoi 80 (top)

Song Saa Private Island 122–125

Stockconnection/Inmagine 42 (top), 73

Tim Hughes/Getty Images 95 (bottom)

Tom Bonaventure/Getty Images 31 (bottom), 32

Tom Bonaventure/iStock 35 (top)

Tugu Bali 45, 148–9, back cover (suite)

Tugu Lombok 25 (top), 158–9

Uma Paro 96 (top) 120–121

Uma Ubud 150–1

Villa Babar 152–3

Villa de daun 154–5

Villa Sungai Bali 156–7

W Perry Conway/Corbis 497 (bottom)

W Retreat Koh Samui 198–9, back cover (bath), 216

Wayne Lynch/Photolibrary 22

Numbers in *italic* denote pages where pictures appear. Numbers in **bold** denote hotel pages.

A

Aberdeen Harbour *42*
acupuncture 75, 111
Adam's Peak 97
Agra 51, 63, 70
Aleenta Resorts & Spa
    Hua Hin – Pranburi **178–9**
    Phuket – Phang Nga **179**
Alila Villas
    Hadahaa 78
    Uluwatu *86*, **106**
Alpine Ascents International 53, 99
Altira Macau 80
    Spa *81*
Aman Spa
    Luang Prabang 160
    Phuket 205
Amankora **118–9**
Amanpulo 29, 103, **172–3**
Amanpuri **204–5**
Amanresorts 118, 138, 204
Amansara 103
Amantaka 50, **160–1**
Amanusa **138–9**
Amanwana *103*
Amanwella **176–7**
Ananda Temple 48
Anantara Golden Triangle Resort & Spa 76, 86
Ancol Dreamland 39
Andaman Adventures 22
Angkor Wat *13*, 46, *47*, 102, 103, 128
Angthong National Marine Park 193
Anjuna Beach 23
Annapurna 53, 94, 95
Ao Nang 56
Apex Base 57
Aqualina restaurant 111
AquaSpa 111
archery 120, 121
aromatherapy 123, 155, 203
Asahan River 54
Asiatique restaurant 147
Athakon Architectural House 129
Auriga Spa 175
Avi Spa 163, *164*
Avillion Port Dickson 22, *102*, **162–5**
AWAY Spa 199
AYANA Resort & Spa *15*, *101*, **140–1**
Ayang River 156
Ayurveda Health Home 77
Ayurvedic treatments 74–5, 77, 78, 87, 121, 169, 186
Azamara Club Cruises 61–2, **110–11**
Azamara Journey 110
Azamara Quest 61, 62, 110

B

Ba Kan Tiang Bay 200
Badulla 71
Bagan 47, 48, 65, 114, *115*
Baguio Highlands 99
Bala's Chalet 97
Balai Seni Rupa 39

Bale Kokok Pletok restaurant 158
Bale Sutra restaurant 148
Bali 13, 24, 67
    resorts 24–5, 85–6, 138–57
Bali Food Festival 143
Balinese massage 139, 142, 145
Banaue rice terraces 99
Bangalore 71
Bangkok 13, 36, 180–1
Banyan Tree
    Bangkok 42
    Bintan 17
    Hangzhou 76
    Lijiang 76, 98
    Phuket *43*, 75, 76, *107*
    Ringha *18*
    Sanya 76
    Vabbinfaru 105
Bar Od 93
BASE jumping *56–7*
Basilica of Bom Jesus 23
Batticaloa 57
Batu Feringgi 27–8
Bau Trang 59
Bawa, Geoffrey 28, 105, 176
Bayon Temple 47
beaches 20–3, 26, 28
Bedulu 146
Beijing 50, 64
Bhamo 65, 114
Bhutan 96
    resorts 118–21
Big Buddha 195
Big Tree Farms 45
Bingei River 54
birdwatching 82, 142, 176, 177
Black Dragon Pool 98
bodyboarding 205
Borobudur 46, *49*
Brilliant Resort & Spa
    Chongqing **130–1**
    Kunming **132–3**
Bukhari restaurant 120
Bulabog Beach 59
Bundala National Park 177
bungee jumping 13, 55
Burj Khalifa *30*
Burma *see* Myanmar
Burma Bar 189

C

Café Batavia 39
Café Chuh-Eum 90
Cambodia
    cruises 66
Cameron Highlands 97–8
Campuhan River 142
Canggu Beach 148
Canton restaurant 135
Capella Singapore **174–5**
Carolina Cottages 99
Datai Bay 26
caving 22, *53*, 56
Cepaka 156
Chakra crystal healing 28, 192
Champassak 66
Changdeokgung 32
Chatuchak Market *36*
Chaweng Beach 195
Chef's Table Seafood & Grill 179

Cherai 58
Cherating Beach 22
Chi The Spa
    Bangkok *75–6*
    Tanjung Aru *80*, 81
    Villingili Island 171
Chiang Mai 98, 182
    resorts 182–7
Chiang Mai X Centre 55
Chiang Rai
    resort **188–9**
China
    resorts 84, 88, 91–2, 98, 130–7
    spas 84, 130–3
China Beach 58
Chinatown Complex 44
Choeng Mon beach 194
Chokra Bazaar 97
Chongqing 64, 130
Chun Lee-Kyung 93
Clipper Odyssey 63
Cloud 9 bar *41*, 135
Club 9 bar *41*, 135
Club Oasis Spa
    Kathmandu 78
    Shanghai 135
Coco Collection **166**
Coco Palm
    Bodu Hithi *13*, *17*, 24, 29, 74, **166–7**
    Dhuni Kolhu 78, **166–7**
Coco Spa 29, *78*, 166
Cocoa Island 29, 102, **168–9**
Colombo 71
COMO Hotels and Resorts group 120, 150, 168
COMO Shambhala Retreat
    Cocoa Island 169
    Uma Paro 121
    Uma Ubud **150–1**
Conrad Maldives Rangali Island *16*, 100, 105
cookery classes 17, 23, 43, 128, 191
Coral Reef Dive Center 21
Costa Cruises 61
Costa Lanta 106
Crossroads Forest Spa 84
Crosswaters Eco Lodge & Spa 84
Crow's Nest Restaurant 163
cruises 18–19, 48, 49–50, 60–7, 110–11, 114–17
Cucina restaurant 135
Cuyo Islands 172

D

DaLa Spa 154, 155
Damai Indah 26
Damai Lovina Villas *85*
Darjeeling 96–7
Darjeeling Himalayan Railway 96
Daswatte, Channa 105
Datai Bay 26
Daulatabad Fort 71
David Brown Restaurant 27
de daun Restaurant 154
Deccan Odyssey 71
deepwater soloing 22
Delhi 43
Deoksugung Palace 32
Desert Point 58

Devigarh Palace 101
Dewi Ramona Restaurant 144
Dharmawangsa, The 39
Dheva Spa 186
dhoni sailing boats 29, *100*
Diethelm Travel 26
dim sum 42
Diva Maldives *104*, 105
dolphins 57, 83, 169, 173, 179
dosha 74–5
Dragon Peak 91
Dragon Valley Hotel 91
Druk Air 120
Dragon Air 120
dugongs 57, 83, 173
Dunhuang 72

E

East Coast Seafood Centre 44
Eastern & Oriental Express 68–70, **112–13**
Eastern Safaris 48
eco-friendly resorts 82
El Nido
    Resorts *83*
    scuba school 83
Elephant Bar 128
Elephant Camp restaurant 189
elephants 176, 177
    training lessons 188–9
    trekking 47, 76, *82*, 86, 98, 195, 203
Ellora 71
Elsewhere... The Beach Houses & Otter Creek Tents 23
Emerald Buddha 36
Everest Base Camp 54, 95
Explore Himalaya Travel & Adventure 53
Extraordinary Weddings 104
Extreme Sports 58

F

Farm Organic Spa, The 80
Firefly Suppers 45
Fish Tail Lodge 96
fishing 84, 98
FJC BaseEuphoria 56–7
flamingos 177
Forbes.com 135
Forbidden City 46, 50
Forest Hot Springs 132
Foster, Lord Norman 174
Four Seasons
    Bangkok 76
    Resort Chiang Mai 76, **182–3**
    Resort Koh Samui 78, **192–3**
    Resort Kuda Huraa 78, 79
    Tented Camp Golden Triangle 17, 43, *83*, 102–3, **188–9**

G

Gaia Spa 191
Galle 28, 71
Ganden Monastery 95
Gangdise Shan 53
Ganges River 63
Gayana Eco Resort 83–4
geisha *48*
Gendeng 49
Genghis Khan 50

Georgetown 27
Ger Restaurant Uuls 93
giant clams 84
Giant Wild Goose Pagoda 72
Gili Islands 159
Ginza Armani Spa 79–80
Gion 48–9
glaciers 98
Glenburn Tea Estate 97
Global Ecosphere Retreats 87
Goa *23*, 71
Golden Chariot 71
golf courses 21, 25, 39, 97
gourmet getaways, 40–5
Grand Hyatt Shanghai 41, **134–5**
Great Wall of China 51, 65, 90, *91*
Green Discovery 54
Grill, The 135
Gua Wang Burma cave system 56
Gulmarg Ski Resort 92
Gunung Leuser National Park 63, 64

H

Hackett, AJ 55
Halaveli wreck 58
Halong Bay 66, 67
Halong Cruises 67
Halong Violet 67
handicrafts 23, 49, 63, 84, 99
Hanoi 66
Harajuku Girls *31*
Harbin 92
Hard Rock Hotel, Macau 80
Heliservices 35
heli-skiing 90, 92, 93
Heritage Network 23
Hermes wreck 57–8
herons 142
highland resorts 95
Highlands Park 92
hill stations 28, 95, 96–7
hilltribe villages 98
Himalaya Journey 95
Himalayan healing traditions 171
Himalayan Heli Adventures 93
Himalayan Mountaineering Institute 97
Himalayas 88, *92*, 94–5
Himmaphan Forest 186
Hin Daeng 201
Hin Muang 201
hjunottsmanathr 13
Ho Chi Minh 66
hobie cats 20
Hoi An 47
Hon Mun Marine Park 21
honeymoon
    origin 13–14
    tips 16–19
Hong Kong 13, 35–6, 40, 42
    Disneyland 30, 39, 81, *104*
Horizon 43
Horizon luxury yacht *60*
horse riding 21, 128
Horton Plains National Park 97
hot-air balloon flights 48, 115, 128
hot springs 89, 90, 130–1, *132–3*
Hotel de la Paix 48

index

Hotel InterContinental Hong Kong 35–6
HotWok 45
Hou Hai Lake 51
Houei Sai 66
houseboats 18, 63
HS Khaan Resort 93
Hua Hin 21, 191
  resorts 178–9, 190–1
Hua Hin Hills Vineyard 21
Hue 46–7
Hue Riders 47
Huei Thamo 66
Hutong 42
Hyatt Regency Kathmandu 78
hydrotherapy 169, 196

I
Iban 26
ice climbing 89
ice sculpture competition, Sapporo 89
Imperial Palace, Tokyo 31
Indera Deria 23
India 18, 40
Indonesia
  cruises 67
  resorts 24–5, 39, 87, 138–59
Inside Japan 101
InterCon Spa 91
InterContinental Beijing Beichen 91
International Snow & Ice Sculpture Festival, 91–2
Intha 114
Iori Machiya Stay 48
Irian Jaya 99
Irrawaddy River cruises 19, 65–6, 114–15
Isla Kite Surfing 59
island hopping 24–9
Island Spa 78
Ithaa wedding chapel 105

J
Jade Dragon Snow Mountain 98
Jahangir 92
Jaipur 63, 70
Jakarta 38–9
Jamahal Private Resort 25
Japan
  hotels 31–2
Japanese Alps 95
Jatiluwih rice terraces 153
Jazz Bar 34
Jen Rei Restaurant 84
Jetwing Lighthouse Galle 28
Jetwing Vil Uyana 86–7
Jialing River 130
Jigokudani Yaenkoen Park 89, 90
Jimbaran Bay 140
Jin Mao Tower 56, 134
Jingdezhen 65
Jinyun Mountains 130
Jungle Bungy 55
Jungle Environmental Survival Training School 59
Jungle Fringe Karaoke & Bar 165
Jungle Walla 56
jungle ziplines 98
JW Marriott
  Hotels 206

Phuket Resort & Spa 206–7
Shanghai 136–7

K
K-2 94
Kabayan mummy caves 99
Kachin 65
Kaeng Krachan National Park 179
Kamigamo Shrine 101
Kanchenjunga 96–7
Kandy 71
Kandy House 104
Kaomai Lanna Resort 184–5
Kaorou Ji 51
Karangbayan 25
Karnataka 71
Kasongan 49
Kata Beach 27
Kathmandu 54, 95
Kati basti 186
kayaking 22, 26, 29, 58, 83, 169, 205
Kemang Icon by Alila 104
Kemiri Restaurant 151
Kerala 8, 71
Kerala Houseboats 63
Khajuraho 50
Khao Phanom Bencha National Park 22
Khao Sam Roi Yot National Park 178, 179
Khao Sok National Park 22
Khao Yai National Park 107
Kikunoi 41
Kinabalu National Park 53
King Climbers 56
King's Cup Regatta 27
Kiong, Arthur 76
Kipling, Rudyard 65
Kitchener, Lord 77
kitesurfing 59
Kobachi restaurant 135
Koh Dok Mai 27
Koh Haa Island 201
Koh Hong 203
Koh Kai Nok 205
Koh Lanta
  resort 200–1
Koh Lanta Yai 106
Koh Phangan 196
Koh Phi Phi 26, 27, 201
Koh Samui 27–8, 196, 199
  resorts 192–9
  spas 193, 195, 197, 199
Koh Tao 193, 196
Koh Yao 203
Komaneka at Bisma 24–5, 142–3
Komodo dragons 67
Komodo National Park 67
Korean ski resorts 88, 90–1
Kota Gede 49
Kowloon 42
Krabi 22
  resort 200–1
Krakatoa volcano 63
Kraton palace 49
Ku Dé Ta 44–5
Kuala Terengganu 22–3
Kuching 26
Kullu Valley 92
Kunming Lake 50–1

Kuta 24, 154
Kyichu Lhakhang temple 96
Kyoto 13, 41, 48, 73

L
Lake Inle 114
Lake Pichola 70
Lake Toba 98–9
Lakeview Spa 132
Lamma Island 42
Lan Tania restaurant 193
Lang Co Beach 47
Langkawi 25–6
Langkawi Kayak 26
Lanna Kingdom 182
Lanna Weddings 101
Lanta Marine National Park 200
Lantern Festival 19
Lanzhou 72
Laos
  cruises 66
  resort 160–1
Lavender Tea House 91
Le Spa du Metropole, Hanoi 78–9, 80
Legend of the Seas 60–1, 116–7
Legian 138
Leon Beach Bistro 144
Let's Sea Hua Hin Al Fresco Resort 21–2, 190–1
Lhasa 54
Library, The 106–7
Lijiang 98
Lingsar temple complex 25
Liquid Bar & Café 181
Lisu 65
Llasa 72
Lombok 25
  resort 25, 158–9
longhouse stays 26
Losari Spa Retreat & Coffee Plantation 106
Love Potion No. 9 80
Loy Kra Thong festival 19
Luang Prabang 13, 49–50, 65, 66, 160
Luang Say 66
Luhur Uluwatu temple 139
Luk Pra Kob 185
Lukla Airport 55
Lumpini Park 181

M
Macau
  spas 80, 81
Macau Tower Sky Jump 55–6
Machapuchare 95
machiya 48–9
Madinat Jumeirah resort, Dubai 79
Mae Phosop 182
Mae Rim Valley 182
Mahamuni Buddha 65
Maharashtra 71
Mai Khao Beach 27, 207, 208, 210
Malacca 22
Malaysia
  resorts 22–3, 27, 162–5

Malé 29
Manali 92–3
Mandalay 65
Mandalay Palace 65
Mandara Spa
  Phuket 207
  Shanghai 137
Mandarin Oriental Dhara Dhevi 12, 186–7
mandi lulur 75
Manor at Camp John Hay, The 99
Marble Boat 51
Marina Bay Sands Casino hotel 44–5
Marine Ecology Research Centre 84
massage classes 191
Matahari Beach Resort & Spa 25, 144–5
Maya Sari restaurant 146, 147
Maya Ubud Resort & Spa 146–7
Mayura Water Palace 25
meditation 78, 86, 203
Mekong Cruises 49–50, 66
Mekong River 19, 49–50, 66–7, 188
Mentawai islands 58
Mir Corporation 73
Mom Tri's Kitchen 43
Mongolia
  ski resort 93
monkeys 22, 26, 89, 90, 177
Moon Bar 43
Mount Apharwat 92
Mount Balwang 91
Mount Batukaru 45, 152–3
Mount Deogyo National Park 90
Mount Everest 54, 94
Mount Fuji 73
Mount Jiu Hua 65
Mount Kilash 53–4
Mount Kinabalu 52–3, 95
Mount Rinjani 159
Mount Teine 91
mountain biking 54
mountain climbing 13, 52–3, 94
Mountain Torq 53
Mountain Tracks 92
Mountain Travel Sobek 95
Moyo Island 103
Mu Palace 98
Muay Thai 57
Mui Ne 59
Muju Resort 90
Mulgirigala rock temple 177
Mumbai 71
Museum Wayang 39
Myanmar cruises 48, 65, 114–5

N
Nagano 89
Nam Ngum River 54
Nanga Parbat 92
Nanjing 64
Nankunshan Park 84
Nanshan Ski Resort 90, 91
National Museum Jakarta 38
Nara 73
Neel Kamal 40, 44
Neka Art Museum 142
Nha Trang 20–1
  Oceanography Institute 21
Nias Islands 63

Nihiwatu resort, Sumba 87, 105–6
Nikko National Park 73
Nong Yao Restaurant 189
North Hot Spring Park 130
North Malé Atoll 167
Nozawa Onsen 90
Nuangyuan 193
Nusa Dua 24, 138
Nuwara Eliya 28, 71, 97

O
Oasis of the Seas 62
Oberoi Amarvilas 51
Oberoi spa 77
Ocean Park Hong Kong 39
off-road buggies 55
onsen 89
Oos River 150
orang-utans 63, 64
Orient Express 68, 69, 112
Orient-Express 65, 112, 114
Oriental Pearl Tower 35
Oum Muong ruins 66

P
Padas River 54
Pagan see Bagan
paintballing 55
Pak Ou Caves 50, 66, 161
Pakse 66
Palace on Wheels 70
Palau 62
Palawan Island 29
Pamalican Island 172
Pandaw River Cruises 66
Pangaea Restaurant & Bar 194
Pangkor Laut Resort 76
Pansea Beach 205
Pantai Chenang 26
Pantai Chendor turtle sanctuary 22
Pantai Pasir Hitam 26
Paradise Koh Yao 202–3
Paradise Spa 202–3
paragliding 96
parasailing 20
Paro Valley 96, 120
Parwathi Spa 145
Patong Beach 206
Peace Hotel 34
pearl cultivation 159
Pejeng 146
Peliatan 146
Pemuteran 144
Penang 26–7
  Butterfly Farm 27
Pendowoharjo 49
People's Square 136
Perlis State Park 56
Peninsula Tokyo 31–2
Petanu River 146
Petulu 142
Pha Peng waterfall 66
Pha Thao 66
Phang Nga 27, 202, 205, 211
  resorts 179, 202–3
Phewa Lake 95
Philippines
  resorts 29, 172–3

Phnom Penh 66, 122
Phra Nang Peninsula 56
Phuket 24, 27
    resorts 179, 204–11
Physiotherapy Hot Spring 132
Pilates 17, 62, 147, 205
Pilgrimage Village, Hue 84
Pimalai Resort & Spa 200–1
Pir Panjal Wilderness Reserve 92
Po Toi Island 42
Pokhara 95–6
Porsea 54
Port Dickson 22, 162, 163
Potala Palace 72
Prambanan temples 46, 49
Prime C restaurant 111
Pulau Dayang Bunting 26
Pulau Singa Besar 26
Pulau Sipadan Resort & Tours 57
Puncak Jaya 99
Puri Le Mayeur villa 148

Q
qi 75
Qian Hai Lake 51
Quan Spa 208

R
Raffles Amrita Spa
    Phnom Penh 123
    Siem Reap 129
Raffles Grand Hotel d'Angkor 102,
    128–9
Raffles Hotel Le Royal 126–7
Rai Leh Bay 56
Raja Ampat and Lembongan islands 67
Ramayana 46, 49, 138
Ranthambore National Park 52
Red Dot Tours 71
reflexology 75, 79, 139, 208
Regal Weddings 101
Regent Singapore 103–4
Rekawa Turtle Conservation Project 177
Remedios, Peter 80
Renaissance Phuket Resort & Spa
    208–9
Resorts World Sentosa 30, 39
Riau Beach 164
rice terraces 99, 153
River Café 146
Road to Mandalay 48, 65, 114–15
rock climbing 22, 56, 117
Rock Spa, Macau 80
Romeo and Juliet restaurant 117
Royal Caribbean International 60,
    116–17
Royal Chitwan National Park 95
Royal Dragon, The 43
Royal Rajasthan on Wheels 70–1
Ruak River 188
ryokan 18, 90
Ryuzushi 40

S
S Medical Spa 76–7
Saffron Cruises 42
sailing 23, 83
Sakura Charters 29

SALA
    Phuket Resort & Spa 27, 210–11
    Samui Resort & Spa 194–5
SALA Spa
    Koh Samui 195
    Phuket 210–11
Samode Palace 101
Samosir Island 98–9
Sanchon 32
sandboarding 59
Sanpatong 184
Sanrio Puroland 73
Sanur 24, 138
Sapporo 88, 89
Sarangkot Hill 96
Sarasin Bridge 208
Sarawak 26
Scarlet Hotel 38
Scuba Dive Vietnam 21
scuba diving 21, 23, 27, 28, 29, 57–8, 83,
    144, 159, 169, 173, 193, 195, 196, 201
Sé Cathedral 23
sea cows see dugongs
Sea Safaris of Indonesia 67
Secret Point 58
Seminyak 138
Sentosa Island 37, 174
Seoul 13, 32–3
Seven Eden Spa 181
Seven Seas restaurant 201
Shanghai 19, 30, 33–5, 40, 41, 64,
    134–135, 136
    Museum 34
    World Financial Center 35
Shangri-La Express 72–3
Shangri-La Hotel Bangkok 75
Shangri-La's
    Boracay Resort & Spa 59
    Rasa Sayang Resort & Spa 27
    Tanjung Aru Resort 80, 81
    Villingili Resort & Spa 14, 60, 78,
    170–1
sharks 27, 57, 169
ShaSa Resort & Residences 196–7
Sheraton Hong Kong 42
Shilla Seoul 33
Shinkansen 48, 73
Shwedagon Pagoda 114
Siam Rivers 98
Siberut Islands 63
Siem Reap 48, 103
    hotels 128
Siguragura Waterfall 54
Sihanoukville 57
Silolana Sojourns 67
Similan Diving Safaris 27
Similan Islands 27
Singapore 13, 37–8, 40, 44
    hotels 38, 174–5
Sipadan Island 57
Siri Sathorn 180–1
Sirinath Marine National Park 208, 210
Six Senses
    Ninh Van Bay 20, 21
    Spa, Tea Factory 97
ski resorts 88–93
Skrang River 26

sky diving 13
Sky Resort 93
Skywalk X 55–6
snorkelling 23, 29, 83, 144, 159, 166, 173,
    177, 205
snow monkeys 89, 90
snowboarding 13, 90, 91, 92
snowmobiling 89
Sofitel Legend Metropole Hanoi 78
Song Huong 47
Song Saa Private Island 122–125
Spa by Mandara 78–9
Spa IV 179
spas 18, 74–81, 84, 99, 117, 123, 129,
    132–3, 135, 175, 189, 193
    couple's 62, 74–5, 78–9, 80–1, 83,
    85, 93, 99, 111, 117, 121, 129, 137, 143,
    156, 159, 160, 169, 171, 175, 181, 185,
    194, 197, 202, 207
Spas by MTM 80
Spirit of Adventure 62–3
Splash Jungle water park 208
Sri Lanka 18, 28
    resorts 28, 85, 176–7
Sri Srinivasa temple 37
St Francis Xavier 23
St James Power Station 27
St Paul's Subterranean River 29
Star Cruises 61
Star Ferry, Hong Kong 35
Strawberry Moment Café 97–8
Subic Bay 58, 59
Subic Bay Aqua Sports/Scuba Shack 58
Sukhothai Bangkok, The 36
Sumba Foundation 87
Sumbawa 67
Summer Palace 50
Summit Climb 53
Sun Mountain 91–2
Sungai Gold 157
surfing 24, 25, 47, 58–9, 166
survival courses 59
Suwit Muay Thai Training Camp 57
Suzhou 64, 65
Swedish massage 75, 133, 139
Sweta market 25
swimsuit history 23

T
Ta Prohm temple 47
Tadoba Wildlife Sanctuary 71
tai chi 17, 133
Taj Lake Palace 40, 44
Taj Mahal 13, 46, 51, 70
Takieb Mountain 191
Takieng restaurant 208
Taktsang Monastery 94, 121
Talise Spa, Dubai 79
Tamil Nadu 71
Tangalle 176
Tanggula Express 72
Tanjong Jara Resort 23
Tanjung Rhu 26
tea ceremony 131
Tea Factory, The 97
Tea Horse Road 38
tea plantations 18, 28, 97
Telaga Tujuh 26

Temple of Heaven 50
tented camps 17, 43, 82, 83, 102–3,
    188–9
Terracotta Army 65, 72, 110
Thagarn Spa 185
Thai Boxing see Muay Thai
Thai massage 75, 133, 189, 191, 208
Thailand
    cliffs 21, 205, 211
    resorts 18, 21, 27–8, 36, 86, 178–211
thalassotherapy 62, 111
Thaleban National Park 56
Thatbyinnyu Temple 48
Thawat Cherdsatirakul 184
Thermes Marins Bali Spa 141
Thimphu Tshechu 96
Three Gorges Dam 64
Tiananmen 50
Tibet 71–2
    Train Travel 72
Tiffany 34
Tiger Hill 97
tigers 52, 71, 107
Ting Li Guan 51
Tjampuhan Valley 150
Tokyo 30–2, 40–1, 73
    Disneyland 39
Tomorrow Square 136
Tonle 66–7
Tonsai 56
Traditional Chinese Medicine 75
trail biking 54, 55
trains 48, 54, 68–73, 112–3
Traverse Tours 54
trekking 94–5
Trincomalee 57–8
Tsangpo River 96
Tsukiji Fish Market 40
tuak 26, 159
Tubbataha Reefs 29
Tugu
    Bali 45, 148–9
    Lombok 25, 158–9
Tumasek Beach 162, 164
Tunku Abdul Rahman Marine Park 83
Turpan 72
turtles 22, 57, 83, 169, 176, 177

U
Ubud 24, 142, 143, 147, 150
Uda Walawe National Park 177
ultralight aircraft 96
Uluwatu 24, 25, 58, 152
Uma
    Paro 96, 120–1
    Ubud 150–1
UNESCO World Heritage site 23, 49, 50,
    65, 96, 98, 114, 115, 153, 160

V
Vang Vieng 54
Varanasi 63
Vat Phou cruise ship 66
Vat Phou ruins 66
Vedana Spa 84
Vegetarian Festival 19
Vertigo Grill & Moon Bar 42–3
via ferrata 53

Victoria Cruises 64
Victoria Jenna 64
Victorian Spa 81
Vietnam 18
    resorts 21, 84
Viking Emerald 65
Viking River Cruises 64, 66
Villa Babar 152–3
Villa de daun 154–5
Villa Sungai Bali 156–7
Villingili Island 170
volcanoes 63, 95, 106

W
W Retreat Koh Samui 198–9
wakeboarding 58–9
Wan Hao Chinese Restaurant 136, 137
Wang Meng 93
Waroeng Tugu 45
Wat Arun 36
Wat Pho 36
Wat Phra Kaeo 36
Wat Saket 36
water sports 23, 27
waterskiing 67, 166
weddings 100–7, 117, 119, 122–3, 140,
    142, 164, 174–5, 186, 192, 197, 200–1
Westgate Mall 34
Wetlands Restaurant 133
whale sharks 57, 83
whales 57, 133
White Hadahaa Tea blend 78
white-water rafting 22, 54, 98
Wildflower Hall, Shimla in the
    Himalayas – An Oberoi Resort 77
windsurfing 23, 58, 205
Winter Carnival, Manali 92
Winter Olympics 88–9, 93
Winter Sonata 90
winter vacations 88–93
wreck diving 57–8

X
Xaisomboun Special Zone 54
Xi'an 64, 65, 72
Xintiandi 136

Y
Yabuli 88, 91–2
Yamuna River 51
Yangtze River cruises 19, 64–5
Yangzong Hot Spring 132
Yangzong Lake 132
Yellow River 72
Yichang 64
Yinding Bridge 51
yoga 17–8, 62, 76, 78, 131, 132, 133, 147,
    150, 169, 185, 193, 203
    Malay style 23
Yogyakarta 49
Yong Pyong Resort 90
Yoyogi Park 31

Z
Zao Onsen 90
Zegrahm Expeditions 63
zorbing 55
Zouk 37